Sacred Revolutions

Contradictions

Edited by Craig Calhoun, Social Science Research Council

Sacred Revolutions

Durkheim and the Collège de Sociologie

Michèle H. Richman

Contradictions, Volume 14

University of Minnesota Press
Minneapolis
London

Published by the University of Minnesota Press
111 Third Avenue South, Suite 290
Minneapolis, MN 55401-2520
http://www.upress.umn.edu

Library of Congress Cataloging-in-Publication Data

Richman, Michèle H.
    Sacred revolutions : Durkheim and the Collège de Sociologie /
Michèle H. Richman.
        p.   cm. — (Contradictions ; v. 14)
    Includes bibliographical references and index.
    ISBN 0-8166-3973-6 (HC : alk. paper) — ISBN 0-8166-3974-4
(PB : alk. paper)
        1. Durkheim, Emile, 1858–1917.   2. Sociology—France—History.
    I. Title.   II. Contradictions (Minneapolis, Minn.) ; 14.
    HM477.F8 R53 2002
    301'.0944—dc21

                                                        2002002097

Printed in the United States of America on acid-free paper

The University of Minnesota is an equal-opportunity educator and employer.

12 11 10 09 08 07 06 05 04 03 02   10 9 8 7 6 5 4 3 2 1

Contents

Preface and Acknowledgments

Sacred Revolutions was motivated by the question informing all my research: How does a culture or social group develop a critical perspective in regard to itself? Correlatively, what are the respective contributions of specialized discursive practices—whether literary or from the human sciences—in the production of an answer?

French intellectual history offers a virtually unique response by means of the long-standing tradition emanating from Montaigne's daring essay on cannibalism. Cultural comparisons fostered a mode of anthropological thinking that allowed thinkers from the Renaissance to the Enlightenment to circumvent censorship and address controversial issues. My contribution to this eminent tradition has been to demonstrate how it was revived and emulated in the twentieth century by the founding figures of modern French sociology and anthropology, from Emile Durkheim and Marcel Mauss to Claude Lévi-Strauss.

Meshing a moral imperative with social critique, the sociological revolution exerted a lasting influence on many major French intellectuals in the interwar period. How they refashioned the ethnographic perspective to be relevant to the social and economic turbulence of modernity is the central issue that I investigate. By following the lead provided by the dissident surrealists Michel Leiris, Roger Caillois, and—especially—Georges Bataille, it was possible to recapture a chapter in the interactions between the cultural avant-garde and the new social sciences culminating in the formation of a Collège de Sociologie between 1937 and 1939. More pointedly, I ask why it is these radical social thinkers and cultural critics forged a *sacred sociology* in order to address issues as diverse as politics, social relations, art, and eroticism.

This was the starting point for an extensive foray into the history of French sociological thought. At the conclusion to my earlier study of Bataille's modification of Mauss's study of gift exchange for his theory of general economy, I was already convinced that his ability to conceptualize collective forms of expression and activity in terms that communicate the unique potential of the social was the most important lesson he derived from French sociology. *Sacred Revolutions* therefore focuses upon the related phenomenon of effervescence. Effervescence signals the continuity between Durkheim and his epigones in the Collège as well as that which in their thought and practice defies ideological or epistemological conventions. Indeed, what is to be made of a phenomenon acknowledged by scholars as distinctly characteristic of Durkheim's thought yet resistant to representation? In order to meet the challenges presented by effervescence to existing disciplinary boundaries, I have implemented the particular model of scholarship developed in my previous work—a synthesis of textual analysis, historical contextualization, and sociological theory required to both explicate and evaluate a topic that had not been the exclusive focus of any other investigation.

Sacred Revolutions thus proposes a chapter in the history of the human sciences while demonstrating the formation of an innovative critical discourse that straddles literary theory, social thought, religious and cultural studies. Indeed, a central argument is that the ethnographic detour signals the need to transgress existing disciplinary and epistemic limits at a particular historic conjuncture. The ideological thrust connecting the various figures represented here is the possibility for collective thought and action in the modern world. With its focus on the controversial phenomenon of effervescence, *Sacred Revolutions* counters the stigmatization of collective assemblies through association with fascism, and vindicates their revolutionary potential with examples drawn from 1789 to May '68.

At all stages of this project I benefited from the advice and collegial generosity of Philippe Besnard, Marc Blanchard, Paul Buck, James

Clifford, Douglas Collins, Randall Collins, Carolyn Bailey Gill, Marcel Hénaff, Eva Illouz, Christopher Johnson, Victor Karady, Marc Manganaro, Bill Pickering, Gerald Prince, Magali Sarfatti-Larson, Susan Stewart, Ivan Strenski, Mick Taussig, C. W. Thompson, Steven Ungar, and Sasha Weitman. I am indebted to them for translating intellectual largesse into concrete expressions of support. Their conversations, recommendations, invitations to colloquia, critical readings, and publication of earlier versions all contributed to the realization of *Sacred Revolutions*. Gwendolyn Wells must be singled out for rescuing the manuscript from my stylistic transgressions. Jonathan Eburne deserves a special word of gratitude for insisting that I accept his brilliant title.

Douglas Armato at the University of Minnesota Press has been an ideal editor: I salute him and his staff for their gracious interactions during a stressful process. My appreciation also extends to Craig Calhoun for welcoming the work of an unofficial sociologist into his series.

I am grateful to the John Simon Guggenheim Foundation for financial support during a sabbatical. Summer research in France was provided by the University of Pennsylvania Faculty Research Foundation.

Finally, I dedicate this book to my children, Isabelle and Julian. They may have presented distractions at every stage of its production, but they are also what made it worthwhile.

Introduction

Why Sociology?

> *The sacred should neither be revered as a vestige of antiquity nor restricted to an experience for primitives.*
>
> Georges Bataille

The impetus for this study was the following paradox of French modernity: that some of the most brilliant intellectual figures of the interwar period would invoke a "sacred sociology" to examine the ambient social and political crises. Indeed, the heterogeneous gathering of ethnologists,[1] philosophers, writers, and artists who convened in a Paris café as a "Collège de Sociologie" between 1937 and 1939 focused upon the relevance of myth, power, and the sacred to the fascist menace. For the cultural iconoclasts leading them—Georges Bataille, Roger Caillois, and Michel Leiris—intellectual activism would counter the paralysis induced by the threat of imminent war. Recognizing that death is the primary catalyst for attraction as well as repulsion, and that the need to mediate it prompts consecration of sacred persons, places, or things, they defined as sacred any movement or cultural form responsible for promoting *unity*.

Edicts issued to mark its inception declared that the Collège would enlist the scientific contributions of the French school of sociology—which at the time encompassed the ethnographic study of so-called primitive cultures—and apply to modern social formations categories usually reserved for societies at a much simpler level of development. These declarations also urged that collective representations derived from ethnography be enlisted without diluting the potentially contagious effects against which their mentors had warned. Participants were encouraged to foster bonds among themselves conducive to sustaining a moral community rather than the looser professional relationships characteristic of a conventional academic or scientific setting. They committed theory as well as practice to exploring manifestations of an active presence of the sacred within modern society and culture. Potentially most controversial was the stated ambition that their activities should have concrete political consequences.

Until the 1973 publication of the collected texts emanating from the Collège, its existence as an entity independent of its contributors was often an object of speculation, so much so that the editor of the anthology was accused of fabrication.[2] Yet in contrast with parallel, covert activities and the review *Acéphale* initiated by Bataille, the Collège was a sufficiently public undertaking for Claude Lévi-Strauss to cite it in his 1945 survey of French sociology as an example of the widespread influence exerted by the discipline.[3] Philosopher and erstwhile participant Jean Wahl also noted the magnetic pull exerted by sociology within the Collège when he considered from a less engaged point of view why the discipline of Emile Durkheim and Marcel Mauss had come to be viewed as the endpoint of intellectual and political trajectories that led to André Breton as well as to Karl Marx and Sigmund Freud:

> Here is this sociology, of which I was never a very devoted follower, taking hold of young minds that are eager for rigor, who think they have found in it an answer to questions that they previously thought could be resolved by surrealism, by revolution, and by Freudianism. We must try to understand this phenomenon, which is itself sociological.[4]

The scholarly goals and historical framework of this study are determined by the ambition to respond to the dual thrust of Wahl's query regarding the significance of sociology as a rallying point and the sociological factors contributing to its appeal. Rather than a historical reconstruction of sociology as a discipline, however, the approach adopted here underscores that dimension of the sociological enterprise that

Wahl did not explicitly address: namely, the qualification of sociology by the sacred.[5] By affixing the sacred to sociology, contributors to the Collège signaled the appearance of a point of view irreducible to its constitutive elements. Thus, the central argument that has guided this investigation and provides its justification is that conventional definitions of the sacred and sociology divorced from the French context cannot account for the production of analyses subsumed under their conjoined terms.

Comparable claims have been made for this period and its exemplary figures. Jean Baudrillard underscored the originality of the critical discourse arising from the melding of perspectives provided by Ferdinand de Saussure's *Anagrammes* and Mauss's *Essai sur le don*.[6] James Clifford's *ethnographic surrealism* captures the revolutionary approach to culture resulting from the encounter between an avant-garde movement and the exploration of exotic cultures Paris provided in the interwar period.[7] Clifford credits Durkheim and Mauss for promoting an ethnographic awareness among the dissident surrealists who first collaborated on the eclectic art review *Documents* (1929–31), to which Mauss contributed, and who would subsequently come together in the context of the Collège. However, in contrast with the German "sexpol" movement's revolutionary syntheses between Marx and Freud or the Frankfurt School's critiques of the new mass culture, the Collège's enlistment of the sacred basis for collective action would at first appear conservative or anachronistic. Nor could the French school's characteristic meshing of sociology with ethnography based upon the work of "museum anthropologists," as Mauss designated himself, claim the heroic aura or scientific legitimacy attributed to the new generation of field researchers in British and American anthropology. Although Caillois and Leiris had been students of Mauss, and Bataille was initially familiarized with his lectures through his ethnographer friend Alfred Métraux, sociology—as Wahl's question indicated—was not an obvious option for the cultural radicals associated with the Collège.

The first response developed here is that the sacred/profane opposition as developed within Emile Durkheim's *The Elementary Forms of Religious Life* (1912) provided the conditions of possibility for an innovative critical discourse, especially among intellectuals who subsumed Hegel within the Marxian reading provided by Kojève, appropriated the surrealist introduction of Freud in France, and challenged the hegemonic influence exerted by the "literary paradigm" within French academic and cultural life. Central to the sociological enterprise since its inception in the nineteenth century, the religio-sacred provided a distinguishing feature of sociology by which to examine such ostensibly nonreligious phenomena as authority, status, community, and personality. Especially noteworthy is the centrality the sacred acquires in the final phase of Durkheim's work, described this way:

> Of all concepts and perspectives in Durkheim the sacred is the most striking and, given the age in which he lived, the most radical. His use of the sacred to explain the cohesive nature of society, the constraint that society exercises upon man, the origins of culture and even of human thought must surely rank as one of the boldest contributions of a positivist non-believer.[8]

For Durkheim, the sacred became the basis for an investigation into what would constitute the central challenge of the sociological project: to discern the *specificity of the social,* the new object of epistemological focus for the nascent discipline he was responsible for formalizing in the last quarter of the nineteenth century. More pointedly, the question as it arises in his vast opus is twofold: how to circumscribe the sui generis nature of the social defined as phenomena that are both external to and independent of individual consciousness and, equally urgent, how to communicate to individuals the nature of that social specificity, especially the possibilities it represents. As a result, the sacred and the social, as Robert A. Nisbet pointed out, "are inseparable: distinguishable but not separable. The sacred, we are justified in saying, is the social carried to the highest possible point of categorical imperative in the lives of individuals and, when carried to this point, it lies in a domain of its own."[9]

One purpose of this study will be to recapitulate Durkheim's trajectory from the early studies of the division of labor and suicide to the final great work, *The Elementary Forms of Religious Life,* in order to demonstrate why and how the latter provided his most accomplished representation of those moments of intense sociality responsible for transforming anomic individuals into a social unit that is conscious of itself as something other than the sum of its parts. The distinctive features of such moments is that they are described by Durkheim as effervescent, and are characterized as an intensification of exchanges leading to the production of virtually all social forms and ideals. Not to be equated with the "consciousness-feelings" Rudolf Otto associated with religious experiences, nor entirely analogous to the eros/thanatos forces described by the Freud of *Beyond the Pleasure Principle,* the unmarked effervescence generated by the gathering of a group is described in their particularity as *social* energies. As such, I situate this study within the lineage of Durkheimian models of interaction that view the creativity of the individual in terms of a circulation of emotional energies within a collective social context responsible for new ideas.[10] Whereas other studies have also argued against the dismissal of effervescence as indicative of a loosening of social bonds, the distinguishing feature of my contribution is to reexamine group effervescence in relation to social upheavals.[11] Paramount among Durkheim's ambitions, sociology's potential influence upon large-scale innovations nonetheless remained a relatively unresolved area of his thought.[12] By highlighting the nature of the metamorphosis that occurs within the individual during the moments of social interaction associated with effervescence, I am able to argue that this transformation constitutes the *precondition* for social and political movements.

Sociology thus became an essential resource for the Collegians when exploring the interface between the individual and the collectivity in the course of social and political action. One of the Collège's founding declarations claimed that an understanding of how the longings of the individual condition are projected into social life provides insights into the etiology of social upheavals that other disciplines would not venture to approach. Conveners of the Collège acknowledged their debt to the French school's basic premises that the whole is greater than the sum of its parts, that the collectivity induces transformations within its participants, and that these transformations are only accessible and sustainable within a *mouvement d'ensemble.* The group becomes the privileged locus for explorations otherwise capable of inducing madness or suicide in the isolated individual. Contributors drew upon Robert Hertz's 1909 study of the bifurcation of the sacred to encompass a virulent, threatening, and powerful left sacred, as well as a right one responsible for order and stability.[13] The Collegians envisioned the sacred as a dynamic force whose ambivalent power of repulsion and attraction could undermine as well as construct the hierarchical foundations of the social order.

The intellectual merits of the Collège's contributions to a sacred sociology are therefore inseparable from its group formation. Whether Hans Mayer's study of the avant-garde political function of nineteenth-century German male clubs or Anatol Lewitzky's exploration of Siberian shamanism, Caillois's admiration for secret societies capable of resisting the "winter wind" or Bataille's endorsement of the social functions of the sacred/profane distinction within the spatial organization of French churches and their courtyards—all pursue the subterranean forces leading to eruptions of collective behavior.[14] Lectures entitled "Sorcerer's Apprentice" or studies of shamanism refer to an interest in the role of individuals in fomenting and/or channeling the nature of explosive forces whose direction is unforeseeable. But the overriding concern was with the possibilities opened by group endeavors, the nature of the transformations effected in collective activities, and their role as catalysts for change. The very suppositions shared by Collegians were faithful to the tenets of the French school of sociology, where individual action is viewed as symptomatic of broader social trends prior to codification within collective norms. Given sociology's bias in favor of the primacy of the social, the Collège was immediately at odds with the liberal tradition of humanistic individualism. Yet sociology also provided the means for the Collège to respond to ambient crises by setting the following agenda: To revise the nature of collective life in the modern world by identifying social equivalents to those rare and fleeting moments to which the individual accords the highest priority. Politically, contributors sought to move beyond the contractual model and rethink democratic atomization without falling prey to authoritarianism. Transformations of this magnitude, however, were understood to be contingent upon alternatives to banal or anachronistic forms of the sacred. Most challenging would be the shared perception that the sacred so envisaged defies representation.

The place of collective representations in social analysis introduces a dimension of sociology that forges a crucial link between the two moments of its history examined here. Indeed, Durkheim's 1895 discovery of the sociological basis for religion is correlated with a thorough revision of his scholarly output until that point.[15] That pivotal moment is evident in the preeminent role he would henceforth grant to symbolic thought and rituals in the promotion of social solidarity.[16] But whereas even recent critics contend that responsibility for the full exploration of the symbolic dimension of social life would fall to Durkheim's nephew and intellectual heir, Marcel Mauss, I argue that *The*

Elementary Forms of Religious Life provides an inadequately appreciated contribution.[17] This claim entails a rereading of Durkheim's magnum opus, especially with a view to the significance of its ethnographic shift to what he described as one of the most primitive societies on record. As signaled by declarations at the time of the Collège's founding, the ethnographic representations of archaic religious life furnished the sociological imagination with possibilities inaccessible within existing social and cultural forms. By drawing sociology into the symbolic sphere, Durkheim was inevitably confronted by two sources of tension and even opposition: one, the external institutional conflict pitting the social sciences against the humanities—especially the longstanding French privileging of literature as the basis for the *culture générale* and moral life of the nation; the other, the internal crisis of scientific legitimation for the discipline he had been instrumental in formalizing. For disciples of sociology within the Collège disaffected from regnant cultural norms, the appeal as well as challenge of the field would be to explore the implications of "contagious" representations in a way even their mentors had resisted.

Historical and Epistemological Frames

The significance of symbolic representations for modern sociology is examined in light of French particularities dating from the sixteenth century. On one side is the intellectual tradition variously referred to as "anthropological thinking" by Lévi-Strauss or by Caillois as the "ethnographic revolution." Spurred by the discovery of the New World, it entails an ethnographic detour—whether real or imagined, documented or experienced—leading to a self-reflexive, often critical stance regarding one's own culture and society. On the other side is the correlation between politics and politeness transmitted by means of what Norbert Elias first described as the "civilizing process."[18] Both dimensions are evidenced in the work of Durkheim and Mauss. One contribution of this reading is to demonstrate the dialectic between them and how they determine the vicissitudes of French social thought to the present.

The epistemological framework is thus provided by the virtually unique phenomenon of the French school of sociology's ethnographically based comparative model derived from cultures often considered at a simpler level of development. This ethnographic dimension has been taken by some as indicative of the deficient state of French field-work in contrast with Anglo-American anthropology. Here, however, it is regarded as a screen that, according to Jean Claude Chamboredon, allows the author to introduce issues otherwise inaccessible within existing paradigms. When applied to Durkheim, anthropological thinking leads to a more pointed position than one that perceives in his reorientation to Australian aboriginal religion the standard methodology of the French school's evolutionary perspective. Instead, the reading now offered seizes upon the foray into the archaic as an interpretive guide to the modern in its potential as an investigative, critical tool. Drawing upon Pierre Bourdieu's contention that sociology functions as a psychoanalysis of the social, the self-reflexive stance inherent to the work of Durkheim, and even more explicitly that of Mauss, is enlisted to explore areas of social life devalued, marginalized, or actively repressed in the name of modernity.

Sociology's ethnographic representations have played a critical role in the revitalization of modern critical and social thought. Historically, the notable precedent is Jean de Léry's 1578 account of his sojourn among the Brazilian Tupis. Unlike travel literature content to remain at the level of observation, or the compendia of exotic practices inventoried by his contemporary Thévet—who eventually devoted his services to the court—the Protestant Léry's depictions of the Tupis were accompanied by denunciations of French society, especially those brutally exploitative and racist representatives from whose aborted colonizing venture he had sought refuge among the Indians.[19] Spain's colonial horrors provoked the condemnations of Las Casas, but the specificity of the French critical discourse was not replicated within other countries or cultures. France's exceptionalism can be attributed to a confluence of factors, especially the monarchy's initial reticence to subsidize official expeditions and its repression of the reform movement that led to civil religious wars. Early contacts with the New World were therefore left to private commercial initiatives or conversion goals, rather than dictated by imperialist ambitions. Initially, the strongest impetus to venture new settlements arose from among the persecuted Huguenots, whose humanistic tolerance toward "savages" was conditioned by ideology as well as experience.[20]

Léry's account of his sojourn among the Tupis enjoyed popular success, particularly among contemporary coreligionists. That it is memorialized in the history of ideas must be credited to Montaigne's famous reflections upon cannibalism. Indeed, that essay provided the template for subsequent works within the sociological revolution by borrowing ethnographic material from contemporary travel relations such as Léry's, or by relying upon interviews with first-hand observers, including natives brought to Europe, in place of actual travel experience, and by drawing upon the sensationalism surrounding controversial issues such as cannibalism to point to equal if not greater "barbaric" horrors among the Europeans. A moral lesson was thus derived from encounters with others, especially in regard to unequal distribution of wealth and political power. Montaigne's revitalization of the Socratic dialogue engaged with a native speaker responsible for delivering subversive critiques, established a convenient means to skirt censorship, and explained the closing jibe of his essay to civilized readers wont to reject the lesson imparted by so-called naked philosophers.[21]

Montaigne's ironic allusion to the possible disqualification of his ideas because their source lacked breeches points to another dimension of social thought and practices responsible for the evolution of sociology in France—the ideal of civility forged in the sixteenth century. The vernacular term *civilité* appears there at the same time that it began to proliferate throughout an increasingly secularized Europe, whose social as well as cultural renaissance necessitated the development of new identities for both enriched middle classes and vestiges of a feudal nobility vying with the monarchy for power. Benefiting from the expansion of markets, the bourgeoisie enjoyed a brief period of social mobility and the added luxury of redefining its values and morality after virtual exclusion from the social *imaginaire* of feudalism.[22] In response to the demand for new codes of conduct, the Dutch philosopher Erasmus provided a treatise on education—*De Civilitate morum puerilium* (1530)—responsible for formalizing and disseminating the code of manners that would exert an especially lasting imprint upon French social behavior. While adapting the central elements of feudal virtues to modern requirements, Erasmus also stressed the cult of intellect over physical prowess by means of which the bourgeoisie could attain social prominence. This strategy of social ascension characterizes the bourgeois struggle for social legitimacy well into the twentieth century, when as recently as in the post–World War II period Bourdieu qualified diplomas from the prestigious Grandes Ecoles as "new titles of nobility." Utilized throughout Europe as a pedagogical manual, Erasmus's work was especially popular in France and reprinted most frequently there. His own advocacy of social change notwithstanding, Erasmus's subtle repudiation of the aristocratic model of behavior disappears altogether from the treatises of his successors in the seventeenth century when the consolidation of absolutism enlisted the cult of manners in its campaign to stymie social mobility. This distinctively French turn of events[23]—wherein politeness or civility is equated with strict obeisance to rank and respect for the centralized government—effectively discouraged the development of a distinctive set of bourgeois values that would challenge the rigid social order.

Despite the undeniable intellectual influence exerted by the critical dimension of anthropological thinking Lévi-Strauss discerns from Montaigne to Rousseau, its ideals remained within a minority discourse until their triumph in 1789.[24] Due to its mixture of social critique, moral imperative, and ethnographic references, the critical discourse's marginality can be contrasted with the educational monopoly enjoyed by neoclassical ideals transmitted through the literary representations forming the basis of the French *culture générale*. With its assumption that human nature was an atemporal phenomenon remaining constant throughout time and space, the classical tradition could reduce the otherness of the "noble savage" to an exotic variant of itself.[25] As a counterdiscourse to the rhetorical tradition of the classics, anthropological thinking was primarily transmitted by means of the new writing form invented by Montaigne—the antigenre (Derrida) of the essay. The essay's use of French vernacular, universalistic claims for the subjective I, and patchwork construction pioneered a radical questioning of traditional seats of authority. Especially targeted were the Church—by pointing to the morality manifested among unbaptized savages—and antiquity, in relation to a New World the venerable ancients had not foreseen.

Like all representatives of the ethnographic revolution who figure in this study, the gentleman Montaigne never envisioned a return to the state of Nature he nonetheless lauded in contrast with his own corrupt society. It would be an egregious simplification indeed to polarize French intellectual trends and figures between an encomium to the noble savage on one side and respect for the civilizing process on the other. Nor can such a clear-cut opposition be said to exist as such within the work of Durkheim himself. For all the thinkers featured here, Nature at best provides a hypothetical zero degree of culture by which to gauge the workings of society upon the individual. For the sociologist, we recall that the social represents possibilities that the individual cannot attain in isolation. The goal of sociological investigation is precisely to explore the specificity or, in Durkheim's favored phrase, sui generis reality of the social. Most important, French intellectual history demonstrates the role of ethnographic evidence in providing a privileged vantage point from which to examine one's own cultural practices or to look at oneself through the eyes of the other, even if, as Bourdieu recently stated, the reference to a foreign culture is no longer explicit.[26]

The dual perspective of anthropological thinking and the civilizing process as integral dimensions of French sociology facilitates our appreciation of the historical vicissitudes of the critical discourse spurred by discovery of the New World in relation to social and intellectual forces allied with the often more powerful—and certainly more familiar to modern readers—notion of France's *mission civilisatrice*. The civilizing process extending from the sixteenth to the eighteenth century must be considered in terms of the social and political usage to which it was put, especially when directed toward an internal pacification of the country. Whether explicitly or implicitly, both phenomena represent reactions to the irreversible destabilization of Eurocentrism effected by contact with the alternative cultural practices recounted by sixteenth-century observers. Subsequent intellectual history would be marked by the efforts to retard that realization by some and to precipitate its consequences by others. Groundbreaking studies by Gilbert Chinard and Geoffrey Atkinson in the first decades of the twentieth century documented the myth of America in French literature and, as one historian proclaimed, "revealed in brilliant detail the fluctuating process by which an idealized New World helped to sustain the hopes and aspirations of the Old until the moment when Europe was ready to accept and act upon America's message of renovation and revolution."[27]

But the scholarship justly praised by J. H. Elliott does not venture beyond the end of the eighteenth century, when representation of cultural others was either developed under the new study of anthropology proposed by the Ideologues or else migrated to literary exoticism. In marked contrast with the criticism emanating from earlier versions of cultural difference, the new discourse, as Henri Baudet pointed out, "seldom seems to be directed against the country or continent of origin."[28] The postrevolutionary demise of this particular strain in French

critical thought was attributed to the triumph of the social ideal cultivated domestically and then disseminated abroad as a universal model.
The "civilizing mission" was further rallied by Napoléon's infamous
declaration to the effect that the *bon sauvage* is ignoble. One of the
motivations for the study proposed here is to examine the fate of anthropological thinking after 1789, especially in relation to the advent
of the social sciences.

Sociology's emergence in the nineteenth century as a French discipline under the aegis of Auguste Comte was followed by a hiatus
dominated by Herbert Spencer in England.[29] Durkheim formalized the
rules of sociological method in the last part of the nineteenth century,
just as he endowed the new science of society with the distinguishing
feature of encompassing ethnography within its purview. For scholars
who assume that the two disciplines refer to distinct and even divergent objects of study, the history of the social sciences in France presents special challenges exemplified by Durkheim's move from the issues of labor and suicide to the ethnography of aboriginal religious
life, culminating in what critics agree to be his most accomplished
work—*Les Formes élémentaires de la vie religieuse*. Despite sociology's long-standing enlistment of the sacred to examine nonreligious
subjects, the preponderance of the sacred/profane dualism in that work
astounded both admirers and critics of this fervent supporter of the
republican secular state. The motives for his shift and its consequences
for the ensemble of Durkheim's work continue to exercise scholarly
speculation (see chapter 1), even though the introduction to *Elementary Forms* justified the ethnographic detour to address contemporary
society in the following way:

> Sociology sets itself different problems from those of history or
> ethnography. It does not seek to become acquainted with bygone
> forms of civilization for the sole purpose of being acquainted with
> and reconstructing them. Instead, like any positive science, its pur-
> pose above all is to explain a present reality that is near to us and
> thus capable of affecting our ideas and actions. . . . I have made a
> very archaic religion the subject of my research because it seems
> better suited than any other to help us comprehend the religious na-
> ture of man, that is, to reveal a fundamental and permanent aspect
> of humanity.[30]

When claiming to examine the crises confronting modern society
through categories derived from archaic cultures, contributors to the

Collège modeled their project upon the tradition set forth by mentors in the French school, notably Durkheim and Mauss. One explanation for Wahl's bemusement at such a tack is that, following Durkheim's death in 1917, sociology went from being a productive and presti-gious field to one attracting few young researchers. Competing ver-sions of Durkheim's legacy can be traced to the posthumous fate of the discipline following his death in 1917, when the mantle of the French school fell to Mauss. Critical assessments tend to concur with Bataille's opinion that Durkheim's nephew remained "generally faith-ful to the precedent of the school's founder."[31] But as Bataille also ob-served, it was not until Mauss attracted a variety of students around 1930 that the ideas of Durkheim were revitalized within the cultural and intellectual avant-garde. Why this newly established tradition foundered to the point where, for most students, "anything seemed preferable to the old Durkheimian sociology," has been explained by the institutional bifurcation of a discipline reflected in the complexity of the master's political machinations and Janus-like persona.[32] Durk-heim's contrasting tendencies were manifested in a subsequent polari-zation between dogmatic university Durkheimians on one side and those who transmitted his legacy through specialized but innovative research on the other. By the close of the 1930s, Mauss lamented the rejection of sociology "lock, stock, and barrel" as mouthpiece for Third Republic ideology by the young intellectual stars Maurice Merleau-Ponty, Jean-Paul Sartre, and Raymond Aron. Wahl's request for a sociological approach remains pertinent, since it compels us to explain how the same field of inquiry could be embraced by one seg-ment of the interwar generation represented by enthusiasts within the Collège, while repudiated by another.

The following criterion has determined the historical and ideologi-cal orientation of our response: to what extent does post-Durkheimian sociology sustain the ethnographic detour in order to reach—as Mauss urged—"archaeological" conclusions?[33] From his global survey of gift exchange, for instance, Mauss derived an array of moral, political and economic, sociological and ethical observations directed toward social reform based upon a melding of the old and the new. Such prescrip-tions are distinguished from other (including more recent) modes of anthropology in the service of cultural critique in that they are not simply constructed out of examples imported from the social practices of one culture to another.[34] Rather, they evolve from the systematic comparison of social forms and meanings encompassing the past as well as present of Western and non-Western societies. Collapsing hierarchical as well as temporal and spatial distinctions, Mauss effected a Foucauldian desedimentation of phenomena that continue to inform modern societies—*"albeit less noticeably."*[35] Sociology's role as psychoanalysis of the social functions through the distancing or defamiliarization offered by the point of view of ethnographic difference turned upon itself. The archaeological perspective directed by *archaic* (the preferred replacement for "primitive") examples extends the ethnographic revolution into an even more explicit form of self-scrutiny, since it explores phenomena that have been segregated, devalued, or even actively repressed. With its willingness to excavate relatively obscure phenomena of social life, sociology counters the occultation of archaic social forms and brings to the fore of consciousness collective representations banished from the social imagination.

In this case, the focal point is the sacred—a phenomenon at once familiar and exotic—dramatically revised within the sociologies of both Hertz and Durkheim. According to early statements, the Collegians envisioned their investigation as a way to understand as well as foment the sort of collective action Durkheim had subsumed under effervescent assemblies. Revival of the sacred to address nonreligious social phenomena allowed him to explore the uncharted realm of a sensibility cultivated by objective, collective—effervescent—experiences. In the course of such assemblies, the closed consciousness is opened onto interaction with others, and this transformation places the individual within the realm of the sacred. In its Bataillian version, modification of the individual's inner economy within collective forms of expenditure leads to intensified communication also qualified as sacred.

The consequences of collective effervescence for solidarity derive from its transformative effects upon the psychic construct of individuals otherwise socialized by traditional exchange relations. The reading of Durkheim presented in chapter 1 will extend that claim to social and political movements as well. It will also demonstrate how *Elementary Forms* facilitated the emergence of certain basic notions found in the Collège. The justification for such a position relies upon a fundamental premise of the sociological perspective: that social forms or structures arising from the tension inherent to the sacred/profane duality, for instance, provide the requisite formal basis to mediate contact with that which is most decisive in human experience. As Bataille would frequently reiterate, his surprising endorsement of the need for prohibitions stems from recognition of their role in structuring transgressions—those moments of upheaval and disruption leading to new possibilities.

This defining moment or experience becomes the focus for my analyses of both Durkheim and the Collège, since the latter's stated purpose was to uncover the source for collective movements in the modern period in forces of attraction and repulsion. In contrast with the socialization inculcated by the civilizing process that historically serviced the ruling elite and especially the state in reinforcing rank and order, the transformations effected by means of collective experience can lead to the effervescent revolutionary moments witnessed in 1789 and 1968. Sacred sociology thus converges with postwar scholarship that draws upon the later Durkheim to reexamine the relevance of the sacred/profane dualism for an understanding of modern society and to develop a new model for cultural studies.[36]

Sacred Sociology: Methodological Considerations

The reading of *The Elementary Forms of Religious Life* in chapter 1 approaches Durkheim's monumental work as a modern exemplar of anthropological thinking. Acknowledged as partaking of that distinctively French hoary tradition dating from Montaigne, *Elementary Forms* nonetheless has not been studied explicitly in terms of its political and social relevance to contemporary society.[37] One explanation for avoiding an approach that would privilege the ethnographic dimension is that its author could be characterized as "a moraliste led to perceive archaic societies through a superficial type of benign reverse ethnocentrism."[38] Another objection is that the ethnographic detour collapses historical specificity, thereby undermining its potential critical thrust. Bruno Karsenti's recent study of Mauss also echoes a widespread belief that Durkheim's only model of social transformation remains *evolutionary* and necessitates a move from mechanical to organic solidarity as described in his early classic study of social organization, *The Division of Labor in Society* (1893).[39] Such readings devalue *Elementary Forms*'s radical potential.

Arguing against these positions in chapter 1, I demonstrate that the full implications of the sacred/profane dualism—the analytical fulcrum of *Elementary Forms*—resides in its displacement of the mechanical/organic developmental model found in Durkheim's preceding work. Indeed, as early as *Division*, Durkheim recognized that the *ideal types* of social relations he correlated with the morphological opposition between mechanical and organic were both necessary. With a more nuanced ethnographic representation of the quality of social relations documenting the sacred/profane opposition, he was able to arrive at a model that assured the viability of the social whole as well as individual access to totality. Among its contributions, the tension fostered by the morphological contrast is responsible for generating the effusion of collective energies Durkheim described as effervescent, and to which he attributed the genesis of religious forms as well as revolutionary action.

It is revealing that in a discussion of *Elementary Forms,* Raymond Aron characterized the passages regarding the effervescent sources of the sacred as "the most categorical expression of the Durkheimian vision," while conceding his uneasiness with this aspect of Durkheim's thought.[40] His discomfort is readily explained by the historical proximity of effervescence to LeBon's descriptions of crowd behavior[41] at the turn of the century,[42] as well as with subsequent associations with fascism.[43] A source of controversy in the earliest reviews of *Elementary Forms,* effervescence in W. S. F. Pickering's otherwise judicious reading of Durkheim's theory of religion, for instance, is nonetheless restricted to the religious domain.[44] Another widespread perception is that the disruptive potential of effervescence is tempered by Durkheim's goal to have it foster social solidarity by means of a civil religion.[45] Despite Durkheim's inability to attribute a specific social cause for effervescent assemblies, and Pickering's own skepticism in regard to their ability to produce new representations, the latter nonetheless concedes that "there is more merit in focussing on effervescent assembly than some critics have allowed."[46]

Directing the present review of the uneasy place of effervescence within social thought is my assumption that recourse to ethnographic mediations at critical conjunctures arises from the constraints exerted upon social criticism rather than from the convenience of drawing upon an established tradition. An important function of the following readings from Durkheim to Bataille is to pinpoint the nature of that necessity, and to examine whether sociology provides the conditions of possibility to respond to certain requirements. The general argument connecting them is that the appearance of anthropological thinking actually *symptomatizes* a crisis at several conjunctures, thereby complementing Chamboredon's reconstruction of Durkheim's trajectory leading to *Elementary Forms.*[47] In that account, he considers the multiple historical layers contributing to the development of Durkheim's problematic and rethinks the question of periodization—how a set of dates or a psychologically determined repression can affect the outcome of a reading. The screen model examines how one mode of discourse or academic reference, such as history, is enlisted to mediate the presentation of a contemporary social issue subject to censorship, whether institutional, psychic, or strategic. Chamboredon does not privilege the ethnographic reference in comparison with others found in the Durkheimian oeuvre. But the screen approach bolsters Bourdieu's contention that from its very inception sociology had to mask its social and political critiques under the cover of a scientific discipline.[48] Following his reexamination of Durkheim's successive proposals and projections regarding the purview of sociology, Chamboredon concurs with other readings: "When one orders these diverse texts sequentially, one is struck by the progressive disappearance of politics."[49] The basis for his conclusion is the absence of any formal analysis of the state, although Durkheim eventually explores the possibility of reinvesting the central government with moral authority. As will be argued here, the screen model recognizes that Durkheim's resistance to explicit political solutions such as socialism does not signal their abandonment since they reappear under the rubric of the sacred.

To complete his evaluation, Chamboredon suggests that a political rereading of Durkheim must take into consideration the oblique social critiques that accompany the statistical analyses of *Suicide,* thereby enlisting a close textual reading method traditionally reserved for literary criticism. While deploring the restrictions imposed upon the social scientist, he encourages the intervention of studies such as this one, whose basic premise is that sacred sociology leads to the production of a discourse that defies existing disciplinary boundaries. Chamboredon also argues that the contributions of the Collège can be viewed as adding a new historical stratum to the sociological problematic regarding the collective basis of social life Durkheim formulated in response to the crises of the 1890s, themselves a distant reverberation of the events of 1789.

Consonant with Bataille's position that it neither be respectfully relegated to antiquity nor disdainfully reserved for primitives, the sacred envisioned as a violently disruptive force of heterogeneous attraction serves as basis for the critique of the allegedly contractual foundations of modern society and politics. In the same way the centrality of the sacred serviced Durkheimian sociology at the turn of the century for its own repudiation of Spencer, so sacred sociology would be enlisted by the Collegians who witnessed the debacle of rational democracy. The political as well as social significance of the ethnographic dimension of *Elementary Forms* constitutes the essential part of chapter 1, "Durkheim's Sociological Revolution." Not all reassessments of the history of anthropology in the service of cultural critique have been as enthusiastic as the call for its revival within the Anglo-American traditions.[50] For George Stocking, the model of otherness as the basis for self-reflection ultimately stymied the development of the study of foreign cultures for their own sake and in their own terms.[51] From France, Tzvetan Todorov's study of anthropological thinking based upon a survey of twelve authors generally respected for their enlightened view of others nonetheless leads to a scathing indictment of their inability to consistently sustain the ideals of *liberté, égalité, fraternité* beyond their own cultural horizon.[52] The problems presented by the ethnographic detour in addressing the nature of modern society are pointed out in chapter 1 and highlight the complexity of Durkheim's relation to a critical discourse that challenged the very criteria for scientific recognition he had himself established.

According to Wolf Lepenies, the discipline of sociology emerged from within the tension between literature (emotion) and science (reason).[53] Durkheim's approach to this classic duality is to assess the respective potential of both domains in furthering his own goal—an awareness of the social. More tendentiously, sociology contested the stranglehold exerted by literary criteria upon all research conducted within the French university. Given the controversies ignited by the new reform movement, Durkheim enlisted the historical screen provided by an overview of pedagogy from antiquity to the early twentieth century. His posthumously published lectures, united under the title *L'évolution pédagogique en France* (1904–5), were often inaccessible in France.

By locating Durkheim's sociological revolution within a counter-discourse to the ideal of civility responsible for affect formation as well as reinforcement of social place, this study claims a connection between works otherwise kept separate by conventional classifications. The social and political ramifications of effervescent transformations according to *Elementary Forms* presented in chapter 1, for instance, are reconsidered in chapter 2 in light of the lectures on the history of pedagogy. The continuity between the two works can be found in Durkheim's examination of the role of *collective representations* in molding the individual's perception of his/her relation to the social whole. H. Stuart Hughes rightly discerned that for Durkheim "the defining characteristics of society were of a subjective order. The *sense* of being a member of a social unit he knew to be the decisive consideration."[54] Consequently, Durkheim shared with other members of the generation of the 1890s, who first examined the connections between individual consciousness and the nature of society, the dilemma of exhausting the mechanistic vocabulary they had inherited from positivism. Durkheim's 1895 revelation regarding the social nature of religion is generally used to explain his transition toward an appreciation of the role of symbols in fulfilling sociology's mission. Missing from this view, however, is the complementarity he perceived between representations and rituals, the latter serving to reinforce the sense of social appurtenance transmitted by more abstract phenomena.

In chapter 2, "Savages in the Sorbonne," the reading of Durkheim directed by the concerns and critiques of the Collège argues that *Elementary Forms* provided ethnographic representations of rituals that enhanced the conscious awareness within individuals of their intrinsic duality as social beings. That function of collective representations is contrasted with the effects of literary images and models exerted by the neoclassical literary culture, whose monopoly within the education system was denounced in Durkheim's overview of pedagogical practices. There he traces the demise of medieval effervescence stimulated by scholasticism to the rise of a lettered society in the sixteenth century, when civility became the distinguishing feature of the comportment and worldview of the affluent bourgeoisie. The perspective borrowed from Elias's study of the political usage of the civilizing process is subsumed within Durkheim's own attacks against the long-standing effects of the privileged position granted to belles-lettrism within French culture. Durkheim's positions are contextualized in relation to the reforms introduced by his colleague in literary history, Gustave Lanson, whom he had invited to address students of sociology. As allies within the new Sorbonne movement, Durkheim and Lanson incurred rightwing attacks against their democratizing reforms. Especially virulent was the campaign against "savages in the Sorbonne" mounted by two young pamphleteers under the pseudonym Agathon. The problematic status of literature in relation to ethnographic representations points to the missing term of literature in Wahl's recapitulation of the trajectory common to Collège contributors. The preceding discussion helps to respond to the second part of Wahl's inquiry regarding the generational nature of sociology's appeal. Agathon's rejection of sociology—especially its ethnographic dimension—is contrasted with sociology's popularity by examining the critical positions fostered by the new social science. The institutional and political confrontations between literature and the social sciences in the first decades of the twentieth century provide the background to sociology's complex fate following Durkheim's death in 1917, when the master's work underwent a variety of transformations that are examined in the concluding section to chapter 2. The contest between the humanities and social sciences questions the authority of any one group or institution to monopolize representation of the social as well as dictate pedagogical practices that form the Western equivalent to archaic rituals. At stake in the outcome is which social agency will exert moral leadership over a nation in transition.

Chapter 3, "Politics and the Sacred in the Collège de Sociologie," begins with a survey of the common themes and concerns within this heterogeneous and often fractious group. The next subsection traces a political reading of Bataille's texts prior to and including those delivered to the Collège. The main innovation here is to demonstrate the consequences of the analysis of the sacred for an appreciation of the ways in which effervescent energies are appropriated and concentrated in certain milieus, social spaces, or figures, rather than being directed toward revolutionary movements. "The Politics of Effervescence" examines sacred sociology's view of the transformative effects of effervescence against the dominant models of collective experience according to the crowd psychology inherited from LeBon and Freud. The goal of this section is to explore the political consequences of the Collège's view of the sacred/profane dualism in terms of transgression rather than simple opposition or contrast. The concluding section to the discussion of the Collège texts, "Politics and Politeness," traces the elitist positions set forth in Caillois's "Winter Wind" to the Dandy, and before, to the ideal of civility. Caillois's model of sursocialization is then compared to passages in Mauss regarding the type of habitus needed for the emergence of "men of the elite." The social and political implications of these positions from Mauss—an activist for socialist causes—

are explained by sociology's need to reconsider its privileging of the collective when confronted with fascist rallies and right-wing violence. The demise of the Collège, due in part to internal rifts between Caillois and Bataille, is exacerbated by Leiris's reservations concerning Bataille's concept of the sacred. The transition to the next chapter is bridged by the revised definition of the sacred as communication and what that entails for the role of literature in relation to the sacred.

In chapter 4, "Sacrifice in Art and Eroticism," the foremost contribution to existing scholarship is to examine the relation between sacrifice and the sacred, especially as conceived by Bataille in his writings on art and eroticism. The discussion begins by taking up the view that the sacred is resistant to representation and then considers the transcription of contact with the sacred Leiris provides in his African journal. Those entries are then compared with his texts on the sacred and everyday life in his address to the Collège, as well as with texts found in *Documents,* a review Bataille edited between 1929 and 1931. A section entitled "Art's Secret" covers Bataille's writings on Lascaux, Manet, and various essays written primarily for *Critique* in the postwar period. "Eroticism and Communication" considers Bataille's texts on the subject, but always from the ethnographic point of view, since the goal is to explain his insistence upon the continued need for interdictions as a social means for gaining access to areas of experience that would remain impossible or prove fatal if pursued in isolation. To complement this sociological perspective, I have included a comparison with both Durkheim and Mauss on the obligatory expression of sentiments, including the violent mourning rituals found in *Elementary Forms*. The conclusion effects a synthesis between the two major topics of art and eroticism via Bataille's posthumously published *Les Larmes d'Eros*.

A postscriptum covering the period from 1945 to the present serves as a general overview and conclusion. The emergence of social movements characterized by effervescence in many major industrialized nations during the 1960s challenged its stigmatization through association with fascism. Such eruptions call for a reconsideration of the centrality of effervescence within the French sociological tradition distinct from the ideological agendas of earlier assessments. The opening argument to this section questions the disciplinary displacement of the sacred from sociology onto anthropology, a move that effectively undermines the importance of social effervescence within modern social formations. The alternative proposed here is to vindicate sacred sociology by means of the example of May '68 and its legacy for social action in France to the present. A summary of the socio-logic inherent to the sacrificial sacred according to Durkheim and Bataille testifies to the viability of a critical discourse with continued relevance for art and eroticism, as well as for politics and social relations.

One

Durkheim's Sociological Revolution

Midway through *The Elementary Forms of Religious Life* Emile Durkheim illustrates the opposition between the sacred and the profane by evoking its particularly violent dramatization among Australian aboriginals. Periodically, clans are called together to celebrate a snake or fire ceremony, so that the dull and torpid existence of the dispersed phase of social life is transformed into a concentrated exaltation of collective energies. The exceptional intensity of generalized effervescence fosters among participants the sense of having reached a qualitatively different order of being: individuals feel, think, and behave in new and unpredictable ways, so much so that for the "new being"

> The decorations with which he is decked out, and the masklike decorations that cover his face, represent this inward transformation even more than they help bring it about. And because his companions feel transformed in the same way at the same moment, and express this feeling by their shouts, movements, and bearing, it is as if he was in reality transported into a special world entirely different from the one in which he ordinarily lives, a special world inhabited by exceptionally intense forces that invade and transform him.[1]

How, questions Durkheim, when experiences like these are repeated day after day, for weeks at a time, could one avoid concluding that the universe is divided into two heterogeneous, mutually incompatible worlds: "In one world he languidly carries on his daily life; the other is one that he cannot enter without abruptly entering into relations with extraordinary powers that excite him to the point of frenzy. The first is the profane world and the second, the world of sacred things" (220).

Such Dionysian verve from the founder of modern French sociology—stereotypically viewed as the staid bourgeois moralist of Third Republic ideology—could not fail to surprise supporters as well as detractors.[2] Durkheim was fifty-four and at the apex of his career when *Elementary Forms* appeared in 1912. A decade earlier, his appointment to the Sorbonne had provoked hostility from the prominent writers Charles Péguy, Romain Rolland, and Daniel Halévy, whose primary allegiance was to Henri Bergson, Durkheim's intellectual nemesis. Vociferous opposition to Durkheim was expressed as well by philosophers and Catholic priests. Despite substantial political differences, sociology's adversaries were united in a common concern that its aggressive combination of rationalism and positivism would be particularly hostile to the spiritual revival they sought to foster in the closing years of the century. In the wake of demoralization from the 1870 defeat, the repression of the Commune, and the dramatic polarizations crystallized during the Dreyfus Affair, advocates for social reunification through spiritual means would perceive Durkheim's positions as anathema. In his turn, Durkheim targeted the spiritualism and esotericism in vogue at the Sorbonne, which was associated with renewed interest in the work of Victor Cousin. Religion, a central research area for sociology during the Paris years, certainly seemed to exemplify the irrationalism to which social science provided a corrective. A Dreyfusard, Durkheim dedicated his teaching to encouraging social solidarity through the transmission of a lay morality that his enemies derided as "dogmatic secular religion."[3]

A six-hundred-page treatise on the religious practices of Australian aborigines by this devoted servant of the secular state was therefore received with as much consternation as praise, despite the fact that the "recovery of the sacred" had been a unique feature of sociology since its inception as a discipline in the early nineteenth century.[4] The motives for Durkheim's shift from the social issues of labor and suicide in his early writings to the ethnographic study of religion nonetheless continued to exercise scholarly speculation, as signaled by one sociologist's recent query: "Why did this highly rational, secular, positivistic Frenchman decide sometime after 1895 to devote nearly fifteen of the most productive years of his life to the exotic cults, dancing, and blood-letting of a primitive people?"[5]

The 1895 watershed refers to Durkheim's self-described "revelation" of the social foundations of religion—an autobiographical statement often invoked to explain the reorientation leading to *Elementary Forms*. The new perspective provided by readings in the history of religion—Robertson Smith among others—is not only credited with marking "a dividing line in the development of my thought," but was so revolutionary "that all my previous researches had to be taken up afresh in order to harmonize with these new insights."[6] Because the manuscripts of the course were never found, scholars can only speculate as to those elements of Smith's study of ancient Semitic religions most likely to have had an impact on Durkheim's rethinking of religion in relation to the social.[7] Another rare personal observation, however, indicates the strong feelings associated with the recent discovery and announces the global claims that would subsequently be made for the social consequences of religion:

> Religion contains in itself from the very beginning, even in an indistinct state, all the elements which in dissociating themselves from it, articulating themselves, and combining with one another in a thousand ways, have given rise to the various manifestations of collective life. From myths and legends have issued forth science and poetry; from religious ornamentation and cult ceremonials have come the plastic arts; from ritual practice was born law and morals.[8]

Yet this capacious definition fails to gauge the revolution in Durkheim's thinking effected since his early vituperations against the repressive nature of archaic religion. With a vehemence capable of fueling his critics' worst suspicions, he forwarded positions consistent with those of the *philosophes*, for whom institutionalized religion was regarded as the requisite external authority for the internalization of mores within the individual conscience. Durkheim's reasoning at that time could be imputed to a rejection of mechanical solidarity fostered by repressive religious practices in segmental societies, where an equally unchallenged *conscience collective* stymies the development of free thought. In the 1899 statement, earlier religious practices are not so much endorsed on their own terms as considered an important methodological tool, because

[o]ne cannot understand our perception of the world, our philosophical conceptions of the soul, of immortality, of life, if one does not know the religious beliefs which are their primordial forms. Kinship started out as an essentially religious tie; punishment, contract, gift and homage are transformations of expiatory, contractual, communal, honorary sacrifices and so on. At most one may ask whether economic organization is an exception and derives from another source; although we do not think so, we grant that the question must be kept in abeyance. (237)

Durkheim's position further complicates the French school's methodological strategy of examining institutions through their earliest forms with the claim that "a great number of problems *change their aspects completely* as soon as their connections with the sociology of religion are recognized" (237). The introduction to *Elementary Forms* is yet more precise regarding the implications of this new orientation since it declares that by means of the study of the religious practices of one of the most primitive societies on ethnographic record, sociology is capable of addressing a problem of continued relevance.

With its assertion that sociology's study of archaic religion is essential to an understanding of the present, *Elementary Forms* exemplifies the French tradition of a critical discourse that refracts contemporary issues through the lens provided by the practices of other cultures. Following his nearly fifteen-year intellectual sojourn among Australian aborigines, Durkheim revitalized on a grand scale the French tradition of *anthropological thinking* Lévi-Strauss first credits to Montaigne. For both, other cultures furnished a screen for their respective fusions of analysis with moral fervor, especially evident in the descriptions of effervescent assemblies punctuating the scholarly exposition of the *Elementary Forms* in a pattern mimetic of the alternation between profane dispersion and sacred concentration organizing aboriginal social life. By means of his engagement with ethnographic material his source—Spencer and Gillen—had relegated to the "wild and savage,"[9] Durkheim extended the conventional boundaries of scholarly prose to reveal the underlying commitments as well as possibilities of his sociological revolution. Consistent with sociology's view that the collective offers possibilities otherwise inaccessible to the individual as well as providing the basis for social cohesion, Durkheim argues that effervescent assemblies are the matrix from which all social forms emerge. He even claims that the idea of religion itself evolves from them. In the course of rituals, the moral sense is heightened and collective representations generated. Conventionally termed ideal, this plane of reality is nonetheless credited with stimulating new and unforeseeable actions.

In keeping with my general argument that recourse to the ethnographic detour signals a crisis in the existing disciplinary/discursive configuration, this chapter demonstrates why and how representations of effervescence and its transformative effects within collective experiences—especially those elementary religious practices presented as the foremost instantiation of the sacred—resolve dilemmas announced in Durkheim's earliest writings. Durkheim's readers recognize that his emphasis upon collective representations signals sociology's appreciation of the ways in which individuals are attached to their society and the contribution of symbolic systems to the consolidation of that bond. Yet none has systematically explored the importance of moments of intensified social interaction within the development of Durkheim's work from the early texts to *Elementary Forms*. One may indeed ask, What it is that occurs within those exceptional periods of heightened sociality externally identified by their particular atmosphere, which Mauss would also describe as effervescent? Can sociology account for the effects of such intensified contact in a way that convincingly justifies the extraordinary claims Durkheim makes for their results, especially in comparison with the inflammatory portrayal of collective action disseminated by the contemporaneous crowd psychologies?

The citation from *Elementary Forms* opening this chapter guides our overview of the Durkheimian oeuvre because it (1) condenses the multiple dimensions of the sociological problematic by first representing the transformative experience induced within the collective rituals or social practices and (2) demonstrates how the morphological opposition between the sacred and profane phases of social life structures the conditions of possibility for such inner transformations to occur. In order to provide this overview, we have highlighted nodal points of tension signaling the questions raised by sociology but whose resolution challenged the discipline's existing parameters. The purpose of this demonstration is to explore the connection between effervescent transformations and the possibility for innovative political and social movements.

Sacred versus Profane

Durkheim's general predilection for expressing broad social issues in dualistic terms does not prepare the reader for the exceptional status granted to the opposition between the sacred and the profane in *Elementary Forms*. Whereas earlier antinomies were often demonstrated to be more apparent than real, this last work traces the identity of religious phenomena to the universal antithesis qualified as no less than absolute and unique: "In the history of human thought, there is no other example of two categories of things as profoundly differentiated or as radically opposed to one another" (36). The language of superlatives is reserved for the opposition, which functions as a comprehensive classificatory scheme extending beyond thought and experience to objects and persons:

> The traditional opposition between good and evil is nothing beside this one. Good and evil are two opposed species of the same genus, namely morals. . . . [B]y contrast, the sacred and the profane are always and everywhere conceived by the human intellect as separate genera, as two worlds with nothing in common. The energies at play in one are not merely those encountered in the other, . . . they are different in kind.[10]

Passage between the two states is possible, but the magnitude of the metamorphosis required to do so is indicative of the heterogeneity separating them. The well-known initiation ceremonies entailing symbolic death and resurrection further corroborate claims for the division between what are virtually two worlds. Such intense differentiation can even degenerate into overt hostility and prompt extreme withdrawal from the profane, leading to the kinds of religious suicide associated with asceticism. Beliefs and rites are directed at establishing and maintaining the distinction, so that the sacred basis for religion is defined this way: "*A religion is a unified system of beliefs and practices relative to sacred things, that is to say, things set apart and forbidden—beliefs and practices which unite into one single moral community called a Church, all those who adhere to them*" (44).

Already in Marcel Mauss's 1906 study (written with the assistance of Beuchat) of seasonal variations among the Eskimos, substantial evidence indicated that the sacred/profane duality corresponds to a universal distinction formalized by every culture between the need for moments of production and expenditure, taboo and transgression, euphoria and dysphoria.[11] The Eskimos, however, offer what is undoubtedly one of the most elaborate versions of the social alternation, since the differentiation between winter and summer is marked upon virtually every detail of material, religious, mental, sexual, individual as well as collective life: names are changed, laws are modified, houses are switched, spouses are swapped, kinship is restructured. Families dispersed during one phase of the cycle into small groups of hunters and gatherers loosely allied by clan affiliations are melded into a community during the other. The long winter months, with everyone housed in common and personalities fused in sexual communion, immerse the Eskimos in sacred festivities rarely sustained in other cultures for such a duration. Despite the correlation between the two social modalities and the seasonal shifts that mark them, Mauss notes that the social pattern is not determined by natural causes. When natives are removed from their initial habitat to areas in which the seasons are not nearly as evident, they nonetheless continue to reproduce the same organizational structure. He is then able to claim that this fact constitutes a scientific demonstration comparable to those of the natural sciences, and thereby conclude that social laws exist at an unconscious level, break with biological or environmental factors, and correspond to universal structures.

By integrating a dimension of concentrated social life into its general cycle so dramatically distinct from the normal realm of activities, the archaic contrast between the sacred and the profane furnished a model of the structural conditions of possibility vital to a delineation of the sui generis nature of the *social*. Indeed, sociology's first scientific requirement was to demonstrate the existence of social "facts" or phenomena as determinants of behavior, feelings, and thought the individual could neither experience nor possess outside of a social formation. But the discipline's claim to legitimacy based upon the externality of the social also burdened it with the paradox of having to prove to individuals the elusive forces acting upon them. From the polemical tone of the second preface to the *Rules of Sociological Method*, the reader infers that the objective nature of social facts as external to and independent of the individual consciousness is the point of greatest resistance the author had to overcome.[12] Consequently, Durkheim escalated his insistence upon the quasi-tangible effects of social phenomena and describes them as currents that he categorizes according to degree of concentration. His elaborate architectonic ranges from the most basic cultural conditioning responsible for the habits or second nature produced in every socialized being from birth, to the unpredictable eruptions of collective energy fostering actions so "unnatural" they may even be repudiated once the exaltation has abated. Between these extremes, the foundation for collective life is constituted through language and economics, indisputably collective social institutions whose totality defies the grasp or modification of any one individual:

> The system of signs that I use to express my thoughts, the monetary system that I employ to pay my debts, the credit system that I utilize in commercial relations, the practices followed in my profession, etc. function independently of the uses to which I put them. . . . Here are ways of thinking, behaving, and feeling that offer the remarkable property of existing independently of the individual conscience.[13]

Despite the ubiquity of the social, its collective origins are not easily understood:

> We speak a language we did not create; we use instruments we did not invent; we claim rights we did not establish; each generation inherits a treasury of knowledge that it did not itself amass; and so on. We owe these various benefits of civilization to society, and although in general we do not see where they come from, we know at least that they are not of our own making.[14]

Equally elusive are the free-floating currents of social life that find expression in assemblies where enthusiasm, indignation, and pity overcome the group without emanating from any one identifiable source: "They come to each one of us from without and are capable of sweeping us along in spite of ourselves." The objective reality of such emotions is confirmed by the resistance mounted against efforts to defy them. Yet the majority of individuals remain unaware of the source of the groundswell even as it is taking hold: "We are dupes of the illusion leading us to believe that we ourselves elaborated what was imposed from without."[15]

Further confirmation that the actions generated by the group are incomparable to any experienced in isolation resides in the disconcerting sense of estrangement experienced once the collectivity has disbanded. In good deeds as well as bad, individuals are led to behave in ways that are at odds with their habitual responses.[16] Moreover, the primacy of the social extends into areas often thought to be safeguarded by the individual as the domain of the particular and private. This assessment of contemporary social practices prompted Mauss to assert,

> Even feelings which appear to be completely spontaneous, such as the love of work, of saving and of luxury, are in reality the product of a social culture, since they are lacking among certain peoples and vary greatly within the same group, according to different social strata.[17]

As collective habits became the central object of sociological investigation, the discipline had to venture into the realm of opinion as well as consider the role of collective representations in their transmission.[18] Credited with a causal function, the common substrate constitutes the intimate basis of social life. Until the advent of sociology, the specificity of a culture was determined by its national spirit or "Geist." What Durkheim calls the *particulier* of a society would henceforth be investigated at the level of the group, and by means of the representations it produces of itself.

But the sociological enterprise can succeed only if it integrates a critical dimension: that is, a scientific accounting of the social basis of identity otherwise occulted by popular "prenotions" reinforced by vulgar opinion and even by philosophy and literature. At the time of *The Division of Labor in Society* (1893), the challenge was considered this way: on one hand, the division of labor had succeeded in liberating individual *conscience* from the *collective conscience,* impeding the full efflorescence of independent speculation. The following passage from the conclusion underscores the process of emancipation:

> The effacement of the segmental type, at the same time that it necessitates a very great specialization, partially lifts the individual conscience from the organic environment which supports it, as from the social environment which envelops it, and, accordingly, because of this double emancipation, the individual becomes more of an independent factor in his own conduct. The division of labor itself contributes to this enfranchisement, for individual natures, while specializing, become more complex, and by that are in part freed from collective action and hereditary influences which can only enforce themselves upon simple, general things.[19]

The individual mind, however, does not necessarily develop the self-reflexive stance needed to appreciate the social sources of actions and ideas so conditioned as to appear to be the spontaneous emanation of individual will and thought. With this arrogation of "unlimited

powers," the anthropocentric modern individual denies the very existence of social phenomena beyond his or her control and is therefore
doubly condemned, Durkheim claims, to their influence. Because the
modern corporate state is also remiss in fostering ceremonies needed
to ritualize the collective origins of civilization, sociology alone reveals
the effects of the social unconscious.

Responses to the challenge presented by social phenomena independent of the individual's *conscience* became central to the aims of
a discipline eager to formalize its scientific basis while also exerting a
moral influence. The convergence of these ambitions appeared in the
earliest works in speculations regarding the impact of the new division
of labor upon the individual *conscience,* an especially fortuitous term
for the sociologist since in French it conveys both morality and conscious awareness. In the Durkheimian lexicon, consciousness signals
recognition of the primacy of the social as well as connoting the process
whereby an individual repudiates the prenotions and collective representations reinforcing the distorted perception that identity, thought,
and values can exist independently of the collectivity. Frequent references to *conscience* can be traced to its modification into a *conscience
collective* and, more fruitfully, to the issue of representations, in order
to demonstrate that it cannot be equated with, nor interpreted as, the
Cartesian cogito extended to the collectivity.[20]

A better appreciation of the complexities entailed by the notion of
conscience in Durkheim's work can be attained by examining the possible institutions and/or social agencies that sociology explored as capable
of stimulating recognition of the social within the inner *conscience*—
whether the division of labor, corporations, the state, schooling, the
religio-sacred, or the sociologist as moralist. Assessment of the potential efficacy of each is gauged in terms of the representations with
which they are associated or can foster. Militating against the sociological perspective are representations of the individual as *homo clausus*
inherited from philosophy, or the model of *homo duplex* promoting a
representation of individuals torn between the conflicting demands of
a sensuous egotistical body and collective moral soul. Without denying
the reality of such a tension, Durkheim pursued a variety of paths to
examine how an awareness of the social unconscious—especially one
that would demonstrate its benefits as well as requirements—could be
instilled within the individual conscious mind. These reflections are
interwoven throughout his early work and cannot be isolated either

thematically or chronologically, but will be examined here in relation to the possibilities presented by the ethnographic detour of *Elementary Forms*.

Accompanying reflections in even the first texts regarding the potential role of various structures as well as agencies to instill a sense of the social are striking expressions of enthusiasm for the sui generis quality of collective interaction. Thus, the 1897 study of suicide examined the relevance of corporate models derived from classical and medieval studies.[21] Banished officially by the decrees of 1789, the corporatist vestiges of the feudal period had already begun to die of their own inadequacies by the end of the eighteenth century. Yet the strong guild tradition, and the renewed call for their revitalization throughout modern Europe, indicate that they undoubtedly fulfilled a function still relevant to the nineteenth century. At several points Durkheim eloquently describes the sense of community he believes flows spontaneously from the sustained contact among coworkers. The Roman model of corporations, for instance, whose religious origins endowed each member with a god, temple, common cult, banquets, and cemetery, reinforced his contention that occupational groups can and must foster a sense of solidarity. Optimism appears further justified because he deems it virtually impossible for men to be associated in work "without acquiring a sentiment of the whole formed by their union, without attaching themselves with its interests, and taking account of it in their conduct."[22]

But Durkheim's sanguine conviction that the division of labor could foster the requisite awareness of the social as a network of interdependent individuals is seriously threatened by another correlative to the fragmentation of professional life—the diminished quality of representations related to cohesiveness. Precisely at a moment when their social contribution had become most urgent, he notes that "[i]t is, indeed, remarkable that *the only collective sentiments that have become more intense are those which have for their object, not social affairs, but the individual.*"[23] This recognition of the congruence between the effects of (possessive) individualism and the nature of *représentations collectives* marks yet another phase in the determination of the sociological problematic: For even if sociological doctrine ascertains the existence of social facts or forces external to and independent of the individual; or, assuming it can demonstrate that the individual is always already part of a social group from which he or she evolves a personal identity, such assertions are relatively ineffectual against the stronger reality of daily life as experienced in individual—and, in modern times, individualistic—terms. Durkheim eschews explanations derived from psychology (i.e., egotism) or an ideology of false consciousness (Marxism), and instead attributes the imbalance to the relative weakness of social representations and practices: "With the exception of outstanding moments, society exists in us in a state of abstract representation, whereas individual forces are concretely felt."[24] The rare moments of exceptional intensity in question refer to instances of spontaneous effervescence or ritualized assemblies capable of furnishing the individual with incontrovertible evidence of the duality of human nature as well as existence, of being both self and other, social as well as individual: "By compressing itself almost entirely into circumscribed periods, collective life could attain its maximum intensity and power, thereby giving man a more vivid sense of the twofold existence he leads and the twofold nature in which he participates" (221).

Durkheim's rhetorical question cited at the outset to this discussion regarding the indigenous experience and its representation of the heterogeneity separating the sacred from the profane must therefore be recognized as a query subtending the sociological perspective: how is it that all cultures have given expression to a universal belief in the duality of human existence, a bifurcation mirrored within the *inner conscience* as well? The very doubleness of religious forces as they have appeared throughout history explains their function as the fountainhead from which all the major elements of civilization have been elaborated. Religion thus proved to be an invaluable resource to the sociologist since the sacred/profane opposition is one of the rare cultural forms to acknowledge and to maintain the fundamental duality in its most intense degree. Religious forces crystallize a tension Durkheim would ultimately seek to formulate in exclusively sociological terms by transferring what he considered the most important discovery of *Elementary Forms*—the "dynamogenic" nature of religion—onto society defined as a system of active forces. But first sociology had to reopen the discussion of the duality on which philosophy had imposed closure when it inscribed the pair within invidious, hierarchical oppositions privileging spirit over matter or mind over body. The two sides of human nature had always been presented so that one dimension was elevated at the expense of the other. Historically, the social side appeared in terms reminiscent of Durkheim's early portrait of religion, as subservient to the common good for which sacrifices were exacted.

This dominant or spontaneous representation in the Althusserian sense of society as a primarily, if not exclusively, exigent force, was addressed in *The Division of Labor*'s description of the medieval corporation, where it is claimed that rites and rituals celebrated a sense of solidarity at the conclusion of work.[25] But just as modern banquets serve a role beyond compensation for the coercion exerted by collective life, so the sacrifices society exacts are relatively minor when compared with the "pain and disorder produced whenever inter-individual relations are not submitted to some regulatory influence."[26] Submission to constraint eventually cedes to the individual's need to surpass himself, for as he learns the charm of this new life, he contracts the

> need for it, and there is no order of activity in which he does not seek it passionately. That is why when individuals who are found to have common interests associate, it is not only to defend these interests, it is to associate, that is, not to feel lost among adversaries, to have the pleasure of communing, to make one out of many, which is to say, finally, to lead the same moral life together.[27]

Regardless of its initial association with the corporation, religion appears destined to play a reduced role in comparison with the occupational group. Not only by dint of work's material benefits, but because one's occupation affects morale as well as mores: "A group is not only a moral authority which dominates the life of its members; it is also a source of life *sui generis*. From it comes a warmth which animates its members, making them intensely human, destroying their egotism."[28]

The 1902 preface to the second edition of *Division of Labor* reasserted the possibility that occupational groups will again play the role of moral exemplars mediating between the ever more powerful state and the dispersed energies of unaffiliated individuals. In this context, Durkheim envisions the sociologist as both diagnostician and social engineer called upon to auscultate the sick body social and to prescribe remedies, even if a single cure eludes him.[29] Whether religion is destined to disappear altogether or remain stabilized in a secondary role to work and science is unclear. Equally vague is Durkheim's indictment of social injustice, but his passions are clearly ignited as he describes the warmth, good spirits, and even intimacy prevalent within small groups whose members initially banded together through common interests, and who ultimately transcend themselves by means of sacrifices for the general good. From the assessment of modern social ills one certainty emerges: that beyond the isolated individual lies the possibility for a sui generis social realm, constituted by the collective energies and shared consciousnesses with and among others. Thus, greater independence for local groups and a concomitant reduction of state power are advocated, even though the only really useful change is one that would simultaneously produce a concentration of social energies. Durkheim favors occupational decentralization under the auspices of reconstituted corporations, despite the fact that their modern format makes it difficult to envisage such loosely bound clusters of rivalrous individuals "elevated to the dignity of moral powers."[30] Society is qualified as *moral* not because it dictates rules and values, but because it succeeds in demonstrating that interdependent relationships are mutually beneficial. Most elusive and least appreciated is that society can be a source of joy.

It is now possible to appreciate the relationship between Durkheim's early texts and *Elementary Forms* regarding the type of social organization most likely to maximize social solidarity. In that final work, the alternating rhythm of sacred versus profane social phases documented among Australian aboriginals further bolstered Mauss's contention that the seasonal morphology of Eskimos instantiated a fundamental law of social organization. This model therefore provokes a significant modification to the earlier developmental one proposed in *Division of Labor*, when organic solidarity was claimed superior to mechanical because it emanates from "a system of different, special functions which definite relations unite."[31] Instead of conceiving the relation between mechanical and organic as one of progression, the concentrated/dispersed forms of social life subsumed within the sacred/profane duality is now recognized as *a pattern that encompasses both within the same culture.*

The conclusion to draw from such a claim is that the heterogeneous realities of the sacred and the profane are complementary, each necessary but not sufficient. The fact that the distinct states of being to which they correspond must coexist rather than supersede each other is indeed consistent with Durkheim's contention that religion responds to permanent needs; therefore, the construction of social reality through the contrastive organization between the sacred and the profane must perdure even in modern society. As noted by James Boon, the Australian tribes were exemplary in a peculiar way, since "they revealed an irreducible basis of solidarity among divisions and thus illuminated the sort of integration that France and modern Europe had lost."[32] The social model of the aborigines satisfies the dialectic between similarity and difference discerned as the basis of all social life, since the ceremony recounted at the outset of this chapter unites members of different clans, and the ritual initially acts out an armed conflict resolved through a generalized exaltation. With its unqualified enthusiasm for collective experience, *Elementary Forms* radically revised the standard account and perception of the duality conventionally postulated as an insuperable conflict between individual and society. The ethnographic examples provided by aboriginal practices serviced sociology's revolution by demonstrating the possibility of meshing the duality of being both self and other, individual and social, with the rhythm of social morphology.

Following both *Division of Labor* and *Suicide,* explicit reference to the mechanical/organic distinction virtually disappeared from the Durkheimian repertoire. Thus, when weighing their impact upon the subsequent development of Durkheim's theoretical prescriptions, critics have been divided in regard to the relative significance of the mechanical/organic typology. For instance, Durkheim eloquently describes at several points the sense of community he believed would flow spontaneously from the sustained contact among coworkers. He also underscores that the full advantages of the division of labor could emerge only from within a common social context. Nisbet qualified this assertion as a turning point in Durkheim's ongoing rebuttal to Spencer's contractual model, since it is here that he explicitly posits the primacy of the social in relation to any personal modifications or specialization it may subsequently undergo—an argument clearly stated in his thesis when he opposed social philosophers "who believe they have grounded society in nature when they have shown that men manifest a vague sympathy for other men and that it is in their interests to exchange services with each other."[33] The tenacity of biases against the collective foundation for individual identity compelled Nisbet in 1966 to restate the Durkheimian position on the social in equally forceful terms:

> What all four works have in common . . . is a social metaphysic and methodology rooted in the conviction that took shape in Durkheim's mind as he wrote *The Division of Labor:* that all human behavior above the level of the strictly physiological must be regarded as either

emanating from, or else sharply conditioned by, society: that is, by the totality of groups, norms, and institutions within which every individual human being consciously and unconsciously exists from the moment of his birth. Social instincts, prepotent complexes, natural sentiments—all of these may indeed exist in man (Durkheim never denied their existence), but viewed against the determinative effects of society on such matters as moral, religious, and social conduct, they are a negligible influence, supplying barely more than an organic base. They are, in any event, impossible to get at—in sociological terms—until all possible consequences of the social have been exhausted. This last point is the major truth so widely overlooked by the individualistic-utilitarian minds of the nineteenth century, as indeed it continues to be overlooked by many even now.[34]

More controversial is Nisbet's further claim that the social in question is constituted through those mechanisms associated with mechanical solidarity:

> [S]ociety—in all its guises, functions and historical roles—becomes for Durkheim, a compound of social and psychological elements that he had first relegated to folk or primitive society. Not only is normal society founded, he would ever after declare, on such traits as collective conscience, moral authority, community, and the sacred, but the only appropriate response to modern conditions is the strengthening of such traits.[35]

Support for this position is garnered from the fact that the very notion of organic disappears from the Durkheimian lexicon in subsequent writings. Regarding these assertions, however, Anthony Giddens retorts, "This is an extraordinary judgment; it is much closer to the truth to say exactly the opposite—that most of the theory established in *The Division of Labour* remained fundamental to the whole of Durkheim's later writings."[36]

What both these positions overlook is that in an unexpected qualification of the evolutionary schema from mechanical to organic, *The Division of Labor* also proposed that "[t]hese two societies really make up only one. They are two aspects of one and the same reality, but none the less they must be distinguished."[37] Explanations for this dramatic modification in Durkheim's thinking can be traced to the importance accorded *secondary groups*—whether spontaneous or intentional—in providing an affective dimension of social bonding. Whereas Nisbet's characterization of the global nature of social determinism is accurate, it must be completed by the role ascribed to group formations or "foyers" fundamental to the realization of the social's potential. Rather than paralyze individuals with evidence of social determinism, the role of sociological intervention would be to accentuate the *possibilities* opened by social forms, especially those collective encounters associated with effervescent moments of intense social creativity and transformation. Early intimations of this position can be found in Durkheim's speculations regarding the effects of the division of labor, valued for its ability to promote a sense of the social whole: "The more we advance, the more societies acquire a profound sense of themselves and of their unity."[38] While the general law may obtain in any group situation, it is particularly apposite to the modern division of labor, where the individual necessarily acquires a sense of place within the greater social configuration:

> This is what gives moral value to the division of labor. Through it, the individual becomes cognizant of his dependence upon society; from it come the forces which keep him in check and restrain him. In short, since the division of labor becomes the chief source of social solidarity, it becomes, at the same time, the foundation of the moral order.[39]

The ascendancy of work over religion appears inevitable, though the most important feature of this example is the nature of group life it proposes. In contrast with the preceding emphasis upon the restraint exerted by the division of labor, other passages offer effusive praise for the benefits of the collectivity, since "[a] group is not only a moral authority which dominates the life of its members; it is also a source of life sui generis. From it comes a warmth which animates its members, making them intensely human, destroying their egotism."[40]

Durkheim suggests that one look not to religion for the experiential source of group affect rediscovered through the corporation, but to the family, where "in the past, as legislator of law and ethics, severity went to extremes of violence, at the same time that it was the place where one first learned to enjoy the effusions of sentiment."[41] The demise of religion is indeed linked to the disappearance of small groups as the fundamental social unit: "Unless the great societies of today helplessly crumble and we return to the little social groups of long ago, that is, unless humanity returns to its starting point, religions will no longer be able to exert very deep or wide sway on consciences."[42] The model of alternation between the sacred and the profane made it possible for

Durkheim to conceptualize a social future in which such groups could exert a critical role without imposing a specifically religious doctrine. Their efficacy, however, derives from the transformations they effect upon the individual's inner *conscience*. Aboriginal ceremonies may provide the exotic trappings of cultural alterity—frenetic dancing, loud music, bizarre cults—but the most exhilarating and radical sense of otherness occurs when individuals are modified by the effects of collective interaction.

Effervescent Transformations

Durkheim considered the sacred's quality of otherness in his earliest reflections upon religion, although he was quick to point out that the characterization did not imply any intrinsic property or transcendent status since sacred significance is added on to persons, places, or things, and sustained by collective belief and ritual. This position is indeed consistent with the fundamental premise dating from the 1895 revelation of the social basis for religion. And in a letter fragment dated 1899 he distinguished religious phenomena from all others according to the social coloration imparted to them. Despite a consensus regarding the sacred status of certain things, the key to religion lies in understanding how they are so designated and appreciated: "Just as we experience things through their colors, etc., so society represents its life and the life of the objects related to it as sacred objects with which it is in relation, as sacred. It colors them with religiosity. Why? the matter is highly debatable!"[43] Religious cults without deities exist, but they all include the special category of sacred phenomena that are identifiable because they are completely distinct *(tout autre)* and irreducible to any others. Religious representations such as myths and dogmas are immediately recognizable since they are the product of collective, sui generis mental states that one would never confuse with the products of individual, private conception.[44]

In the same way that constraint was a characteristic of social facts in the early definitions, so "obligatoriness" is used to distinguish religious phenomena at this stage of analysis. Moreover, in keeping with their imposed status, religious phenomena are given a formal definition reasserting their social origins and establishing consistency with the fundamental Durkheimian postulate that sociology exists because the realm of the social manifests a reality all its own: "Society has its own way of being and, therefore, its own way of thinking. It has passions, habits and needs which are not those of individuals and which place their mark on everything that it conceives."[45]

What this definition fails to clarify is how to distinguish the sacred from the social. Indeed, a critical challenge arises when attempting to establish criteria that would account for the inviolability of certain social beliefs—the French Revolution or Joan of Arc, or even progress. Because they are obligatory and universally held, the sacred status of such ideals places them closer to religion than to law or general morals. A variant of these positions surfaced in Durkheim's earlier discussions of the sacred, since an initiation to sacred things generally coincided with the socialization of the individual who acquired a "new" nature and became a "new" being upon entering the religious life. Whether one can therefore assume a displacement of the religious initiation by a secular *rite de passage* is left open. Less doubtful is the experience of alterity accompanying the sacred, and traceable to "the exceptional intensity of the forces it is supposed to reveal."[46]

Durkheim's gloss on effervescent assemblies further clarifies their relevance to an understanding of the sacred's social function. First, effervescent experience as the source of religion is corroborated by the fact that "what is properly called religious activity in Australia is almost entirely contained within the periods when these gatherings are held" (220). Second, the erroneous assumption that the sacred dominates among the most elementary religious forms is upset by evidence that prayer and ritual occur daily in advanced societies, whereas in the Australian pattern one finds that apart from the celebrations of the clan and tribe, the time is nearly all filled with lay and profane occupations. Most important, the alternation between the sacred and the profane in the social life of the Australians "brings out the link between the two phases. Among the peoples called civilized, on the other hand, the relative continuity between them partially masks their interrelations" (221).

The caveat is necessary because the progressive blurring between the sacred and the profane in the modern world has rendered largely imperceptible the relation between the two extremes. At stake is nothing less than insight into the parallel dualities of human nature and existence. It was therefore imperative that an investigation into the sacred reinstate the stark contrast it offers with the profane—a contrast acutely evident in the elementary form of aboriginal social and religious cycles. Commenting upon the exaggerated intensity of the communal months among the Eskimos, Mauss concluded that the extreme polarization of social life "inflicts a violence upon the individuals' *consciences* that they can sustain for only brief periods, and that a time comes when they are obliged to slow down and partially withdraw."[47] Durkheim retained from this observation that the violence of the polarization is *necessary*, in that it provides a mechanism for dramatizing the difference between the profane and the sacred. This sense of otherness marked by violence becomes internalized when sacred and profane things "form two distinct and separate mental states in our consciousness, just as do the two forms of life to which they correspond" (243). The value of the sacred, then, is to impress upon the inner consciousness a heightened awareness of the social.

This is also the conclusion Henri Hubert and Marcel Mauss reached in their essay on sacrifice as early as 1899.[48] The overarching movement of the authors' review of the institution as well as the anthropological theories seeking to account for it is to shift from purely external considerations of the religious rite—directed to the propitiation of archaic gods—to its intimate penetration of participants. With the retreat of gods in the evolution of society, the role of sacrifice as gift gave birth to sacrificial rites, so that the gift evolved to a form of homage, and from there to a sacrifice carrying the connotations of abnegation and renunciation. Other functions such as the sense of solidarity Robertson Smith ascribed to a communal meal also fell into desuetude. Thus, beyond the impressive complexity of rites and rituals of sacrifice they examined, the authors extricate one dominant role for sacrifice: it is the primary means of communication between the sacred and the profane within the new social space defined according to their opposition.

Several consequences of this assertion require additional clarification. One is that the opposition between the sacred and the profane is permeable. Unlike Durkheim's conception of the dualism as absolute, Hubert and Mauss argue that the structure of sacrifice includes a *mediating* dimension to guarantee passage and/or contact with the divine. Sacrifice itself confers a sacred otherness onto the victim chosen to transmit a sacred element to the profane or the inverse, since "it is indifferent to the direction of the current that moves through it."[49] Enlisted to serve a variety of ends, the sacrificial mediator between the sacred and the profane also acquires autonomy as a sacred foyer or nucleus of energy as a result of the collective forces invested in it. As such, it radiates an aura beyond the immediate goals for which it had been intended, thereby affecting a broad spectrum of social things that derive sacred protection or benefit from it.

But why the elaborate mediations, whether through the form of an animal or human victim? Because the very power of the life force associated with the divine—however beneficial—is so concentrated as to prove fatal. Indeed, for the sacrificer who attempts to follow through the ritual on his or her own, death is a certainty. In light of this ambiguity of the sacred, the sacrificial victim must undergo a process of sacralization in order to serve as conduit between the sacrificer and the divine, even though it is not protected from destruction. In agreement with Durkheim, the authors point out that the sacred is not an intrinsic quality, but the result of the consecration bestowed upon it by the ritual. Among earlier explanations, a common error was to assume the religious nature of a sacrificed object, animal, or person, and to then interpret the significance of the act of sacrifice itself as a modality of propitiation, abnegation, and/or or redemption. For Mauss and Hubert, sacrifice is only one ramification of a more general process of *consecration* whereby arbitrarily designated objects are subjected to a transformation by means of the sanctions or taboos surrounding them. Once labeled sacred and accepted as such by the gods, the victim can serve as substitute for the agent initiating the sacrifice who is thus redeemed.

The sacred/profane social alternation also offered a solution to the need for a sociological position regarding the duality of human nature, a dilemma set forth in 1909. The context for the debate is the ever-present Durkheimian linkage between morality and conscience. Initially, the mystery of human duality—of being both self and other, internally oriented and externally driven—was formulated as a potential conflict between incompatible demands driving divergent forces. In *Division of Labor,* the divided consciousness correlates with two modes of social being ultimately viewed as necessary complements if society is to overcome its crisis of cohesion. Yet in *Suicide,* the pull toward individuality is portrayed as antagonistic to the forces leading to the collective: "One, the collective force, tries to take possession of the individual; the other, the individual force, repulses it."[50] For Durkheim, the very notion of society necessitates a sui generis supra-individual reality: "In this sense, sociology lacks an object, it is an abstract psychology. One must understand that the social is an original synthesis, resulting from the combination of individual consciousnesses."[51] Under reflections regarding the formation of a moral ideal at once distinct from and superior to the individual, he then announces themes that would be central to the study of aboriginal religion: the possibility to explore and to explain the duality of self/other, elevated to the primary object of sociological investigation. Recognized but left unresolved by Kant, and subject to the errors of philosophy as well as early sociology, the *conscience collective* raises the possibility of a synthesis to be distinguished from the average individual.

It is in this context that Durkheim first mentions effervescent assemblies, where the individual is swept away by a collective élan and even the most ordinary citizen becomes capable of extraordinary deeds. Whether the French Revolution, the war of 1870, the Socialist Party, or the Dreyfus Affair, the process entailed is the same: ideals are generated beyond any one conscious mind and fixed by means of special mechanisms, whether emblems, dates (anniversaries), public festivities, or special loci (pilgrimage sites). While ideals may be incarnated in ordinary persons and not only great figures, the foremost social device for their consecration resides with things, so that contact with them maintains the sensation of collective exaltation. The absence of rites and festivals marking the renewal of collective experiences reflects the lack of new ideals in the modern period.

The reading of Durkheim's early work presented thus far has been determined by the perspective on social cohesion provided by the sacred/profane duality and the description of effervescent gatherings that communicate a sense of the sacred's specificity. Such passages in *Elementary Forms* make it possible to argue that reference to Australian aboriginal practices provided the most striking rendition of the sacred experience the sociologist could enlist in defense of the transformative benefits of collective life and, more controversially, of its effervescent quality—"collective thought transforms everything it touches. It fuses natural orders and combines contraries; it reverses what one might regard as the natural hierarchy of being. It eliminates differences and differentiates between what is similar."[52] Vivid descriptions of ebullient aboriginal ceremonies were essential in substantiating Durkheim's final blow at the stereotypical view of the affective basis for religion in fear and trembling or weakness and dependence. Natives are appreciated not as hapless victims of self-induced nightmares, but as artisans who fashion totemic beliefs out of elation. Only later in the evolution of religious thought do the terrible and jealous gods appear. Nor can modern religions provide the requisite alternatives since "[t]hese continue to depict us as tormented and suffering." By contrast, admiration is expressed for the "crude cults" of "inferior" societies, since they alone "breathe forth and inspire joyful confidence."[53]

Illustrations of elementary forms of religious life also encouraged Durkheim to jettison vestiges of his earlier emphasis upon constraint as a defining characteristic of archaic religion and, therefore, of mechanical solidarity. Because the "social soul" consists of a few relatively simple notions and feelings, the individual easily bears it within his *conscience*, so that he is actually following his nature rather than submitting to external coercion. Despite local variations in religious forms and practices, the underlying unity of religious experience resides in the extraordinary élan experienced by the individual. Herein resides the commonality among diverse religious phenomena—the isolated individual is endowed with an added sense of confidence and sometimes even courage, transported by an objectively verifiable surge of force because it is the outcome of a sui generis reality of collective gatherings. The ritualistic aspects of crude cults foreground a fundamental feature of religious life often overlooked or demoted to a secondary status within the modern evolution toward a personalized relation between individuals and their deity. Repetition of rituals constitutes an integral part of religious life by revitalizing the memory of extraordinary sensations:

> In fact, anyone who has truly practiced a religion knows very well that it is the cult which stimulates the feelings of joy, inner peace, serenity, and enthusiasm that, for the faithful, stand as experiential proof of their beliefs. The cult is not merely a system of signs by means of which the faith is outwardly expressed; it is the sum total of means by which that faith is created and recreated periodically. (420)

The relation between representations and rituals depicted in the opening passage to this chapter is indicative of a crucial interaction, since the ideas and images that individuals form of the sacred emanate from the repetition of cries and gestures that eventually lead to a rhythmic chant and harmonized motions. Ceding to the collective movement, participants attain another "level of being" (Lévinas) inseparable from its bodily basis, thereby demonstrating how rituals inculcate an experience of human duality, of being both self and a social other—undoubtedly one of the most fundamental yet intractable dimensions of the sociological project it needed to represent. Here, too, one can discern another dimension of the contribution made by the ethnographic detour to the modern sociological imagination.

Indeed, when considering the relation of *Elementary Forms* to Durkheim's work as a whole, it is possible to argue that its daring representations of effervescent ceremonies and their ritualized reenactments provide a bold and dramatic rendition of the theme of small group warmth and intimacy sketched in the margins of the first social studies. Certainly the language of this last major work offers a concentrated version of the vocabulary of forces and currents deployed throughout the preceding texts. Ostensibly derived from the natural sciences, the imagery seems particularly well suited to the intensity and alterity of effervescence. Steven Lukes nonetheless reproves the "metaphorical and polemical" style as undermining the very scientific pretensions Durkheim sought to legitimate through their use since, he argues, "*Elementary Forms* is not about the impact of collective forces, but about the social origins of beliefs and rituals, the interpretation of their meaning and symbolism, and their consequences for individuals and for society as a whole."[54] By borrowing terminology from the natural sciences and particularly from the new theories of thermodynamics, Durkheim appears to invalidate his claim to be describing the sui generis reality of the social. But we have already seen that there is no qualitative distinction between the sociohistorical instances of creative effervescence and those consecrated as sacred. Lukes's insistence that Durkheim's language is purely metaphorical or analogical robs it of the material impact and transformative jolt Durkheim took as evidence of religion's reality: "This system of conceptions is not purely imaginary and hallucinatory. . . . [T]he moral forces they awaken are quite real. . . . This is the dynamogenic influence that religions have always exercised upon men."[55]

The "moment of conversion" brings to level-of-conscious awareness the otherness that is called sacred resulting from the concentration of *social energies*. Distinct from the productive forces fundamental to Marxist theory, or the sublimated sexual drives of Freudian psychology, social energies constitute the specificity or sui generis object of sociological analysis. One of the most significant revelations of the Australian ceremonies is that the process itself of gathering together induces the unusual intensity of sensations: "The very fact of the concentration acts as an exceptionally powerful stimulant. When they are assembled, a sort of electricity is formed by their collecting which quickly transports them to an extraordinary degree of exaltation."[56] Society, Durkheim argued, can exist only in and through individuals, since it is nothing other than assembled and organized individuals. More problematic is the fact that society "cannot penetrate individual *consciences* without stimulating an entire system of *sui generis* representations that express it, that is to say, without adding to our individual being a new psychic being."[57] These representations induce an altered state of consciousness by means of physical rites and rituals from which their effect is inseparable.

The Ethnographic Detour

Durkheim's explanation for his research shift to the religious practices of one of "the most primitive societies on record" reasserts the sociological revolution's heuristic value: "The most bizarre or barbarous rites and the strangest myths translate some human need and some aspect of life, whether social or individual" (2). Fire ceremonies and snake-worshipping rites dramatize religion's function as a representational system that articulates the relationship of individuals to a greater social body: "[R]eligion is first and foremost a system of ideas by means of which individuals imagine the society of which they are members and the obscure but intimate relations they have with it" (227). Despite its ability to address specific issues, science cannot usurp religion in providing a sense of the totality. Without some representation of the part to the whole, individuals are threatened by anomie and the collectivity risks dissolution. In the absence of periodic renewal of the social covenant, moral values and ideals lose their hold, since they are fundamental to the sense of connectedness, or what Durkheim initially called the individual's *dependence* upon society. Cultures are differentiated by their particular means of envisaging this relationship and the forms they develop to represent it. Within each successive phase of Durkheim's work the contribution of representations to the social as well as psychic realms received greater attention. Initially conceptualized as leading to a *conscience collective*, they evolved from the status of an epiphenomenon of social concentration to being endowed with relative autonomy, capable of influencing and modifying the substrate in which they are grounded. One reason for their growing centrality is that the intensified portrait of socially conditioned ways of being and acting they propose is claimed to be superior to individual states of consciousness, since they concentrate the countless individual representations that contributed to the formation of each of them.

As early as *Les Règles de la méthode sociologique* (1894–95), the notion of representations was enlisted to define sociology in terms of its specific object—the collective forms of social life. The standard "error" of psychology as well as philosophy, however, was to reduce society to a substrate constituted through individuals envisaged *ad seriatum*. And by its second edition (1902), *The Rules of Sociological Method* argues that all of social life is constituted by representations. The status of representations is ambiguous in this initial phase of Durkheim's thinking, given their tendency to mirror the distortions to which all prenotions prior to scientific examination are subject. Although the sociologist may use them to gain access to the *mentalité* of a group or milieu, they are inadequate without an accompanying demonstration of the relation between a particular group's mindset and its social sources. These inadequacies are always described in terms of each profession's partial relation to the social totality: Between 1890 and 1900 lectures posthumously published under the title *Lessons of Sociology,* for instance, restate the need for professional morality to guide the expanded nature of the group with the following rationales: "For as society expands its domain, . . . [t]he individual can embrace but a small portion of the social horizon," or "the more society overpowers the individual, the less his awareness of the social interests it is nonetheless essential for him to take into consideration."[58]

One of the central ideological issues addressed by *Elementary Forms* is the basis for religion's enduring authority within the modern world. For its investigation, *Elementary Forms* proposed an evolutionary perspective by means of the Australian totemic system. Against the animist and naturalist explanations, which refused a religious designation to totemism because it is devoid of reference to human gods or divinities, Durkheim offers the novel reinterpretation that totemism illustrates the most basic yet complete form of religious practice. Because totems meet the criteria for all sacred objects, it was possible to reinscribe them within the vast indigenous cosmology structured along the sacred/profane axis. At the antipodes to Sir James Frazer's propensity to regard religion as intimate and personal, the key to Durkheim's analysis of the totemic principles resides in the notion of force, characterized as an anonymous sensation identified by its exceptional capacity to bolster the individual's ability to confront the adversities of daily life. Subsumed within the indigenous term *mana,* the forces in question are not metaphorical, but appreciated as exerting an undeniable material influence. Imbricated in the religious or sacred dimension is the social role played by the totem as emblem of the clan to which each member pays homage out of respect, not fear. When carrying out obligations to the totem, each individual sustains and consolidates the social bond. The totem itself is first and foremost a name, and as such confers upon the clan a purely social identity irrespective of consanguine filiations. Family ties are replaced by attachments forged through moral obligations. The term *mana* designates the untranslatable power of a force circulating within the group and endowing each individual with supernatural powers.

Force, argued Durkheim, is a notion originating in religion which philosophy and science borrowed. Comte rightly made metaphysics heir to theology, but he erred by concluding that the idea of force was destined to disappear because its mystical origins undermined any claim to objective value. To the contrary, the reality of religious forces is indisputable according to Durkheim, despite the mediocrity of the symbols used to transmit them. As a symbol, the totem is therefore dual, uniting both "force" and "society" in a material form bearing no intrinsic ("natural") relation to its ultimate significance. Whether vegetable or animal, this arbitrary incarnation becomes the material and accessible embodiment of the clan's need to distinguish itself from all others. But if in fact it is the symbol of both god and society, how is it that they are not one? Like a god, society maintains its members in a situation of dependence and, because of its special nature, orients them toward specific goals. Although it occasionally feels like a god of greater strength, society exacts respect and devotion because of its moral superiority.

Durkheim's explanation for the confusion of force, deity, and society within the symbolic totem rests with the native's inability to recognize that transformative forces are actually the product of assemblies of associated individuals, even though he certainly feels himself transported beyond himself to the point of living a life other than his ordinary one. The need to attribute the feeling to some external source explains the prevalence of totems and their sacralization as the visible body of a god. The final answer as to why the clan effects the transfer of collective energies to the totem relies upon earlier critiques Durkheim leveled against the inadequacies of even contemporary morality to communicate a view of the societal ensemble. By contrast, the totemic object functions as metonymic device, as a part substituting for the whole that lies beyond the group's conscious grasp:

> The totem is the flag of the clan, so it is natural that the impressions the clan arouses in individual consciousness—impressions of dependence and of heightened energy—should become more closely attached to the idea of the totem rather than to that of the clan. The clan is too complex a reality for such unformed minds to be able to bring its concrete unity into clear focus. Besides, *the primitive does not see that these impressions come to him from the group.* (222, emphasis added)

Recourse to archaic religious models to illuminate contemporary social problems therefore highlights the following dilemma: Whereas the transformative effects of effervescence are undeniable, *the propensity of the group immersed in their disorienting alterity is to attribute the collective energies generated by their contacts onto an external object or person.* Restricted neither to so-called primitive societies nor to non-Western modes of thought, the phenomenon of displacement is also manifested in modern political life, when individuals feel themselves acted upon by forces whose origins they cannot discern: "But the ordinary observer cannot see where the influence of society comes from. It moves along channels that are too obscure and circuitous, and uses psychic mechanisms that are too complex, to be easily traced to the source" (211). Illustrative of the modern version of such *simplisme* is the sacralization of individuals who have no claim to respect other than the powers invested in them through social consensus: "A clear indication that this apotheosis is the work of society alone is that society has often consecrated men whose personal worth did not warrant it" (215). Even the enigma of sacred things is therefore revealed to be collective ideals that have been affixed to a material object, just as the deification of the individual in Western culture occults the social basis of its identity.

The relevance of the ethnographic detour to the political and social context of *Elementary Forms* can be detected in the illustrations of creative effervescence it provides. It is striking that minimal attention is granted to historical illustrations of creative effervescence, though several appear in the text prior to the examples supplied by religious practices, among them, the famous night of August 4 during the French Revolution, when aristocrats went against their own interests and committed, in Rivarol's well-known phrase, a "Ste Barthelémy des propriétés." In earlier works, such as the study of pedagogy examined in chapter 2, the Carolingian revival and even the Dreyfus Affair are cited as moments when energies united in a common cause overflowed in creative, even sacrificial gestures, because individuals were brought into more intimate relations with one another, meetings and assemblies were more frequent, relationships were consolidated, and the exchange of ideas intensified. The transformations brought on by effervescence are indeed dramatic, as witnessed during the 1789 Revolution, when the most mediocre and inoffensive bourgeois could emerge either a hero or executioner.

It is revealing that Durkheim then slipped from the prototypically social situation to an explanation of how it receives a religious attribution: "And the mental processes are so clearly the same as those at the root of religion that the individuals themselves conceived the pressure they yielded to in explicitly religious terms" (213). Not surprisingly, his main illustrations of the Crusades and Joan of Arc leave open the possibility for an ideological interpretation of both. Given the aggressive Action française campaign to sacralize the maiden of Orleans—including violent attacks against the Sorbonne professor Thalamas for his exclusively historical interpretation of her actions— the examples of naive displacement in totemism previously discussed can now be read as Durkheim's politically motivated tactic to expose the right-wing shift from social causality to a religious origin in his own day. The reading of *Elementary Forms* developed here therefore suggests that Durkheim's work must not be taken so much as a study of religious forms *stricto sensu* as a demonstration of the tendency to mistake social phenomena for religious ones.

It is now also possible to argue that the ethnographic/religious frame itself functioned as a screen for his retort to the critics who denounced his arrival at the Sorbonne a decade earlier in 1902—those intellectual and literary leaders of the Third Republic who were convinced that the regeneration of the socially fragmented order would take place through a spiritual or religious revival of the most traditional sort, thereby placing them at the same level as the indigenous inventors of totemism for whom religion was the solution to the "overly complex" problem of society. The central political lesson of *Elementary Forms* is that social energies will be returned to the collectivity following the demystification of certain opinions, deities, or persons erroneously regarded as the source of well-being society alone provides.

The advent of sociology as a new science of man heralded at the conclusion to *Elementary Forms* signals the need for an innovative discourse that must mediate apparently contradictory requirements, on one side to implement the scientific defetishization of social life, and on the other to preserve the religious function as safeguard of the sacred forces it has historically transmitted through representations and rituals. Unlike Marx before him and Freud after, Durkheim never doubted the reality of religious effects and argued that their moral tonus was incontrovertible. His concern with the basis for religion's continued authority in the modern world must be situated within the broader discussion of whether any other collective representation could compete with—let alone usurp—its moral dominance. *The Elementary Forms of Religious Life* claims that the social exerts its ascendancy through the mental pressure of moral suasion. But in seeking to appropriate for society the authority of other institutions, such as religion, Durkheim also highlighted a strong parallel at the experiential level between religious and social forces. His demystification of projections that occult the social must therefore be distinguished from his recognition of the value of the arbitrary but necessary symbols and representations in which every group concentrates the experience of effervescence as a communicative device. The emblem or totem reawakens those same forces when society guarantees its survival through periodic rites and ceremonies. In a break with the classical mimetic model, representations are ascribed the creative capacity to exert a formative influence upon the mind. What distinguishes one social group from another is the form through which the collectivity sustains and transmits its relation to a distinct, separate, and extraordinary domain designated as sacred.

Durkheim at his most radical reasserted the need for collective life and its transformative consequences because the very possibility of society is contingent upon individuals consolidated through a symbolic system. These claims explain the intensified focus upon symbolic systems and modes of representation in Durkheim's later writings, even though that concentration incurred the criticism that his work progressively abandons its social and political commitments for an anti-materialist idealism.

The position developed here is that this move indicates the sociologist's realization that the political values and socialism he supported could not survive in a democratic system without some effect at the level of inner consciousness, as reflected in the assessments of various potential agencies capable of fulfilling such a role. In *Suicide,* for instance, one finds, "Individuals are made aware of society and of their dependence upon it only through the State."[59] "Moreover, the State is too remote from individuals; its relations with them too external and intermittent to penetrate deeply into individual consciences and socialize them within."[60] With a growing appreciation of its collective basis, religion also received an increasingly positive reassessment, possibly a reflection of the reorientation in his thinking that Durkheim attributes to the 1895 revelation. Erroneously imputed by traditional psychology to individual fears or the "reverence inspired . . . by mysterious and dreaded beings" religion cannot be reduced to individual states of mind. Like law, morals, customs, political institutions, and pedagogical practices, it falls under the purview of collective life examined by sociology. Most important, religion exerts a social function since "[r]eligion is in a word the system of symbols by means of which society becomes conscious of itself; it is the characteristic way of thinking of collective existence."[61]

Whatever the specific agency examined—division of labor, the state, corporations, religio-sacred, or the sociologist as moralist—the importance of its role remains constant. At stake is the fact that with the scientific unmasking of the projective forms of alienation, a *sharper consciousness* will evolve into conscience in the moral sense. The readiness to assume the responsibilities incumbent upon every citizen may not necessarily follow without some positive representation of the individual's relation to the social whole. The complexity of Durkheim's relation to religion—reflected in his study of its abiding authority—resides in his concession that it, more than any other cultural system, has been able to transmit that representation effectively. For this reason, we have attempted to nuance Bernard Lacroix's earlier conclusions that *Elementary Forms* mounted a *machine de guerre* against all religion, in contrast with his indictment of only those that have stifled the collective nature of religious life as socially based integrated experiences. We recall that the earliest texts lament the decline of modern celebratory social events and collective representations that would sustain within the minds of individuals their debt to society while communicating the enhancements unique to the social:

> In general, social things are felt in terms of the moral constraint they exert, as just acknowledged. However, they also possess *another dimension, virtually opposite to that one,* which consists in a comforting and beneficial effect, but which is less appreciated because less obvious and easily discerned. (211 n. 6)

The examples derived from the ethnographic detour allowed Durkheim to approximate a description of the social in which individuals arrive at an appreciation of their mutuality in ways that transcend conventional reciprocity or contractual relations subject to rationalized calculus, thereby acknowledging their dependence upon a social formation to which they owe both the possibilities for self-realization and the accomplishments of civilization. The social enhances the individual's ability to withstand the adversities of everyday life—a moral tonus providing sustenance within the relative isolation characteristic of profane, dissociated individualism. Durkheim's university thesis of 1892 endorsed Rousseau's conceptualization of the collective will precisely because it does not subjugate others to a state of what Durkheim would consider immoral dependence. Talcott Parsons noted in 1937 Durkheim's frequent references to the individual's dependence and distinguished between two analytically different types—economic and emotional—but justified his abandonment of the issue because, he claimed, it ultimately lies at the periphery of Durkheim's systematic theorizing as well as of his own.[62] Yet in lectures of the 1890s, the distinctively sociological notion of a *liberating* dependence appears, a succinct formulation of the shift away from grounding the effect of social structures in constraint to an appreciation of their capacity to induce social creativity as well as cooperation. As an alternative to the individualism that equates wholeness with self-sufficiency, the division of labor is credited with enhancing personal capacities within the collective framework, leading Durkheim to question why it is generally assumed that "there be more dignity in being complete and mediocre, rather than in living a more specialized, but more intense life, particularly if it is thus possible for us to find what we have lost in this specialization, through our association with other beings who have what we lack and who complete us?"[63] To be a person in this particular sense is to be an autonomous source of action; correlatively, activity becomes richer as it becomes more specialized. Durkheim envisaged each contribution in relation to individuals "coordinated and subordinated to one another around some central organ which exercises a moderating action over the rest of the organism."[64] The rationale for enthusiastic participation is that in-depth concentration on one task or area of expertise enhances the individual's sense of accomplishment while simultaneously promoting cooperation among workers.

Compatibility between specialization on the one hand and the superior achievements of the collectivity on the other was most evident in the ambitious research enterprise the sociologist organized in conjunction with the publication of the review *l'Année sociologique* (1896). Personal accounts indicate the existence of greater diversity and looser ties among contributors than generally assumed. Mauss's perception of those years of collaborative effort eloquently attests to the modified notion of individual gratification and identity obtained from participating in a project beyond the reach of any one scholar: "I cannot divorce myself from the work of a school. If there is any identity, it is immersed within voluntary anonymity."[65] Mauss's statement appears to corroborate a widely held view among scholars that the kernel of the Durkheimian problematic, including the midlife shift to religion, can be charted as a movement away from constraint to *moral voluntarism* as the foundation for solidarity.[66] But whereas the primary reference for this argument is Parsons's voluntaristic theory of action, it is noteworthy that Parsons himself cautioned against the simplified opposition between voluntarism and constraint which he attributes to utilitarian individualism:

> Individualistic modes of thinking are so deeply embedded in our culture that such confusion is very difficult to avoid. For the usual distinction between voluntary adherence and constraint carries the connotation of the utilitarian dilemma. Yet this is just what Durkheim has transcended. He has precisely distinguished, as the utilitarians did not, between voluntariness and arbitrariness. While, on the one hand, adherence is voluntary, on the other, that adherence is binding on the individual. But it is binding not from physical necessity, but from moral obligation.[67]

Jeffrey Alexander's account of the move toward voluntarism argues that the break of 1895 was already symptomatized in essays dated as early as 1893, when Durkheim recognized the inadequacy of constraint as an externally induced basis for social order, thereby necessitating a major and thorough transformation in his thinking.[68] Alexander's is the most extreme position among those who have argued for some degree of discontinuity, since he insisted that the reworking of the social model entailed a rewriting of all of the essays and studies that predate 1895. The relation of individual to society is revised accordingly in each successive phase, leading to an increasingly subjective view of the affective basis for social cohesion. Despite Parsons's caveat, however, Alexander's reading continues to rely upon an unproblematized use of the individual/society classical antinomy, which, as argued above, was considerably challenged by the transformations effected in the course of effervescent assemblies.

Ethnography thus furnished the sociological imagination with representations of the experience Durkheim could otherwise but advocate or announce:

> If today we have some difficulty imagining what the feasts and ceremonies of the future will be, it is because we are going through a period of transition and moral mediocrity. The great things of the past that excited our fathers no longer arouse the same zeal among us, either because they have passed so completely into common custom that we lose awareness of them or because they no longer suit our aspirations. Meanwhile, no replacement for them has yet been created. (429)

From this standpoint, their potential effect would be to demonstrate how rituals activate a new structure of sensibility by playing an expressive and aesthetic role complementary to the cognitive or ideological functions also attributed to religion. It is now possible to appreciate the impact of dramatized effervescence upon readers otherwise inured to moralizing exhortations to greater social conscience and examine why, for Durkheim, all these dimensions of the social are virtually inextricable.

Conclusions

In the final analysis sociology must replace religion, since the gods of other societies cannot satisfy our own. The heuristic potential of the elementary forms of religious life resides in the sense of elements or basic units from which future practices may evolve. Discussions of the meaning of elementary in Durkheim's title tend to oscillate between the possible connotations of "early" or else "primitive." But the interpretation suggested here is consistent with sociology's claim that science creates its objects, which the new discipline did when it replaced the individual with a collective one—the social.[69] Durkheim extolled the power of the religious imagination to transform the collective sentiments of everyday experience into objects worthy of respect. In a parallel gesture, he exhorted the sociologist to help society overcome its crisis of moral mediocrity by envisioning feasts and ceremonies conducive to social regeneration. However, by moving beyond documentation of what is to speculative extrapolations of what might be, Durkheim strained the very limits of the project he had established. That sociology must respond to historical exigencies through evolutionary modifications would also be consistent with a discipline distinguished by the burden of its social mission.

These concerns inform Durkheim's last writings, an unfinished treatise on morality he hoped would provide the capstone to his entire oeuvre.[70] The prospect of scientifically formulating moral precepts and final goals led to a science of morality distinct from sociology. "Moral" is favored over the academically recognized *moeurs,* because the latter is restricted to a catalogue of past behavior. Like Minerva's owl, science arrives too late to participate in the social process, whereas art alone projects beyond the immediate: "Any discipline that looks toward the future can be said to lack an object: consequently, it deserves the name of art, rather than science."[71] The perception of a temporal disjuncture between changing values expressed through collective representations and the inertia of institutions constitutes Durkheim's closest approximation to a theory of conflict and transformation: it also explains his move toward collective representations as recognition of their ability

> to accelerate or retard the momentum for social change, so long as the social system is functioning effectively. Only when it begins to break down, do the old values and ideals get challenged in any consequential fashion: Durkheim's conclusions about the role of collective representations in social process together with his conception of structural differentiation, I believe, provide the outlines of a fruitful theory of social change and suggest the direction of future work in the development of such a theory.[72]

From *Division of Labor* to *Elementary Forms,* the overarching continuity/evolution model is inflected with crises precipitated by anachronistic structures reaching their point of obsolescence. Yet these are also the transformative moments of effervescence when individual actors contribute to the general ferment by combining creative energies. The inadequacy of the movement/stasis schema to allow for social agency on the part of groups as well as individuals other than as reagents within the structural crisis is at least partially confronted in the final meditations on morality. As Jean-Claude Filloux pointed out, Durkheim's sociological project had always been motivated by the belief that it would exert a social influence, whether by dint of its very existence or through more explicit practices, thus "his way of convoking other sociologists, of acting by means of books, of lectures, of writing for popular education, as well as the importance he granted to the teaching of sociology in the philosophy classes and within the Normal Schools."[73] Such external manifestations of sociology's engagement—often less sympathetically perceived as evidence of its imperialist ambitions—belie the inner agony of Durkheim's search for a definition of and expression for sociology within the confines of one discipline or science.

It is now possible to argue that the sources of Durkheim's predicament were internal as well as external. The first can be traced to the self-limitations imposed at the time of sociology's initial conceptualization, and the latter to the role the discipline could exert as a moral force. The tensions they highlight are manifested as early as Durkheim's inaugural lecture to his first course on social science (published 1888), where sociology's scientific status is made contingent upon its restriction to "the description of social facts and things as they exist, in an effort to simply understand them."[74] Eschewing the speculative dimension of *ars politica* ("how they should be organized in order to be as perfect as possible")[75] as well as the prescriptive role of political philosophy—what societies "ought to be *[doivent être]*," sociological observation must, as Rousseau insisted, first detect the very constitutive movement of the group: "Before examining the act by means of which a people elects a king, it would behoove one to examine the act by which a people becomes a people."[76]

With its explicit repudiation of the Spencerian contractual model, Durkheimian sociology discerned the possibility for cohesion at the moment when *the group becomes conscious of itself qua group,* and when individuals acquire a sense of the nature of their relations to the social whole—both realizations rendered possible by the intensity of a transformative experience associated with those moments of hyper-sociality modeled upon the sacred. The projection beyond the self compelling individuals to effect the painful externalization required for *homo clausus* to acknowledge the social basis for identity is, therefore, qualified as nothing less than *moral:*

> Everything which is a source of solidarity is moral, everything which forces man to take account of other men is moral, everything which forces him to regulate his conduct through something other than the striving of his ego is moral, and morality is as solid as these ties are numerous and strong.[77]

The uncertainties haunting Durkheim's early speculations with regard to the nature and function of the sociologist attain some degree of resolution in his final writings. Assuming the role previously ascribed to the state, corporation, or religion, the figure of the moralist emerges in his last essay as agent provocateur of the sociological revolution. Incorporating sociology's polemical thrust as critic of traditional morality willing to take on standing assumptions regarding the notion of private property at odds with his socialist commitments, the *moraliste* no longer waits for the disparity between values and institutions to erupt in overt antagonism.[78] With the crucial qualification that he is able to do original work, to be immersed in what is new, the sociologist may actively intervene in preparing the conditions of possibility for transformations in moral doctrine. In keeping with the sociological view that innovation emerges from the collectivity, he seeks alternatives to academic discourse by scanning the currents of social forces for subterranean traces of values, representations, and ideals in gestation:

> Proverbs, popular maxims and non-codified customs are no less sources of information. Literary works, the conceptions of philosophers and moralists (you observe that I do not exclude them), direct our attention to aspirations that are only at the stage of attempting self-realization.[79]

The moralist thus performs a social maieutic by bringing to the fore an emergent morality prior to its crystallization in socially sanctioned forms, since it is through him that "minds acquire an awareness of themselves and manage to express themselves in a reasoned way."[80]

Further insight into the continuity of the critical role played by the process of heightened consciousness within the sociological project is provided by a post–*Elementary Forms* 1914 address, where the distinguishing feature of any future religion will be the "awareness" of its social origins. Even if the actual form for such a projected religion is unforeseeable, the sociologist is nonetheless able to predict from which social forces it will emanate. Despite a general reticence to refer to specific class identities, Durkheim now declares,

> All that matters is to feel below the cold morality which casts its pall over our collective life, the sources of warmth which emanate from within our societies. *One can go even further and assert with some accuracy in which region these new forces are especially in the process of formation: they are the popular classes.*[81]

Prompted by the misunderstandings surrounding his thesis on religion, Durkheim's final communications repeat that in view of the massive disaffection from institutionalized religion and the paucity of collective ideals, sociology must address the fact that the requisites for a viable social life will inevitably be overpowered by individual needs. Breaking with the conventional view of social life as contingent upon renunciation or sacrifice, sociology posits the model of a voluntary attentiveness. As a faculty of intellectual vigilance stimulated by social intervention—"awakened in us only by the effects of society"—the process connoted by *volontarisme* underscores Durkheim's wariness of representations prior to critical scrutiny: "one must suspend the spontaneous course of our representations and impede the conscience from giving in to its natural movement of dispersion; in a word, one must counter our strongest propensities."[82] The obligation to counter the spontaneous representations of the social, whether derived from one's lived relation to reality or those mediated through education—institutional as well as familial—explains the importance attributed to pedagogy within the Durkheimian corpus examined in the following chapter.

Access to the unconscious "treasure" of social life transmitted from generation to generation provides in itself verification of sociology's scientificity. Occulted by the French constitutional *simplisme* for which teaching practices since the sixteenth century are held responsible, the collective dimension of being was also distorted by the persistence of philosophy to deny reality to any object other than the individual. When traditional eighteenth-century political philosophy examined social life, it considered only the restrictions it could devise in order to limit the inevitable demands required of the individual by the collectivity: "Under these conditions, all sociological issues consisted in understanding how individuals can exist without mutually impinging upon one another or at least as little as possible. Such is the nature of political philosophy in the eighteenth century which, until quite recently, was also our own."[83] To upset this dominant trend and liberate sociology from an ideology of accommodation provides sociology with its central impetus. It also explains recourse to the ethnographic distinction between the sacred and the profane for representation of a qualitatively distinct experience of the social.

Sociology's concern with the internalization of a certain representation of society as the basis for collective morality nonetheless has been correlated with an effacement of its political involvements. A counterargument in Lacroix assimilates the political to a definition of the social that refuses to reduce politics to a specialized set of activities or class of persons, thereby encompassing within its purview both the nature of social relations and the ideological dimension of how they are represented. The preoccupation with the discipline's ability to intervene in the symbolic order at the level of representations is acutely evident in the attention devoted to issues of pedagogy, most notably in a series of lectures Durkheim delivered during the academic year 1904–5 in which he offers a celebration of the social, intellectual, as well as spiritual accomplishments of medieval effervescence.[84] The ninth-century Carolingian renaissance is characterized as a period of liberation from extreme material want, and the ambient effervescence associated with the rise of an altruistic morality, intellectual inquiry, and social as well as geographic mobility. With its particular fusion of reason and faith, scholasticism is upheld as an ideal basis for learning subsequently displaced by the literary culture servicing the needs of a newly enriched bourgeoisie.

Effervescence may be envisioned as a crucial dimension of social solidarity, but its effect within modern society nonetheless remains contingent upon the revival of those moments "when our societies once again will know hours of creative effervescence during which new ideals will again spring forth and new formulae emerge to guide humanity for a time" (429). Durkheim's explicit projection into the future signals what we have claimed to be the source of an internal crisis for the sociologist eager to direct the course of social events—a goal underscored in the final plans for a sociology of morality. The mutation of the sociologist into moralist also reflects the pressure exerted by an external phenomenon—the displacement of the social by the more acceptable and politically neutralized category of the moral which, following the Dreyfus Affair, had become the means by which the new intellectuals imposed their opinions. Although committed to positions often critical of the government, these men framed their adversarial stance in moral terms so as to convince the general public that they were indeed above partisanship. Chamboredon therefore extends the phenomenon of screens beyond Durkheim to a generalized occurrence that emerged from the nexus of political and social problems subsumed under moral:

> The crisis is not only political; it is social in two senses: the crisis linked to class antagonisms and the crisis, more profound and the foundation for the first, of a society whose old order collapsed (based on rejected absolutes, whether religious faith, royal absolutism or despotism), and is not replaced by a new order of reason grounded in new principles. The difficult period of establishment of the new Republic, following the imperial demise, reawakens the questions born of the long reflection regarding the crisis of French society inaugurated since the French Revolution. . . . *What is in fact most striking in the political discourse around 1870 and 1880 is the extent to which the social crisis is both present and masked, often dissimulated under the image of a political and moral crisis.*[85]

It is plausible to argue that sociology's evolution to the point it is defined in 1906 as the study of opinion and representations actually reinforced Durkheim's political commitments. Lacroix made the strongest case for the connection between politics and collective representations by pointing out that however innovative in comparison with Durkheim's early writings, *Elementary Forms* fulfills the reinterpretation of politics intimated as early as *Division of Labor* and then the *Lessons on Sociology*.[86] Such a reading is consistent with the one presented above: The political lesson of *Elementary Forms*'s sociological revolution was not for a return to the cults of archaic religion but that the continuity between the archaic and the modern resides in their shared inability to discern the laws of the social. This realization justifies the development of sociology with the sociologist-as-moralist at its helm. The contradictory role of sociology in relation to representations relevant to the future was resolved in terms of a position toward the present, with a commitment to understanding the status quo in such a way as to foresee the future development of collective representations in relation to regnant aspirations.

The political impact of representations resides in their centrality to opinion since "everything in social life rests on opinion, including science itself. To be sure, we can make opinion an object of study and create a science of it; that is what sociology principally consists in. Still, the science of opinion does not create opinion, but can only clarify it and make it more conscious of itself" (439–40). And no more critical area of influence exists than the one dictating what is considered sacred, or respected as a source of moral authority. Indeed, the political dimension of these issues is most salient if we recall that the integration of belief with behavior is a central tenet of the portrait of religion provided in *Elementary Forms*. Even if, according to a post–*Elementary Forms* address (1913), Durkheim deplored the randomness of some actions stemming from belief, he nonetheless reasserted their indisputable reality for the individual.

The conclusion of *Elementary Forms* makes it evident that Durkheim's interest in religion's epistemological status was inseparable from the sociologist's ambition to have his discipline acquire the requisite moral authority to impose a view of the social that would foster modes of solidarity relevant to the transformations of fin-de-siècle France. Among the means at religion's disposal, the religious imagination, Durkheim observed, is capable of transmuting banal things into sacred objects. Steven Lukes has noted that none of Durkheim's interpreters and critics seems to have elaborated his appreciation of the "expressive" aspect of religion.[87] Lukes himself astutely underscored those passages of *Elementary Forms* describing the recreative and aesthetic element of religion, when rites are compared to dramatic representations, games, and art forms. The challenge of the sacred/profane duality was not to rationalize the opposition of the two categories, but to communicate the distinctness of the sacred resulting from the expression of collective energies. That Durkheim enlisted a religious imagination is consistent with his argument that given the ludic nature of rites, religion would constitute the foremost source of most aesthetic forms:

> Indeed, as I have shown, although religious thought is something other than a system of fictions, the realities to which it corresponds can gain religious expression only if imagination transfigures them. . . . So the world of religious things is partly an imaginary world (albeit only in its outward form) and, for this reason, one that lends itself more readily to the free creations of the mind. Moreover, because the intellectual forces that serve in making it are

intense and tumultuous, the mere task of expressing the real with the help of proper symbols is insufficient to occupy them. A surplus remains generally available that seeks to busy itself with supplementary and superfluous works of luxury—that is, with works of art. (385)

Durkheim's caveat that the representational economy of the ritual be safeguarded from reductionist interpretations ("The worshippers are seen jumping, whirling, dancing, shouting and singing, and they are not always able to assign a meaning to this turbulence") is consistent with the opposition he stressed between the sacred and work or any utilitarian criteria. But even if he resisted ascribing a specific meaning to expressions of collective energies, his admiration for their role in social communication is beyond question. Thus, the potential of religious symbolism to stimulate action is extended to all collective representations: "An individual or collective subject is said to inspire respect when the representation that expresses it in consciousness has such power that it calls forth or inhibits conduct automatically, irrespective of any utilitarian calculation of helpful or harmful results" (209). But whereas it would be relatively feasible for sociology to investigate and document the effects of social conditioning in inculcating habits, behavior, and even ways of thinking, it was of another order of difficulty—and controversy—to assess the impact of collective representations as stimuli of action, particularly in relation to moments of social upheaval. and it explains, I have argued, his recourse to the ethnographic detour.

An earlier screen that facilitated the transmission of social critiques was Durkheim's required course on pedagogy for future teachers. The indictment of *simplisme* figures prominently in his review of those practices he held responsible for the distinctively French brand of learning—a valorization of style over substance, the apotheosis of great men over respect for contributions of the collectivity, and abstract generalities over specialized, concrete, scientific, and/or historically based knowledge. Beyond the teaching of literature, the cult of rhetorical prowess is viewed as an egregious symptom of *simplisme*, his code word in this context for the national deficiency that upholds a model of universal and immutable human nature transmitted by the neoclassical, literary *culture générale*. Propelling the historical panorama of pedagogy from Greek antiquity to twentieth-century Germany is a concern with how early schooling transmits a particular representation of the social. Pedagogical practices must therefore be recognized as part of the rituals that complement collective representations within the socialization process. The French cult and culture of literature is examined for its sources in the sixteenth century and directly related to the social transformations of that period. Durkheim's denunciations of *simplisme* also obliquely point to contemporary conflicts raging within the university between the social sciences and defenders of the elitist literary-based general culture that reached their paroxysm with the campaign waged by two young men in 1911 against sociology as embodiment of the new Sorbonne spirit.

In the chapter to follow, the discussion thus far of the sociopolitical implications of the ethnographic detour will be complemented by an analysis of the institutional reverberations provoked by sociology's introduction of "savages" into the Sorbonne. As self-designated spokesmen for the "generation of 1914," Henri Massis and Alfred de Tarde accused the new discipline of usurping the moral precepts imparted through literature to preceding generations and replacing them with the mores of Botocudo Indians. The fact that they carried their campaign against the new discipline to the chambers of the National Assembly indicates the extent to which the polemics provoked by the sociological revolution galvanized the entire nation.

Two

Savages in the Sorbonne

In the introduction to *Elementary Forms,* Durkheim espouses the revolution effected by ethnography within sociology and repudiates its enlistment as a *machine de guerre* against religion. His caveat points to precedents in the history of French ideas, when the discovery of New World denizens exhibiting a morality without benefit of Bible or baptism delivered a metaphysical shock tantamount to the first European realization that "God is dead."[1] Ensuing legends from Montaigne to Rousseau centered on noble savages and fueled a critical discourse directed against the authority exerted by the Church and the social hierarchy it sustained through political alliances with the monarchy. Unfettered by formal constraints within the essayistic antigenre modeled by Montaigne, anthropological thinking survived censorship for the next two hundred years by means of the exotic conceit. After 1789 representations of cultural others migrated to a new mode of exoticism compatible with the expansionist policies of the Third Republic. Whereas the new literature associated with colonialism omits reference to the country of origin, the self-reflexivity characteristic of anthropological thinking displaced primitivism onto medievalism:

> Just as the eighteenth century popularized the use of primitive materials—the whole vogue of exoticism, for example, which so

strongly undergirded natural law models—for purposes of contrast with the present, so, now, the nineteenth century began to utilize medieval materials for comparative purposes.[2]

In the same way that *Elementary Forms* fulfilled a heuristic function by establishing an explicit continuity/evolution between the archaic and the modern, so the examples derived from medievalism offered more than historical exoticism:

> As the monumental studies of von Gierke, Fustel de Coulanges, Rashdall, and Maitland make clear, interest in the Middle Ages was harnessed to scholarly search for the institutional origins of European economy, polity, and culture. The Middle Ages could be the basis of idealization and utopia for the nineteenth century—as in the writings of Chateaubriand, Sir Walter Scott, and others down to William Morris—but it could also be a mine for some remarkable researches in history and the social sciences.[3]

That Durkheim would first enlist reference to the Middle Ages to represent effervescence in his pedagogy study can also be attributed to the disparity between the impressive quality of French historical studies at the time and the deplorable state of ethnographic research. Among antecedents to the new social science, Broca's *Société d'anthropologie de Paris* of 1859 was initially restricted to physical anthropology and only later expanded to include "sociologie ethnographique." Charles Letourneau's ethnography was equally deficient due to its strong reliance upon nonscholarly travel literature and neglect of antiquity in favor of an idealized version of Indians. Nor could Durkheim endorse Letourneau's preferential treatment for primitive peoples—an indulgence he reproved as "simplisme révolutionnaire" despite its sincere indignation against social injustices.[4] This form of inverted idealization, he argued, posits a hypothetical political and social tabula rasa consistent neither with Marx nor with socialism, but symptomatic of a nostalgic primitive communism from which he was careful to distinguish his own socialist views.

Most instructive for the future symbiosis between sociology and ethnography was Durkheim's adamant repudiation of Letourneau's uncritical prescription of archaic examples as panacea for modernity's discontents. Heir to the eminent intellectual tradition emanating from Montaigne to Rousseau, modern French sociology nonetheless required a method for which Anglo-American anthropology was the most obvious existing model. Indeed, British social anthropology's scientific legitimacy by means of fieldwork leading to the monograph of one geopolitical group underscored early French ethnography's lack of direct contact with other peoples. The French alternative—a product of social and intellectual influences explored below—was to pursue a comparative approach. Introduced to the techniques of statistical analysis in the course of his collaboration with Durkheim on *Suicide* (1897), Marcel Mauss, for instance, followed his uncle's shift to ethnography sometime after 1895. His volumes of review articles— covering information gleaned worldwide—helped to maintain French ethnography on a par with other nations at a time when French researchers had little access to government-sponsored expeditions.

By the time of the essay on sacrifice (coauthored with Henri Hubert in 1899) Mauss's work exhibited the characteristics of the French school by focusing on a single topic—magic, the person, the gift, prayer, or even the nation—based upon the data gathered by others. This reliance upon derived information was justified by the low level of analytical development of the original material in its country of origin and further legitimated by Mauss's remarkable command of languages. Mauss himself attributed the continued inferior quality of French field ethnography into the first decades of the twentieth century to the virtual ban from 1815 on of all studies unrelated to the classics. Besides the obvious paucity of government subsidies for expeditions, ethnography's lack of development could also be ascribed to the passivity of academics in the nineteenth century who refused to challenge the influence exerted by a pervasive resistance characterized by Mauss this way: "A sort of generalized, stubborn, reactionary social opposition set itself against the progress of the science of man: ethnography, auxiliary to anthropology, is still, like the mistress science, relegated to the sidelines of the French scientific movement."[5]

The overarching purpose of this chapter will be to explore the social basis for that opposition. To do so will allow us to examine the fate of Durkheim's sociological revolution during the interwar period (see chapter 3), including the political implications of the ethnographic detour argued in chapter 1. We first consider the institutional repercussions of introducing a distinctively French mode of sociology informed by ethnography into the university system. Sociology's reliance on ethnography had the effect of elevating the latter from its inferior status, but the symbiotic relationship also exposed the new discipline to criticism from various quarters. The counterrevolution examined here was provoked by the "Agathon" authors—Henri Massis and

Alfred de Tarde—in defense of literature as the primary cultural system responsible for the moral values of the nation. This reaction undoubtedly reflects a veritable contest between sociology and literature whose institutional reverberations are directly traceable to Durkheim's ambitions. But the discussion of the role of literature in the formation of French national identity must also be situated in light of sociology's critiques (see conclusion to chapter 1) regarding "partial" forms of knowledge that occult the social basis of individual as well as collective being.

Indeed, the tendency to mistake social phenomena for individual realities is not restricted to the vulgar consciousness. Durkheim discerned its prevaricating role in the early texts of sociology itself, since even Comte confused concepts with *les choses,* the actual phenomena of social origin. So it is not surprising that a scientific enterprise as recent as the one proposed by Durkheim would have to tackle the distorted representations of social life in order to impose the new objects of the discipline—the external and unconscious phenomena nonetheless amenable to scientific analysis. It is certainly difficult to totally evacuate all vestiges of psychological origins from sociological explanations, yet this is precisely what he sought:

> Traditionally, a certain religious feeling, a certain minimum of sexual jealousy, filial piety, paternal love, etc., was considered innate to man and was used to explain the origins of religion, marriage, and family. But history demonstrates that these inclinations, far from inherent to human nature, are either lacking within certain social circumstances, or manifest such variation from one society to another, that the remainder left when such differences are eliminated, and which can only be considered of psychological origin, is reducible to something vague and schematic which leaves behind the facts that one must explain. These sentiments are therefore the product of collective organization rather than its basis. *Even sociability has not yet been proven to be instinctive.*[6]

The realization that even sociability is not a given prompted the centrality granted to the role of representations in each succeeding phase of Durkheim's thinking. The importance allotted to religious ones, however, did not preclude his criticism of the potentially reactionary role played by representations—especially literary—within a culture.

A crucial factor in the development of sociology was the preponderant influence exerted by letters in the cultural, intellectual, and even political life of the nation. Recognition of this privileged status—

unique even among European cultures—provoked Durkheim to elaborate a critique of its institutional consequences for the French school system. His motivation for devoting such seriousness to the issue of pedagogy must therefore be appreciated as a way to undermine the extension of letters to the literary paradigm—"that quasi-monopolistic way of seeking knowledge and model for all scholarship outside the natural sciences"[7]—which exerted a stronghold within the French university system until the end of the nineteenth century. Wolf Lepenies confirms the French bias by pointing out that even scientific treatises were ultimately judged by stylistic criteria. Until the advent of reforms initiated by Durkheim and his allies in the new Sorbonne, the acquisition of a general culture whose foundation was literary remained the primary criterion for assessing an educated individual. The introduction of empirical studies and the methods derived from history allowed the emergent social sciences to effect a break with standards dictated by the literary paradigm. Concurrently, the world of letters, spurred by the Dreyfus Affair, split into several camps, most notably into the opposition between the worldly literati cultivated by predominantly right-wing salons, and the engaged intellectuals with a literary background bent on exerting moral—that is, political—influence.

The second goal set for this chapter is to discern the basis for sociology's appeal within some groups and its rejection by others. To do so, we follow Durkheim's lead by examining the sources for those reactions in the nature of the social and moral *habitus* fostered by the influence of schooling responsible for the civilizing process since the Renaissance in conjunction with the development of a "lettered" society. It is significant that the first major discussion of effervescence is found in Durkheim's study of pedagogy. Those lectures provide our narrative with a historical perspective regarding the counterrevolution sparked by sociology's entry into the Sorbonne among stalwarts of belles-lettrism as the primary cultural vehicle of French national identity. We recall that the philosopher Jean Wahl had speculated that the explanation for sociology's appeal among Collège cohorts might be traced to a generational phenomenon, but noted that even that explanation would be subject to a sociological analysis. Because of the close correlation in France between school and society, teaching practices serve as a barometer of social change in relation to the entrenched forces militating against innovation. These multiple perspectives provide the needed framework in which to trace the erratic manifestations of the sociological revolution from the sixteenth century to the present.

Pedagogy and Politics

Sociology's renewal after twenty years of repression and censorship was propelled by the widespread conviction that the national defeat of 1870 reflected negatively upon the inferior standards of the French university. Among the Prussian victor's strengths were more advanced scientific methods, including those of the social sciences Durkheim had admired firsthand. Yet his own thwarted patriotism during a childhood in Alsace-Lorraine was rekindled by the ambition that sociology, "daughter of '89," would attend to the crises afflicting fin-de-siècle France, such as tensions in social relations manifested in real strikes and the symbolic growth of worker unity in conjunction with the development of the socialist party. Both developments were especially threatening to the ruling elites, whose political hegemony had been seriously fractured by a series of notorious confrontations, including the Panama scandal, the divorce between church and state, and, most dramatically, the Dreyfus Affair. This historical conjuncture allows one to appreciate that the emergence of sociology—far from attributable to Durkheim's brilliance alone—was indeed overdetermined.

Jean-Claude Chamboredon contends that curiosity for the history of religions as well as for ethnography in the 1890s reflects a displacement within Durkheim's scientific references which, as in the study of suicide, were previously dominated by "moral statistics." This shift was paralleled by a modification within the nature of the problems guiding research as well, so that the social question of class conflict was subsequently regarded as a primarily *moral* one—"the crisis of the modern moral conscience [la crise de la conscience morale moderne]"—within industrial society, and more precisely, as manifested within divisions of the bourgeoisie rather than along strict lines of class: "The specific social problematic of *Suicide* thus reflects the passage from the *Division of Labor in Society* to the division of moral work within the bourgeoisie. One could discern in this shift the origins of a theory of stratification modeled upon that of castes."[8] It is tempting and somewhat justified—especially given Durkheim's avowed predilection for delivering a university prophetism—to read into the focus on morality both the culmination of earlier career tendencies and the desire to compete with the successes of post-Dreyfusard intellectuals. Unlike other intelligentsia, French intellectuals, however politicized, were distinguished by their literary formation. This qualification is significant because it reflects the enduring respect garnered by the rhetorical tradition despite the desacralized status of the writer by the close of the nineteenth century.

It is therefore plausible to argue that the search for a discourse on society invested with the objectivity of science gained a strategic importance for French elites, even if it is not possible to establish strict correlations between those attracted to the new social sciences and specific social milieus. Within the university, a contest for domination erupted between the new disciplines and those united by a common adherence to the lettered paradigm. The introduction of empirical studies and the methods derived from history allowed the emergent social sciences to effect a break with standards dictated by the lettered paradigm. In his pedagogy study, Durkheim documented the historical antecedents to what Lévi-Strauss characterized as a "normative humanism" at the level of secondary education, whereas the struggle for sociology's institutional implantation was being waged within the universities. In the traditional curriculum, rhetoric and the cult of eloquence were promoted over dialectics or logic, French over any foreign languages, and the exceptional event, person, or thing over the collective quotidian. The institutional reproduction of this hierarchical and nationalistic notion of culture and learning was reinforced by the prestige of secondary education crowned by the *Baccalauréat,* to the detriment of the poorly funded and understaffed state university system. The biases of classical humanism were manifested at the university level in the domination exerted by philosophy, responsible for dictating the repertoire of themes to which theses were directed.[9] Followed by classical languages and letters, then French and some French literature up to the eighteenth century, the range of acceptable objects for study conformed to an aristocratic vision of high culture. Even science was not immune to the influence of literary criteria, to the point where their immixture became a hallmark of French scholarship. Priscilla Clark has commented that Buffon's famous "Discours de réception" to the Académie française in 1753 (also known as "Sur le style") expresses perfectly

> the fascination of the French with their language and the belief that
> the manipulation of language by which literature is defined likewise

determines the quality of intellectual work. . . . The precedence of form over subject is not simply a habit of long standing but a deep conviction that the intellectual qualities to be found in writing are as valuable as, perhaps even more valuable than, the content of the work.[10]

Despite the intellectual ferment of 1789, new institutions capable of implementing its many innovations were not established. In the first decades of the nineteenth century, repercussions of the Revolution were evidenced in the attempts made to revise the curriculum by unseating letters from their preeminence. Yet more difficult to usurp was the centrality granted to Latin in all secondary studies, a bias rationalized by the conviction that an "uncontested affinity" existed between Latin and Christian thought. Durkheim credits Victor Cousin in the early part of the nineteenth century for providing students in the fourth form with the possibility to expand their exclusively literary instruction with some scientific courses. Until Victor Duruy, however, students continued to be divided between those who opted for Latin and Greek or Latin and sciences. The focus on rhetoric and the perfection of circumstantial writing was to characterize French secondary school studies until the final quarter of the nineteenth century.

Durkheim's personal antipathy to the dominant literary culture dates from his secondary school studies and is manifested in the mediocre results of his earliest exams at the Ecole Normale Supérieure.[11] He also suffered a serious personal crisis, gradually resolved following a trip to Germany where he was able to admire the organization of university studies that placed sociology on an equal footing with other sciences. Unlike the university at Bordeaux, where he had begun his teaching career, the Sorbonne introduced the new discipline through the channel of its traditional courses in pedagogy, reflecting the academy's refusal to grant the new science of society complete parity with other disciplines. First published in 1938, Durkheim's lectures on pedagogy dating from 1904–5 were virtually impossible to locate until being reissued—significantly—in 1969. Sociology's aggressive campaign to impose itself in relation to neighboring disciplines or powerful ideologies, including Marxism and Bergsonism, have been amply documented. But the writings on pedagogy must also be taken as evidence of yet another dimension of the sociological revolution: the conflicts between social sciences and traditional literary culture accompanying sociology's implantation in the French university system.[12]

This overarching institutional framework is of continued relevance because the early polemics underscore the distinctively French reverence for literature, in de Bonald's summation, as "the expression of the whole of French society," the role of formal education in reinforcing that assumption, and the convergence between the two in the production and transmission of a certain perception of the social.

Indeed, the most vociferous reaction to sociology's implantation in the symbolic center of French intellectual life was expressed nearly a decade following Durkheim's appointment to the Sorbonne in the 1912 pamphlet, *L'esprit de la nouvelle Sorbonne*.[13] Penned under the pseudonym "Agathon" by the relatively unknown Henri Massis and Alfred de Tarde (Tarde was the son of the sociologist Gabriel Tarde, who had engaged in heated polemics with Durkheim and did not use the aristocratic "de" revived by his offspring), the screed impugned sociology for the betrayal of an entire generation no longer able to derive spiritual guidance from modern education. Still viewed as a Teutonic invasion, sociology is held responsible for the onslaught of foreign jargon and, therefore, the demise of the superior clarity and logic of the French language.[14] With its purported aversion to all that is individual, and exclusive valorization of the group, the "sombre determinism" of Durkheimian sociology elicited reactions similar to those provoked by the alleged structuralist dissolution of Man nearly half a century later. Fueling Agathon's animus is the extension of sociology's central tenets to literary studies, especially the perception that they "fortify fanatical authoritarianism, the disdain for individualities, the cult of specialization, the refusal of all real philosophical culture, [which are] the characteristic traits of our new literary instruction."[15] In order to situate these remarks, a brief review of the specific positions expressed by Durkheim in regard to literature is revealing.

The key maxim summarizing Durkheim's pedagogical doctrine is that the formation of the mind is determined by the things it studies. And the striking characteristic of French classical culture is that it offers only one object—"Man." Not men and women in their concrete historical and social diversity, engaged in the activities that sustain the material basis of society, but "man" as an artificial, exsangue construct whose human nature remains a constant throughout time and space. An abstraction from the already eviscerated figures inhabiting seventeenth-century literature, this prototype is thoroughly devoid of social, ethnic, and even historical specificity. All aspects of classical learning thus conspired to convince young people to believe in constancy and invariable traits, so that when variations were presented they were reducible to a superficial local color that leaves intact an "eternal, immutable, invariable and independent" human nature. The profoundly anticomparatist—and therefore antisociological—biases of classical pedagogy produced a condition of "infirmity" that left students insensitive to what is variable in history. By the way it was taught, literature formed the core of a humanistic worldview whose *simplisme* was so pervasive that *"the entire French moral and intellectual temperament bears its mark"* (emphasis added).[16]

The possibility to conceive of social facts at once external to and independent of the individual would remain inaccessible to the point of view fostered by classical humanism in philosophy as well as literature. Durkheim therefore directed his critique of the sources of French *simplisme* during the classical period to that other emblem of French culture and intellect—Cartesianism—responsible for the abstract individualism and general detachment from local culture that was emulated well into the eighteenth century. If the French invention of sociology arose as a reaction to the dramatic loosening of traditional social ties following 1789 and an enduring Cartesianism, it is because the latter's ambiguous legacy fostered both a respect for reason's ability "to translate into clear notions the most complex and unstable of [social] realities,"[17] as well as the tendency to confuse "distinct" ideas with their simplification: "I mean that outrageous simplisme, that mathematical spirit, which produces in us a natural penchant to deny reality to anything that is too complex for our mental framework" (316). To counter the mental and social closure imposed by the combined effects of Cartesianism and classical humanism, Durkheim advocated a comparative approach to the study of culture. Regarding the place of literature in future curricula, he proposed that literary studies be revised to include sociohistorical contextualization, just as the classical canon be expanded to include manifestations of popular culture. And in a tacit attack on the romantic myth of the solitary genius, he pointed out that the sciences he wished students to cultivate can only advance cooperatively.

To further such reforms, Durkheim endorsed professional support between sociology and literary studies by inviting the representative of the new literary history, Gustave Lanson, to address sociology students on that very topic. Significantly, the lecture was not held at the

Sorbonne, but at the Ecole Pratique. From the perspective of literary studies, the innovative program in which Lanson set out to recontextualize works within their original historical setting provided a salutary break with the ahistoricism of classical humanism, but was also dauntingly ambitious. To move literary criticism beyond the prevailing impressionism required the application of methods of documentation borrowed from history as well as sociology. Lanson insisted that literature break with the humanist's determination to extrapolate modern models of comportment from the classical repertory since literature should be envisaged as the expression of an individual who has transmuted personal values into social, that is, collective, goals. Even lyric poetry, conventionally offered as the model of emotive effusion, "does not escape this general condition of the literary work."[18] Durkheimian terminology is especially apparent in Lanson's conclusion that literature be treated as a "social fact" and great authors perceived as symbols of the collective life of the nation.[19] With an image favored by Durkheim, writers are compared to *foyers* "that concentrate at one point in time the rays emanting from the collectivity, and then return them, diversely combined and modified, back to the collectivity."[20]

The convergence between sociology and literary history provided Lanson's ambitious projects with a scope no less comprehensive than the one established for sociology. Encompassing an inquiry into the nature of literary culture in France and its effects on the life of the nation, it also proposed to include forms and manifestations of literary activity in the different periods, regions, and classes of France. The historical break with the primacy of the classical period, coupled with the sociogeographic decentralization from the bourgeois Parisian intelligentisia, would take into account the methods of transmission and reproduction of literary contact: "Diffusion throughout the country, penetration toward the people, here are two series of phenomena whose detailed study would be of capital interest."[21] The democratizing impulses guiding Lanson's reforms of literary studies were manifested in areas of method and organization as well as content. Spurred by a combination of Dreyfusisme, republican patriotism, and the model of collective professionalism advocated by Durkheim in the name of social solidarity, Lanson unseated classical rhetoric with a new attentiveness to the historical context of literary production and reception. Virtually all of the reforms advocated by Lanson in the early 1900s were aimed at reducing the function of social discrimination exerted by the university.[22]

Henri Massis and Alfred de Tarde propelled their counterrevolution against sociology to the chambers of the National Assembly. That two young students could be so effective reflects the tumultuous social upheavals at the turn of the century resulting from the process of democratization and modernization associated with the effects of industrialization, large-scale rural migration, influx of foreign workers, and the transformation of capitalism. Sociology was a favored target since it was held responsible for undermining the aristocratic heritage of neoclassical culture. Though ultimately unable to turn the tide of democratization, Massis and de Tarde's mobilization of public sentiment and political support demonstrated the concern generated by the changes in the nature of French literary culture dating from the early part of the nineteenth century, which certainly accelerated in the closing decades, and for which their *simplisme* held sociology responsible. The "invasion" of politics into the literary domain generally correlated with the Dreyfus Affair indeed represented a nearly absolute reversal in relation to the preceding period, when from 1848 to approximately 1880 the segregation of artists and writers from the political realm was virtually complete. Because of their new involvement, literary figures became engaged intellectuals who set the terms of debate for the population at large. Yet, as Christophe Charle remarked:

> [T]his mutation in the mode of participation, while recouping social losses from the former prestige enjoyed by purely literary activity, exacted its own costs. . . . Literature thus falls from the academic to the political sphere, the man of letters becomes an intellectual, which is to say a professional like any other, the spokesman *no longer for the totality of a culture, but for the particularity of a group, of an institution, of a cause.*[23]

When Lanson collaborated with Durkheim in 1904, neither could claim significant political clout. Three years later, Lanson's influence had succeeded in usurping at least one stronghold of ancien régime bias within the university. From 1880 to the turn of the century, only a "unique" exam covering Greek and Latin existed. By 1902 modest reforms had managed to provide for both a common part and a few options, whether in letters, philosophy, or Greek. But in 1907 the first-level degree *(licence)* was split into four distinct possibilities. With the crucial loss of the "common" section, Agathon appeared justified in declaring that with one fell swoop the test of general culture was abolished from the literary exam. In alliance with Brunot, eminent historian of the French language, Lanson attempted to accelerate democratization by proposing a *licence* as well as *agrégation* in letters stripped of any requirements in the classics. A degree in modern letters certainly would have lifted a very real social barrier at the university level. Defeated by representatives of the provincial universities, Lanson then concentrated his energies on bridging the gap between the secondary and postsecondary systems. He took his mission directly to schoolteachers by giving classes at the "popular universities" and by lecturing at the Ecole des Hautes Études. While all these endeavors were consistent with Lanson's republicanism, his colleague in history, Seignebos, voiced another motive: the fear that literature, symbolic of ancien régime élitism, would be marginalized by the democratic forces mobilizing the "new spirit." In all of his articles proselytizing reforms between 1902 and 1907, Lanson himself eschewed any such utilitarian considerations and maintained the ideological high ground. His commitment to the democratic method of collective work remained steadfast throughout, and his adherence to the two sources of his position— Dreyfusisme and the Durkheimian organic division of labor—provided the basis for his critique of individualism and elitism within literary studies, especially evident in "dogmatic" or "impressionistic" criticism.

As such, the new direction of literary studies dovetails with the social division of labor Durkheim advocated. Between 1909 and 1911 four volumes of the *Manuel bibliographique de la littérature française moderne* were published. Containing 23,000 references, as well as two hundred pages of supplements that appeared in 1914, Lanson's handbook provided the basis for the capacious project of literary history he had already adumbrated. With the rationalization that the most modest scholar can provide some contribution to a coordinated mode of research, Lanson, like Durkheim, encouraged greater specialization among academics as an antithesis to the classical general culture and philosophy as practiced in France: "From Descartes to Bergson, French philosophy shared the prejudices of French literary culture against specialization and the technical vocabulary associated with it."[24] The spirit of Cartesianism is also responsible for the intellectuality of French literary study.

It is possible to argue that the success of the Agathon pamphlet can be traced to its ability to offer a clear-cut division between opposing factions beyond the university that encompassed French culture at large. For one historian, Henri Massis and Alfred de Tarde characterized French society as locked in a debate

> between the *esprit de géométrie*, represented by the Sorbonne, and the *esprit de finesse*, the true spirit of French culture, ably represented by Henri Bergson at the College de France. For Agathon, the *esprit de géométrie* was identified with secular rationalism, Cartesianism, and positivism; it shunned general culture and emphasized scientific methods. The *esprit de finesse*, on the other hand, emphasized the spontaneous, the intuitional, the metaphysical, and was responsible for all that was best in classical culture.[25]

Not surprisingly, Durkheim figured in the camp of the Cartesians, thereby underlining an existing rivalry between him and Bergson, and this is indeed the standard view of Durkheimian sociology perpetuated well beyond the Agathon controversy. The alleged suppression of spirituality by the new Lansonian literary history decried by Agathon is imputed to its Cartesian roots. But in reality, it is the powerful effects of the rhetorical tradition—denounced by Durkheim—that produced the strongest impact:

> Descartes's actual influence is considerably more problematic, for the influence of the classical rhetoric taught in the Colleges of the ancien régime and subsequently in the lycées was equal to, if not greater than, that of any putative Cartesianism in fostering what Pascal—not Descartes—called the *esprit de géométrie*. Classical rhetoric, moreover, was an influence with direct connections to literature and literary culture.[26]

Indeed, in teachings seven years prior to the Agathon pamphlet, Durkheim reproved the global effects of Cartesianism on French thought and culture. Epitomizing the "esprit du grand siecle," Descartes's universal mathematics was derided as *simplisme* systematized.[27] The consequences of Cartesianism's exclusive definition of reality in terms of homogeneous extension were felt well into the eighteenth century, when "abstract individualism" was elevated to a universal conception of human nature. With their nationalist attacks against sociology as purveyor of an imported—Teutonic—jargon that replaced the inherent "clarity and logic" of the French language, the Agathon authors confirmed the bias against the demonstration of the *collective* sources of culture, which proved to be the major impediment to the sociological revolution:

This is why he who undertakes to react against this superficial simplisme in order to remind what is the true place of the individual in
society, abuts against feelings and prejudices that are still highly sen-
sitive. Since such a conception of collective life cannot be reduced to
one of those systems of clear ideas that animate our French temperament, they believe that they have done it justice with a disdainful dismissal as a Germanic importation.[28]

The Agathon campaign brought to public attention the animosity
generated by sociology among cultural elites competing for control over
representations of the social transmitted through the educational system. Within the secondary schools and university, the struggle was irreducible to an opposition between disciplines and methods, since no one
group or individual was indifferent to the benefits—couched in terms
of a quest for moral ascendancy—at stake in the competition. This institutional battle found its ideological expression in sociology's research
into the nature of authority—how one discourse or agency is responsible for the production and transmission of representations and rituals that foster a particular morality. Ideally, sociology's contribution
would be to counter the decline of social altruism and solidarity under
the impact of possessive individualism.

Medieval Effervescence

The example for a moral, intellectual, and social transformation proposed by Durkheim's pedagogy study is the effervescence stimulated by
the Carolingian renaissance. With the consolidation of feudalism and
liberation from extreme material want, the resultant ferment among
European peoples took the form of scholasticism. This early renaissance was characterized by physical as well as social movement among
nomadic monks who effected pilgrimages, attended synods, and generally spread their learning throughout a Christianized Europe more
"cosmopolitan" than would become possible with the advent of nation-
states. Durkheim credited scholastic effervescence with undermining
social hierarchy by supporting schools and lodging for the poorest
scholars, just as he claimed that the Crusades fostered a high degree of
social and geographic mobility. The outburst of effervescence is traced
to the internal dissonance sparked by scholasticism's admirable fusion
of "religious ardor and scientific enthusiasm" (85). Whether incarnated in one man, for example, Abelard, or characteristic of the epoch,
scholasticism is responsible for introducing reason into faith, thereby

injecting a creative tension into the entire period. Durkheim also viewed it as promoting a dialectical mode of reasoning whose logic is infinitely more practical, realistic, and socially directed than any of the literary and rhetorical formalisms that succeeded it. Philosophy can be formulated in isolation whereas faith or belief *(la foi)* requires a social milieu. As the *Elementary Forms* concluded, faith above all is "warmth, life, enthusiasm, enhancement of all mental activity, uplift of the individual above himself."[29]

By means of scholasticism, the pedagogy study offers a refutation to the basic principles of neoclassical education and rhetorical training that immured French students within a worldview diverting the best minds away from empirical science and the material realities for which they were ill prepared. Among its pernicious consequences, French education impeded the ability to grasp the nature of social laws directing collective behavior at the antipodes to the social milieu of literary salons and even the political activity available to French elites within their restricted experience. Alternatively, Durkheim placed the sociological revolution he sought to effect through pedagogy under the aegis of medieval effervescence. The following areas illustrate its transformative potential.

Foremost among them, the possibility for social life to emanate from concentrated *foyers* of energy bearing a close resemblance to the sacred groups of *Elementary Forms* is the one to which Durkheim most frequently returned. Durkheimian sociology's characteristic disregard for class distinctions is generally explained by an overriding concern with cohesion and solidarity. In place of a class-based analysis, however, the point of view directed by effervescence leads to a general repudiation of traditional social categories and challenges the assumptions upon which nation-states and even kinship relations are constructed. In response to the contention that Durkheim's notion of the social hypostatizes a process or movement, his definition of society connotes a totality that is always already divided, just as there exist neither "natural" groups nor superior social forms to be maintained. While arguing in favor of the revival of corporate groups, the preface to the second edition of *Division of Labor in Society* rejected any concept of a biological basis for solidarity: "But we have often had the occasion for showing that consanguinity has not the extraordinary efficacy attributed to it."[30] That same work also alluded to the social transformations rocking *la vieille*, predominantly rural France, whose resistance to centrifugal "cosmopolitan" forces were reflected in the profound rifts that would bring the country to the verge of civil war during the Dreyfus Affair. Regarding the diminished capacity of a traditional geographical locus to elicit allegiance, Durkheim commented,

> These geographical divisions are, for the most part, artificial and no longer awaken in us profound sentiments. The provincial spirit has disappeared never to return; the patriotism of the parish has become an archaism that cannot be restored at will. The municipal or departmental affairs affect and agitate us in proportion to their coincidence with our occupational affairs. . . . There is thus produced a spontaneous weakening of the old social structure.[31]

Another explanation for the political as well as intellectual appeal of medieval scholasticism as a screen for Durkheim's social critiques is to compare it with the campaign to reassert the idea of a true France emanating from conservative Catholic forces. Reacting to the demise of traditional social structures, they shifted their focus from explicit political rhetoric to cultural phenomena, such as public monuments, historical works, schooling, and even the social sciences. The true France movement also sheds light on the problematic status of ethnography at the time. Bolstered by the domestic focus of Louis Marin, it reasserted the influential notion that the roots of French culture are embedded in rural, hierarchical society, where tradition prevails and the sources of patriarchal authority remain undisputed.[32] The nascent discipline of cultural anthropology converged with this ideological perspective when trying to convince French people of their dual identity, of possessing origins in the "petit pays" compatible with the destiny of eternal, potentially greater France, that is, the French colonial empire in full expansion. Instead of encouraging tolerance and diversity within an increasingly cosmopolitan nation of immigrants, the strategy of the true France forces was to reduce the cultural as well as geographical space separating inhabitants of the metropole from those of the new territories.[33]

With his invocation of the medieval model, Durkheim demonstrated how it is that effervescent gatherings exert their maximum influence precisely because they explore forms of collective existence resistant to conventional sociological classifications. If, as one commentary argues, the inception of Durkheimian sociology can be contextualized within a "recherche de la société perdue," then surely it must be evidenced in the quest for alternative, innovative groupings or assemblies.[34] Durkheim's commentators have speculated upon the experiential sources of his notion of effervescence—whether Bastille Day celebrations, the ferment of the Dreyfus Affair, or the socialist ideas exchanged at the Ecole Normale mentioned in his writings—without arriving at any definitive conclusions. I would argue that the Dreyfus Affair should be singled out for providing a privileged contextual reference on at least two counts: by provoking as well as crystallizing social divisions that did not conform to standard sociological expectations; and by stimulating the development of *ligues* and associations that broke with established political party lines.[35] Beyond the atomization of individuals, Durkheim perceived new configurations whose political ramifications could be discerned in their ability to sustain collective action. The role of effervescence in fostering moral unity among loosely federated nations within the Carolingian empire is correlated with a cosmopolitanism more effective than any encountered in turn-of-the-century France. Indeed, the medieval (Christian) version is contrasted with the late-nineteenth-century global constitutional cosmopolitanism—an ideal applicable to all Frenchmen that for Durkheim reflects the French proclivity to generalize from its narrow nationalism to the universal. Traces of his Dreyfusard engagement can also be detected in this barely veiled response to the contemporary usage of cosmopolitanism as an anti-Semitic code word for Jews. As urban denizens, they were reproached for allegedly lacking a long history of attachment to French soil and for maintaining ties to international capital that would impede faith to their "adopted" nation.

By means of the object-lesson provided by scholasticism's particular melding of reason and passion, the pedagogy study also introduced the possibility for the *inner transformation* associated with the sacred effervescent assemblies that subsequently would appear in *Elementary Forms*. Whereas antiquity adhered to a dispersed mode of education dictated by a variety of disciplines, the advent of Christianity ushered in a period of concentration which regarded the child as a whole: "Teaching, as we have already noted, is a product of concentration. For it, dispersion is death" (137). Directed toward the totality of the student, it aims for a new habitus or *disposition constitutionnelle* fostering a "taste for the free life, varied, with the accidents and irregularities it implies" (145). The shift from dispersion to concentration may have replaced one extreme with another, concedes Durkheim, but was still preferable to the education of antiquity, which did not address the *état profond* of the child and provided only for an external armour, "whose different pieces were forged by different masters of instruction, and whose goal was to attain various talents." The really effective educator reaches for this deep state—in order "to create a general disposition of the mind that will lead one to consider things in general under a determined light" (37). The revolution he advocates is compared to the more familiar notion of a conversion:

> True conversion is a profound movement by which the soul completely turns toward a new direction, changes position and disposition, and consequently modifies its point of view toward the world. Since this change does not entail the acquisition of a certain number of truths, it can occur instantaneously. (37)

To be Christian, then, is not so much a matter of familiarity with certain rituals or traditional beliefs, since "Christianity consists essentially in a certain attitude of the soul, in a certain habitus of our moral being" (37).

Thus, beyond a *prise de conscience,* the sociological revolution entails a modification of the individual's moral disposition or ensemble of values and ideals. We recall that Durkheim's earliest writings correlated the nature of social formations with a type of awareness or conscience. Subsequent reflections upon the moral nature of education offer a more developed typology of figures, claiming that when tradition prevails and rules and order predominate during periods of stability, one encounters individuals of "solid reason and robust willpower" (114–15). A "cold" physiognomy also mirrors the inner rigidity and successful self-containment of such model citizens. However, periods of transition such as the one Durkheim is addressing—when Europe had to confront what he qualified as perhaps its most serious crisis to date—require the formation of open and generous persons capable of spontaneous élans or sacrifices proferred with joyous abandon. In characteristically prophetic language, the sociologist declares that failure to do so condemns the nation to a veritable moral depression menacing to its material existence as well.

The explicit relation established in the preceding passage between inner transformations and social change confirms the political reading of the *Elementary Forms* presented in chapter 1, where it was argued that effervescence provided the sociologist with the possibility to represent the complex process that conditions the possibility for individual actors to engage in collective action. By locating the model for effervescence in the Middle Ages, the pedagogical study fulfilled its own heuristic mission by establishing clear parallels between the early modern period and the crises besetting a belatedly modernizing France. Traces of the immediate historical context are most evident within the pedagogy lectures by means of a contrast Durkheim establishes between the demise of medieval scholasticism and the development of Renaissance humanism, both epochs characterized by a generalized increase in affluence. But rather than evolve the expansive morality the sociologist would prescribe for the social crises besetting fin de siècle France, the emboldened sixteenth-century urban bourgeoisie directed its challenge—albeit through emulation—to the social ascendancy of the feudal aristocracy. In place of the intellectual ferment of the scholastic dialectic—with its particular fusion of ardent faith and reason Durkheim so admired—the Renaissance revamped a medieval model of manners and values honored by chivalric codes. One hundred years before Molière's incarnation, the *bourgeois gentilhomme* is depicted by an anonymous sixteenth-century observer: "Pride was heightened in all social states. . . . The urban bourgeois sought to dress like the nobility . . . and the village people imitated the bourgeois of the cities."[36] New markets facilitated French aspirations to Italian luxury, reflecting a social mentality eager to eschew the rigors of medieval scholastic asceticism and abnegation. In its place was favored an elegantly refined culture, distinguished above all by its literary qualities. Durkheim argues that the standard account of the resurrection of classical texts by Renaissance humanism is belied by the accessibility of Greek and Roman literature throughout the Middle Ages. More accurately, literary works had been marginalized rather than repressed by the scholastic bias against texts that would undermine Christian hegemony. If, as claimed, the Renaissance discovered them, it was because they were deemed useful to the promotion of virtues and vices identified as its own. The exaltation of literature in sixteenth-century France is inseparable from the consolidation of new social elites, whose support provided a strong impetus to a literary production that reflected their taste and ideas until the middle of the eighteenth century. In sum, the new book-centered learning disdained action, ignored practical needs, and cultivated rhetoric as the exemplification of intellectual luxury.

Throughout Renaissance Europe, social mobility required new models of comportment. France was distinguished by a flowering literary culture and lettered society that fulfilled the mission of socializing educated elites according to the values and worldview subsumed under the notion of civility. Durkheim ascribes a central role in this process to Erasmus's treatise—*De Civilitate morum puerilium*—since it was destined for pedagogical usage. Following its French publication in 1537 and enjoying many translations and reeditions, Erasmus's work found an especially enthusiastic reception in France, where it appears to have enjoyed the greatest success by rapidly becoming a classroom text responsible for the transmission of the spirit of a polite society bent on indulging "its new refinements, delicate pleasures, and mannered joys" (230). The ambitions of the new social groups found expression in the development of an effete epistolary milieu extending beyond French borders. Within polite society, the very notion of letters must be taken literally, since writing and exchanging them engaged the energies of literate persons dispersed throughout Europe. Correspondence replaced conversation and letters took on the characteristics of literary extracts. Destined to be read by more than one person, they circulated from one major urban center to another. Although not professional by modern standards, the network of *gens de lettres* was virtually closed by its elitist biases.

If, as Durkheim argued, morality originates in the awareness of one's dependence upon society, then the literary life's inordinate esteem in France promotes a distorted perception of that relation:

> For a polite society is one where the harshness of self-interest is dissimulated by a generalized sympathy, and where one lives a sort of imaginary, slightly idealized life, far from the realities of an existence from which one seeks momentary respite, and where the spirit can relax and renew itself. (231)

The limitations inherent to a strictly literary corpus—truncated to facilitate the abstraction of virtues—were further narrowed by the pedagogical practices of the Jesuits.[37] Exerting a virtual monopoly on education by the end of the sixteenth century, the disciples of Loyola carried to an extreme tendencies present in the French methods of teaching by (1) total confinement and control of the pupil, housed and fed away from external influences, including family; (2) domination reinforced by the assignment of one student per teacher, responsible for constant supervision; and (3) immersion in Latin to the exclusion of French. The latter prompted one shocked observer to deplore the deficiencies in their maternal tongue among Jesuit instructors.[38] Their version of the literary canon consisted of few, if any, works read in their entirety, since the goal was not a broad exposure to the variety of genres, but rather a narrow emphasis upon oratory. Eloquence was the supreme art whose mastery marked the high point of all studies and rhetoric its crowning glory. The distinguishing feature of a literary culture is its mediated relation to natural as well as social reality, and Durkheim reserves praise only for science, where objective, disinterested study directs students toward the world at large.

Recourse to the medieval model of effervescence is therefore also explained by its explicit contrast with the development of French society from the sixteenth century onward. For the sociologist, the central commonality between France at the dawn of the twentieth century and the Renaissance resides in the ambiguous moral status of the bourgeoisie. The behavioral foundation for their morality was provided by Erasmus's sixteenth-century treatise on civility, when France, along with the rest of Europe, underwent a dramatic shift from medieval/feudal courtesy to renaissance civility. French social history, however, deviated from that of her neighbors. Norbert Elias traced the specificity of French social life to the frequent contact between the bourgeoisie and court society. Unlike its isolated German counterpart, for instance, compelled to formulate a distinctive identity, the French bourgeoisie's exposure to court society allowed it to derive fundamental ideals and values from the nobility. In its turn, the aristocracy witnessed the expansion of its ranks without having to compromise its lifestyle and privileges. However, what seemed like a mutually beneficial strategy backfired for the bourgeoisie, as evidenced in the very limited degree of social mobility actually effected during this prelude to absolutism. A particularly effective deterrent to the social ambitions of subsequent generations was that the new code of behavior became associated with the observation of social rank. Whereas Erasmus himself had not hesitated to include social jibes and irony, those signs of a spirited critique disappear from the manuals of his successors. By the next century, a distinguishing feature of and contribution to absolutism is that *strict obeisance to social distinction becomes the very hallmark of civility:*

> *The most exact observance of differences of rank in behavior became from now on the essence of courtesy,* the basic requirement of *civilité,* at least in France. The aristocracy and the bourgeois intelligentsia mix socially, but it is an imperative of tact to observe social differences and to give them unambiguous expression in social conduct.[39]

Elias's claim that the civilizing process emanated from courtly society as part of the internal pacification policy adopted by the monarchy has been challenged by historian Robert Muchembled, who sees its sources in the educated elites of the cities.[40] Unlike the rebellious nobility, the bourgeois of the "bonnes villes" remained faithful to the king, and in exchange for their support some were promoted to the rank of *noblesses de robe.* Muchembled also underscores the privileged role of literature in developing a worldview compatible with courtly ideals. Indeed, against a long-standing assessment of literature as the privileged instrument of bourgeois expression—however veiled—he insists upon its early appropriation by the nobility, equally eager to find an outlet for its rivalry with both the ambitious bourgeoisie and an imperious prince bent upon consolidating an absolutist monarchy that left little room for decentralized power or aristocratic sovereignty.[41] That the pen could be mightier than the sword was not an exclusive metaphor for the strategy of bourgeois. It also reflected a reconversion among aristocrats whose ranks had been decimated by forebears willing to salvage their threatened hegemony through sacrificial duels. Thus, by combining both traditional force and written stratagem nobles propagated a new ideal in representations consonant with their interests. The king also manifested political finesse by enlisting literature in his orchestration of power alliances among the various factions vying for his favor.

The parallel evolution of cultural and political forms followed an elusive trajectory that one historian detected in the distinctively French correlation between politeness and politics:

> In the course of the first half of the XVIIth century, the king gradually acquired the central position of fulcrum within a powerful social mechanism, balancing between the aristocracy and the urban forces in ascension. Politics was thus brought forth in France under the cover of politeness, which from then on oriented all social aspirations toward the monarch as supreme model, ultimate goal, and indispensable guarantor of a social equilibrium constantly disrupted, that it was his task to reestablish.[42]

By demonstrating the "persistence of old régime"[43] values and ideals well into the twentieth century, Muchembled also bolsters Elias's contention that sociology must draw upon history in order to assess the present. The civilizing process (Elias) produced the distinctively French phenomenon of an awareness of social boundaries reinforcing hierarchical distinctions and a distorted sense of the social, which gradually expanded to become the worldview of an entire nation:

> Stylistic conventions, the forms of social intercourse, affect-molding, esteem for courtesy, the importance of good speech and conversation, articulateness of language and much else—all this is first formed in France within courtly society, then slowly changes, in a continuous diffusion, from a social into a national character.[44]

From this period of intense affect formation it is also possible to date the overlap between sociology and psychology. The attention drawn to the myriad details of outward appearance catalogued by Erasmus—whether bodily carriage, gestures, dress, or facial expression—is justified by a more philosophical consideration of their reflection upon the inner person. With the conviction that there exists a congruence between appearance and personal quality, another dimension was thus added to the definition of *civilité:*

> In order to be really "courteous," . . . one is to some extent obliged to observe, to look about oneself and pay attention to people and their motives. *In this too, a new relationship of man to man, a new norm of integration is announced.*[45]

In the following century, the impact of this mode of observation upon the evolution of psychology is manifested in treatises dealing with the *science du monde* oriented to the needs of the courtly upper class.

In light of the entrenched tradition of the *science du monde* transmitted by manuals dating from Erasmus, and the extreme codification of behavioral norms they reflect, the question arises as to their combined effects upon the formalization of sociology in the last decades of the nineteenth century. The aspects of education Erasmus encouraged would be dismissed as outer habits in contrast with the moral disposition indicated here. This explains how, by means of the pedagogy study, one could argue that Durkheim touched at the very core of the moral habitus of the civilizing process in France and the concomitant literary formation to which students were initiated and kept captive, in the sense of being actively impeded to explore the world around them, whether through scientific exploration, direct observation of the natural world, cultural comparisons, or contact with the material realities they would eventually inhabit. The social confinement to which they were subject, by dint of isolation, fostered the mental and experiential closure of the *simplisme* to which their exclusive literary-rhetorical

instruction was the most salient contribution. By claiming that a sociological approach to literature devalued the great men of history and by
accusing Durkheimianism of scandalously displacing the centrality of
literature as source of moral and spiritual guidance with the example
of savages, the point of view expressed by Agathon summarized all the
characteristics of the French constitutional *simplisme* against which
Durkheim had directed his animus in the pedagogy course.

It is now possible to appreciate the uneven history of the sociological revolution in relation to the civilizing process and how both form
responses to the decentering of the Old World. Externally, Renaissance
affluence subsidized vast expeditions primarily for the purpose of developing new markets whose products could titillate the palate of a
jaded court society. But they also carried along with their cargo observers and sometimes actual specimens of noble savages, whose lifestyle and social habits revealed a morality developed without Christian revelation. The legends and treatises they inspired provided a
critical challenge to the exclusive claims to civility cultivated among
courtesans and their imitators, so it is noteworthy that whereas Erasmus enjoyed the greatest success in France, it was also there that the
sociological revolution ultimately exerted the most political influence. By the end of the eighteenth century, however, traces of the critical tradition inspired by contact with newly discovered peoples were
absorbed by the claims to universalism propounded within the ahistorical *simplisme*. The civilizing process expanded beyond French borders with the consecration of Western superiority as the universal
model of civilization, and its long-range effects facilitated the conquest
of other nations:

> an essential phase of the civilizing process was concluded at exactly
> the same time when its consciousness of the superiority of their own
> behavior and its embodiment in science, technology, or art began to
> spread over whole nations of the West.[46]

By the nineteenth century, this mindset contributed to the demise of
the self-reflexive and critical discourse associated with the sociological revolution. The conservative cultural anthropology buttressing the
Greater France compaign represented a continuation of the Enlightenment nationalistic representation of a universal civilization and was
denounced as such by Mauss as late as 1930:

> Naturally, what is meant by "civilization" is always Western. It is ele-
> vated both to a common ideal and to a rational basis for human

progress. With the addition of optimism, it becomes the condition for happiness. The nineteenth century confused the two ideas, and took "its" civilization for "the" civilization. Moreover, each nation and each class did the same.[47]

The imperialist mode of consciousness among eighteenth-century elites to which Elias referred can be contrasted with Durkheim's position to the effect that "society is the stronghold of all the riches of civilization."[48] An enduring national trait, the French concept of civilization, was described in 1932 by Curtius:

> To the Frenchman the word *civilisation* was both the palladium of his national idea, and the guarantee of all human solidarity. Every Frenchman understands this word. It inflames the masses, and under certain circumstances it has a sacredness which exalts it to the religious sphere.[49]

Curtius also underscored French literature's preeminent role in the production and transmission of collective representations that were regarded as a unifying national force until World War II.

Thus far, we have reviewed Durkheim's critiques of the role of literary culture in formulating the dominant representations of social behavior in France. Especially targeted is the authority bestowed upon the pedagogical practices responsible for their transmission. The convergence between the sociological contributions of Durkheim and Elias demonstrates the ritualized correlatives to (literary) representations in the civilizing process by means of which children were socialized from the earliest ages to manifest in their outward comportment a social identity reinforcing distinctions within a rigid hierarchy as well as submission to a centralized government. It was thus possible to appreciate the emergence of sociology as a legitimate discipline in relation to those discourses competing for the definition of the social in France since the sixteenth century: on one side, the prevailing official occultation of the social basis for culture and identity through the promotion of an ahistorical pedagogical *simplisme;* on the other, a critical challenge to those presuppositions presented by means of ethnographic detours. The depiction of this opposition avoided a dichotomization between civilizing process and primitivism by citing the example of effervescence derived from scholasticism. In keeping with the overarching thesis of the present study that the sociological revolution responds to a crisis by revitalizing the ethnographic detour, chapter 1 concluded that Durkheim's recourse to it was prompted by his perception that fin-de-siècle France lacked affirmative representations of the collective nature of social being. At stake politically as well as socially was the need for a morality capable of reversing traditional biases against work and specialization that would also be consonant with the social legacy of noblesse oblige and altruism inherited from the feudal aristocracy. For the sociologist it meant promoting representations of elementary forms of social life that would move individuals beyond the Spencerian contractual model, preferably by means of an inner transformation antithetical to the existing goals of educational practices influential in the moral as well as psychological formation of the nation. This dual perspective provides the groundwork to explain why sociology would exert a powerful intellectual attraction for some students while provoking savage debates among others.

Sociology—A Generational Phenomenon?

"Historical generations are not born; they are made. They are a device by which people conceptualize society and seek to transform it."[50] But as historian Robert Wohl then queried, which people? Following the pamphlet directed against the Sorbonne, Massis and de Tarde claimed their positions to be representative of their generation, as revealed through interviews conducted among cohorts between the ages of eighteen and twenty-five attending the most prestigious Parisian lycées and grandes ecoles. With the sponsorship of the French daily *l'Opinion,* their findings were published under the title *Les jeunes gens d'aujourd'hui* (1913). Massis subsequently conceded to the fabricated nature of his inquiry, closer to a literary version of generationalism than to any scientific or statistically determined study. For all the talk of newness, the specific political and social content identifying the young men of 1912 reflected greater continuity with the past than change. Drawing on established religion, an ideal of republican mysticism from Péguy, and the educational status quo, the conservative positions advocated by Massis and de Tarde reinforced the reigning prejudices and fundamental lacunae Durkheim had deplored as a congenital national deficiency. Since no one set of characteristics emerged from contemporary debates, however, the popular notion of a generational identity lacked definitional consensus. Yet the generational conceit serviced Massis and de Tarde by creating the idea of a group whose restricted social base need not necessarily invalidate the generalities they had selected to proffer about it. From a historical and comparative point of view, their example was singled out as epitomizing the particularly narrow social experience of the French literary milieu. In his cross-cultural comparisons among European nations, Wohl concluded:

> The fact was that in 1912 "philosophical and literary" French youth were especially and dangerously divorced from the social realities of their own country. The most sensitive among them confessed that they suffered from a seemingly unbridgeable chasm between dreams and possibilities for action. Only outside France, and preferably in the colonies, could a young bourgeois intellectual . . . discover "reality."[51]

Significant transformations, Massis and de Tarde argued, are not manifested by means of doctrines and philosophies, but in the character of individuals. By insisting upon the common bond of character traits, Massis and de Tarde were probably more accurate in discerning the basis for the shared sense of generational identity than those writers and philosophers who tried to tie it to a doctrine. The description they provided of a secret *entente*—based upon similarities in feelings and modes of action—had the advantage of shifting focus away from common ideas without taking the next step, which would have been to relate the basis for their bond to common social origins or the intellectual and moral habitus inculcated by the French secondary system:

> All products of an elitist educational system, all "heirs" to French culture, accumulated property, and positions of leadership in society, they shared what Barrès called "prejudices, a vocabulary, and objects of disdain." They had read the same books, been trained by the same teachers, developed the same ambitions and expectations, and worried over the same problem of French decline.[52]

The group Agathon purported to represent identified itself through differentiation with the immediately preceding "generation of 1885" (with which they associated Barrès). But the historical longview perceives their commonality as the product of the civilizing process initiated in the sixteenth century and then generalized in the eighteenth to the entirety of French society, so that by the postrevolutionary period it could be promoted as an ahistorical model of French culture shorn of class origins.

Historically, the Agathon pamphlets did little more than provide a compendium of both the critiques against sociology that had accumulated since its inception and, most important, the successes. Indeed, sociology's increasing appeal was noted as early as 1904 by Henri Hubert—close friend and frequent collaborator of Marcel Mauss—who nonetheless feared the dilution of its scientific rigor by a new generation of "magicians."[53] Mauss's response to the Agathon authors was predictably sociological, dismissive of them as young bourgeois who, beyond their own "specious, duplicitious and tendentious way of thinking, reflect the state of mind characteristic of their milieu."[54] Significantly, Mauss addresses his own readers as "comrades"—a reflection of his extensive socialist commitments—whereas the Agathon diatribe, he continues, reveals traces of a utilitarian philosophy guided by cynical practices passed off as pragmatism and religious adherence dictated by tradition rather than belief. Though accurate, Mauss's characterization requires added nuance in order to circumscribe those factors that account for the polarized reactions elicited by sociology within the same demographic cohort and social milieu. Since at the time only 2 to 3 percent of the eligible population in most European countries possessed a secondary education, those who had breached the baccalaureat barrier were considered members of the cultural elite, even if that social level provided more symbolic than real capital. A key element in predicting sociology's appeal among those competing to exert influence beyond their immediate circle can be found in their relation to the symbolic order by means of the collective representations that crystalize a particular cohort:

> Although the concept of a "generation of 1914" suggested the possibility of a mass formation that would cut across classes, it is also true that this idea was the creation of, and had its most direct reference to, a specific social group: literary intellectuals. Not a social class in their own right, these intellectuals were distinguished by their possession of a secondary education and their activity as the creators of the symbols and images with which members of other social groups interpreted and gave meaning to their lives.[55]

Durkheim claims that sociology's contribution to the formation of critical alternatives to the dominant lettered paradigm—especially among philosophy students who accounted for the first generation of crossovers to sociology—resides in its scientific approach to the social:

> In this sense, a veritable revolution has occurred within the minds of our students. The political question which used to enthuse them, now leaves them cold and indifferent. The more or less greater freedom of the press, the relations between Church and State, those re-

lating to executive and legislative power, etc. no longer interest them. To the contrary, everything relating to the internal organization of society, its moral structure, everything that touches the nature of the family, property, the relations between diverse social organisms, awakens in them, and especially among the brightest, a veritable passion.[56]

The political aspirations of sociology are more explicit in Durkheim's accompanying observation that the majority of sociology students are not destined for academic positions but instead those that involve the political life of the nation.[57]

The most aggressive as well as concrete statement of sociology's potential critical thrust occurs in Robert Hertz's preface to his seminal study of collective representations relating to the cultural distinction between left and right. Published in 1909, and therefore contemporaneous with the Agathon pamphlets, it highlights the ideological basis for the social fractures within French society which were ultimately of greater significance in predicting reactions to the new discipline than the generational differences claimed by Massis and de Tarde. The Hertz essay provides a consistent enlistment of ethnographic material to demonstrate that social facts are arbitrary, subject to change, yet necessary. The religious polarity established through the sacred/profane dualism is invoked to explain the overarching opposition between right and left responsible for distinctions made in the human body, spatial organization, religion, politics, and the social hierarchy. Because the right/left dualism is so ubiquitous as to appear both universal and natural, Hertz deliberately sets it within a social perspective that demystifies virtually all explanations in terms of nature or biology:

> The right hand is the model and symbol of all aristocracies, whereas the left hand is that of all plebians. . . . Every socal hierarchy claims to be founded on the nature of things; in this way, it stakes claim to eternal truth and avoids the innovations of the future.[58]

It is also the conclusion to which he arrives following a circuitous detour through the myriad cultural manifestations of the right/left distinction, since the very slight biological advantage of the right side cannot justify the intensified cultivation it enjoys in most societies:

> Along with Aristotle, who claimed the ethnic superiority of Greeks over Barbarians, men, troubled by the demands of feminists, allege a "natural" inferiority of women. Similarly, the preeminence of the right hand is a direct result of the organism's structure and owes

nothing to convention nor is it subject to shifts in opinion. Yet, despite appearances, little in nature either clarifies or provides decisive evidence regarding the reasons for the attributions to the two hands.[59]

Hertz's wide-ranging ethnographic examples illuminate a volatile topic of immediate social interest, thereby fulfilling sociology's commitment to drawing conclusions relevant to the present. The dependence upon existing data, however, had the perverse effect of discouraging original fieldwork, which some came to regard as a deficiency within the French school:

> The Durkheimians' recourse to borrowed data poorly concealed their inability to conceive of sociology as an empirical and autonomous discipline capable of gathering and elaborating its own givens. Durkheimian epistemology thus placed sociology in the situation of a science of syntheses, dependent upon its primary material from auxiliary empirical disciplines, such as ethnology, but also demography, history, or moral statistics.[60]

But whereas the lack of new empirical research may be indisputable, it is also possible to argue that with his critique of the authority exerted by literary representations as the basis for an entire *culture générale*, Durkheim explored the very underpinnings of French culture and society and the role of collective representations in retarding the momentum for change (Bellah). Well into the eighteenth century, blatant discrepancies between the objective successes of bourgeois in the political and economic realms and their social marginalization were reinforced by collective representations perpetuating anachronistic images of a socially idealized past. While effectively propagating new theories, even the bourgeois philosophes remained hapless in the face of pervasive stereotypes and clichés embedded in the collective imagination of the popular classes as well. Lacking validation through representations that would transmit a sense of their distinctive values and contributions, the bourgeoisie relied upon the conventional codification of distinction through a semiosis of wealth:

> The visible signs of wealth which appear in reception rooms (mirrors, tapestries with woven motifs, paintings whose themes are as carefully noted as the nature of the tableau or their frames), are the direct expression of a lifestyle, and translate at once a certain level of revenue and social ambition.[61]

Durkheim's excoriation of the literary-based general culture draws from a pervasive antipathy to Jesuit practices. That he targeted the

Jesuits and not all religious influences is carefully stated in his comparisons between France and countries such as Germany and England,
where the Reformation was responsible for sweeping changes. The
needs of secular society, for instance, were met in the pedagogical innovations instituted through Martin Luther's insistence that schooling
move beyond discussion of ideals. In France even Montaigne's humanistic "horror" of an exclusively bookish formation advocates contact
with nature but skirts any mention of technical or practical training.
Only with Rousseau is the humanistic stronghold on pedagogy seriously loosened, since he, like other Protestants, understood that "things,
an essential factor in our intellectual life, must also be at the corner-
stone of education" (331).

Missing from the preceding panorama of French literary and intellectual life, however, is the curious but important contribution offered
by Jesuit travel relations to the goals of the sociological revolution.
Subsidized by the monarchy as part of a counterreformation policy to
increase the ranks of Catholic subjects, Jesuit fathers were shipped to
the New France territory in search of souls to convert. Eschewing
force, the priests undertook to communicate with the natives, resulting in prolonged periods of contact that would allow them to acquire
a working knowledge of Amerindian languages and mores. Required
to report to their superiors on the state of their progress, the Jesuit relations provided detailed information whose ethnographic value is still
highly valued. For their contemporaries, the adventures of the priests—
who often voluntarily sought sainthood by risking their lives or torture by enemy tribes—constituted highly entertaining reading under the
guise of edification. By the time of their political break with the Holy
See, the Jesuits had provided some two hundred volumes of accounts,
ranging from the most formulaic statements to more self-consciously
literary narratives which could rightly be viewed as protonovels, enjoying widespread readership among the educated elites of the seventeenth century.

Modern readers biased against the Jesuit social experiments or *re-
ducciones* in Latin America satirized in Voltaire's *Candide* will find
it difficult to appreciate the complex contribution to the sociological
revolution played by Jesuit accounts of their New World experiences
a century earlier. Indeed, in soliciting financial support for far-flung
missions, the fathers would have to muster their proverbial rhetorical wiles to overcome a fundamental paradox: that the heathens to

whom they ministered were both in need of conversion and worthy of it. From the earliest explorations and persisting well beyond actual direct contact, debates regarding the actual status of the humanity of the "savages" were a staple of the writing dealing with Amerindians. The conclusions of such commissions were critical, since they could alternately serve to rationalize forced colonialism by some or lead to more enlightened policies by others.[62] To win over skeptics, Jesuit missionaries furnished complex portraits such as the famous one by Père Lejeune in which a compendium of Amerindian vices was counterbalanced by an enumeration of their virtues.[63] Among the latter, one finds interjections of praise for the superior qualities of the indigenous populace in comparison with Europeans. Although such entreaties garnered needed support, they also had the unforeseeable consequence of supplying Libertine positions with evidence that morality could prevail without institutional reinforcement: "Praise for the good savages— intoned for the greater glory of God—was turned against their unwitting admirers."[64]

Not only did the vast quantity of information provided by the Jesuits furnish religious free-thinkers with ammunition, it also encouraged the sort of critical reflection associated with the sociological revolution upon a host of social, economic, and political issues. The circulation of Jesuit relations was expanded in the following centuries by means of anthologies they had compiled and distributed as quasi-devotional literature meant to inspire virtuous thoughts among schoolchildren. Early twentieth-century scholars demonstrated the impact of Jesuit relations by juxtaposing excerpts from the relations with treatises critical of the status quo.[65] Documentation of that influence— significantly encouraged by Gustave Lanson himself—then became an integral part of student manuals in the history of French ideas and literature.

One reason for including Durkheim's pedagogy study in the current overview of his work is that it contrasts the fierce institutional rivalry between literature and the social sciences with the convergence between his positions and those of Lanson. More exactly, Lanson's method—often derided by the forces of postwar New Criticism—is reconsidered in relation to the sociological revolution in which he opted to participate. As late as 1941, for instance, Lucien Febvre deplored the fact that Lanson's projected social history of French literature had not materialized. In contrast with monographs that cater to the cult of individual authors, its portrait of the anonymous reading public would have broadened the conventional tableau of the literary life of the nation. Similarly, Lanson sought to decentralize literary activity from Paris to the provinces. Whereas the concentration of French literary life in Paris is obvious, less appreciated is the role played by centralization in the political control of writers exerted by the Sun-King, whose benevolent as well as munificent support of the arts—especially literature—constitutes yet one more myth sociologists have sought to dispel. To describe the situation of writers at once elevated to a position of prestige while beholden to an enlightened despot, Alain Viala coined the expression "confiscated consecration" to capture the esthetic and ideological compromises their newly attained situation also imposed.[66]

Against the monopoly exerted by neoclassical literature, Durkheim conceded a special role to popular writing and representations, or to those works of literature in which the embryonic forces of future sensibilities and moral ideals exist in gestation (see chapter 1). Whereas in *Division of Labor in Society* most literature was equated with the anachronistic forms of the collective *conscience*—or else so individualized as to no longer be relevant to large sectors of the population—myths and legends are now upheld as illustrations of mental processes "which provide greater insight into the nature of intelligence than reasoned operations" (376). The appearance of *Elementary Forms* (1912) signaled Durkheim's most controversial exploration into the "irrational": the attempt to conceptualize the transformation of the "sensible" realm into a collective domain of representations from which emanate fundamental categories and even scientific concepts.[67] The collective order, he proclaimed, demonstrates that the principle of non-contradiction believed essential to the formulation of all (Western) thought can be, and systematically is, violated in a variety of representational systems or other cultural logics. Myths, for instance, far from constituting local eccentricities or aberrations in relation to a supposed broad evolutionary trend toward heightened rationality, often exert greater influence than their scientific counterparts:

> In myths one encounters beings that are both themselves and other, who are at once single and double, spiritual and material. The idea that a substance can be infinitely divided without being diminished, and while remaining whole in all aspects of its matter, is fundamental

to all sorts of beliefs and practices that one finds among a variety of peoples, and which have not disappeared. (373)

Myths thus service two fundamental premises of Durkheimian sociology: the first contends that individuals are dual. Both self and other, social as well as individuated, they nonetheless suffer from the misguided assumption that that relationship is fundamentally adversarial. According to conventional wisdom, only those willing to unquestioningly submit to sacrifices are able to momentarily palliate the experiential sense of dividedness. The second part of the description of myths corroborates Durkheim's paradoxical contention that the specialization of the modern division of labor can both enhance the individual as well as the totality, since each element of the "infinitely divided" social contributes to a whole greater than the sum of its parts. In the same discussion, he further distinguishes between a logic directed toward the understanding of things, and one that seeks to account for the relation of humans to society. Myths, he concludes, would not exist if earlier peoples had understood the social origins of their existence, thus providing a striking illustration of the parallels between archaic totemism and modern philosophy. By placing the archaic and the modern on a continuum, Durkheimian sociology broke with the point of view of Lucien Lévy-Bruhl, who studied "primitive pre-logical thought" on its own terms but always as distinct from that of moderns.

The scandalous implications of Durkheim's positions were not lost on the Agathon polemicists, for whom they represented a betrayal of the French literary tradition's ability to provide the collective representations for French youth and society by replacing them with the morality of "savages," since in sociology "the mores of Botocudos and Iroquois savages appear most frequently. . . . Under the influence of M. Durkheim . . . [m]orality, known academically as the Science of Mores, is no more than an auxiliary of historical sociology."[68] Massis and de Tarde rightly discerned that in the ethnographic definition of culture suggested by E. B. Tylor in 1871, for instance, the connotations of high culture developed within the civilizing process cede to a broader, more comprehensive view of culture or civilization in the widest ethnographic sense to include knowledge, belief, art, morals, law, custom, and any other capabilities and habits acquired by the individual as a member of society. Their reaction represents a continuation of the collusion between social and intellectual opposition to ethnography cited by Mauss as the main explanation for its inferior development in France throughout the nineteenth century, a persistent stagnation evidenced well into the first part of the twentieth century that was reversed only with the reforms initiated by the new Sorbonnards:

> From then on, the debate regarding primitive societies takes place within the highest echelons of the university establishment, such as the French Society for Philosophy or within philosophical reviews, thus consecrating the culmination of a trajectory that led ethnology from a position of marginality to the summit of academic honor (as symbolized by the 1935 creation of a chair specifically for Marcel Mauss at the Collège de France).[69]

The relevance of ethnography's institutional status to the sociological revolution is considered in the section to follow.

Sociologie à la Française

French sociology of the 1920s and 1930s, according to one American observer, offered the "bizarre" profile of being indistinguishable from anthropology, an allusion to the enduring effects of Durkheim's recourse to ethnographic data.[70] As Mauss proclaimed in a review of Alfred J. Kroeber's *Manual of Anthropology* in 1925, "We need ethnologists as well as sociologists: the former provide the data, the latter illuminate it."[71] Acknowledging this distinctive trait of the social sciences in his own culture, Lévi-Strauss referred scholars seeking an explanation for it to Kroeber's speculations regarding the ideological and political sources of the two fields. Though historically coeval, sociology and anthropology were rapidly invested with divergent goals in the Anglo-American traditions, leading Kroeber to hypothesize that the disciplines had sprung from differing impulses. Sociology's appeal resided in its commitment to social integration whereas anthropology provided alternative models to critics of their own society. These distinctions appear corroborated by sociology's appearance following the upheavals of 1789 and the long-standing assumptions regarding Durkheimian sociology's conservatism. The latter are belied, however, by the alternative genealogy of sociology in the anthropological thinking that Lévi-Strauss, for one, traced to the sociological revolution initiated in the sixteenth century, whose ethnographic detour delineated a privileged discursive space where controversies could be addressed. Its reappearance in the twentieth century under the aegis of modern sociology should be recognized as symptomatic of the constraints exerted upon scientific discourse as well.

In the case of Durkheim, we have seen how the possibilities offered by collective experiences subsumed under the notion of effervescence tested the very disciplinary boundaries he had initially imposed. Effervescence also carried Durkheim to the antipodes of his public persona. Resolved to objectify the experience of the social as a *prise de conscience* of joyful interdependency capable of inspiring the moral outburst witnessed in 1789, he also conceded that effervescent transformations could be perilously labile and responsible for the "sublime or the savage" scenes of the Revolution.

Following Durkheim's untimely death in 1917, the mantle of the French school fell to his nephew and frequent collaborator, Marcel Mauss. As former students or admirers of Mauss's teachings, Roger Caillois, Michel Leiris, and Georges Bataille examined the nature of social attraction and repulsion in the modern period to both understand and foment the collective actions Durkheim had associated with effervescent assemblies. Clifford's rereading of the period, in terms of the "ethnographic surrealism" or sui generis nature of the point of view forged during this period, helped to liberate Durkheim from the long-standing clichés of the staid bourgeois moralist or secular priest that stymied innovative Durkheimian scholarship in France more than elsewhere.[72] But Clifford's seductive phrase (Jamin) has also been faulted for diverting studies of the period away from a less enchanted view of the actual workings of ethnology at a time when the discipline was still groping for an autonomous identity, funding for explorations was scant and university positions few.[73] Indeed, none of the views just indicated explains how it is that the pervasive enthusiasm for the innovations of Durkheimian sociology among students at the turn of the century—to the point of being perceived as a threat to conservatives—was by the late 1930s rejected as Third Republic ideology by the generation that included Raymond Aron, Maurice Merleau-Ponty, and Jean-Paul Sartre.[74]

An appreciation of these polarized responses is further complicated by accounts of the period that emphasize Mauss's efforts to wrest ethnology from sociology's grip in order to establish it as an independent field of inquiry. As such, ethnology would be capable of encouraging the fieldwork conducted by other countries in possession of fewer colonial territories than France. With the 1925 establishment of the Institut d'Ethnologie by the socialists Lévy-Bruhl, Mauss, and Paul Rivet, French ethnology could redirect research efforts away from the politically conservative school of anthropology developed by Louis Marin at the turn of the century. Marin's notion of a Greater France encompassed the colonies as well as the metropole in an assimilation of modernism to cultural domination and held out a strong appeal to the right-wing forces of the Third Republic. Marin legitimated his opinions by means of an indigenous ethnography of French peasant life directed toward staving the rural exodus to the cities, thus preserving the landed basis for true French identity. As a scholar-activist, he was influential during the Poincaré, Reynaud, and then Vichy governments until he fell out of favor and fled to London. This unfamiliar phase of French anthropology counters the traditional hagiography on Durkheim as easily triumphing over the reactionary Agathon obstructionists prior to World War I.[75]

Assessments of sociology in the interim war period are further complicated by the metamorphoses of Durkheimianism following the master's death. Between 1920 and 1940 the considerable body of knowledge developed by the Durkheimian school represented an intellectual project of vast dimensions not readily classifiable under one rubric or agenda. Sociology was subject to a variety of academic, social, and political usages, which also account for the polarized responses it evoked at the end of the thirties. We have already considered the extent to which Durkheimianism was molded by its relations with a host of external forces, not least of which was the ambivalence manifested within the academy itself, as evidenced in Durkheim's appointment to the Faculty of Letters' section on pedagogical training. Without a full-fledged degree program to its name, sociology amounted to only one *certificat* which, from 1920 on, was taught within the framework of morality and sociology, and equaled one-fourth of the philosophy *licence* (first-level diploma). The paucity of chairs in sociology—only four in the entire system and often not identified as such—explains one assessment of sociology's institutional standing as a "semi-failure."[76] The most visible manifestation of sociology's growing intellectual prestige during this period can be traced to its paradoxical situation of being both influential and dependent upon neighboring disciplines, since among the heterogeneous Durkheimians one finds psychologists, historians, linguists, ethnologists, political scientists, and even a large number of jurists and economists within the law faculties, whose conservatism contrasted with the progressive republicanism of the new Sorbonne.

The widespread dissemination of sociology thus entailed its *effets pervers,* the consequence of an appropriative process whereby certain aspects of its contributions were enlisted to enhance the position of academics within their respective disciplines. In the same way that Bourdieu discerned a "strategy of conversion" among academics such as Lanson—trained in philosophy and literature but who appropriated the methods of the new social sciences to boost a failing career—Johan Heilbron has examined the complex maneuvres among the next generation of academics threatened by the power of attraction exerted by the newer disciplines. The paradoxical result was that heightened recognition of sociology was accompanied by reinterpretations that were significantly divergent from the work of Durkheim himself, but modulated to meet the respective needs of a variety of fields. The familiar association of Durkheim with positivism, for instance, is not substantiated by a reading of his works but emanates from one strand of appropriation. Another strategy attempted to salvage spiritualism in the early part of the century by placing Durkheim alongside Bergson. A final example of the distortions inflicted upon Durkheim's positions can be found in Célestin Bouglé's 1922 *Leçons de sociologie sur l'évolution des valeurs.*[77] By designating the study of values as sociology's primary goal, it was able to espouse "philosophical spiritualism" while denouncing as a social menace the socialism Durkheim and Mauss supported.

The social images of Durkheimianism during the interwar period are therefore inseparable from the political usage to which it was put. Sociology's scientific cachet was enlisted in the formulation of a new political philosophy inspired by "republican patriotism" and disseminated by courses in applied sociology in the primary schools or an elective one at the secondary level. Moreover, sociology's university interpreters reduced the problematic nature of the collective representations Durkheim and Mauss had come to consider the central focus of their investigations to the exclusive role of providing solidarity, cohesion and integration based upon shared values and norms.

By 1927 Bouglé described sociology as having its center nowhere and its circumference everywhere. This was an important consequence of the dispersal of the collective effort characteristic of the *Année sociologique* and with it any attempt at maintaining consistency within the sociological project. The first generation of Durkheimians presented a united front stemming from common social, geographic, and academic backgrounds that was consolidated by the opportunities offered by university expansion following the Dreyfus Affair. This appearance, however, masked underlying discord between the university professors and specialized researchers that erupted into overt division after World War I. Heilbron attributes this ideological differentiation to their respective institutional conditions: university sociology, for instance, could be taught only in conjunction with another discipline, obliging professors to maintain connections with the philosophy section from which Durkheim had sought autonomy. University sociology was thus associated with the moralism of the republican establishment. By contrast, researchers such as Mauss, François Simiand, Maurice Halbwachs, Hubert, Marcel Granet, Louis Gernet, and Hertz were all identified as socialists. University professors were more disposed to accept administrative responsibilities and benefited from the savoir-faire that accompanies superior social pedigrees. A readiness to conform to the standards dictated by the lettered paradigm also bolstered their professional successes.[78]

The exclusive concentration upon the Bouglé version of the sociological paradigm within the university establishment exacerbated the rift with the researchers and culminated in the divergence of the university version of sociology from ethnology. A telling consequence of the split is that "techniques of the body," for instance, one of Mauss's signature subjects, disappears from the roster of topics relating to the contemporary world. Mauss enjoyed a small but devoted following among students at the Ecole Pratique des Hautes Études, those for whom ethnology represented a break with university sociology to offer "something new, linked to exoticism, to the world of art, or simply to studies of archaeology, history of religion or oriental languages."[79] It would be a distortion, however, to conclude that either group represented a less adulterated version of Durkheimianism, since both directions highlight ambiguities present in the master's own strategy,

> according to a logic of conceding all in order to have the essential accepted (and perhaps in order to have himself accepted as well). This is undoubtedly why he was perceived as an ascetic, scrupulous, disinterested individual and, at the same time, as the great manipulator of the new Sorbonne, adept at playing the university game of power.[80]

Conversely, Heilbron points out that the identification of the division between university professors and researchers remained an undeveloped chapter in the history of sociology because of the widespread image of the Durkheimians as a closed dogmatic school—a view polemicized by the right at the turn of the century, revived within the "generation of 1930," and then passed on as intellectual doxa.

In contrast with the repudiation of sociology among those youth Agathon claimed to represent, another generation of scholars declared their fervent adherence to the version transmitted via the teachings of Mauss. Following extensive collaboration prior to Durkheim's death in 1917, and without renouncing major elements of the French school's contributions, Mauss gradually distinguished his own work by providing the institutional framework for ethnography to develop as an autonomous discipline. Despite a personal lack of field experience, he devised a manual that guided several generations of French ethnographers. But even Durkheim's endorsement of the symbiotic relationship between sociology and ethnography did not guarantee ethnology immediate entry into the circle of legitimate university disciplines at the same time as sociology. The terms *social science* and *sociology* appeared in 1886 in a course offered by Durkheim at the Faculty of Letters in Bordeaux, whereas ethnology had to wait almost fifty years for comparable recognition. The *certificats* in ethnology first awarded in 1926–27 remained worthless unless used to complete a degree in either philosophy or sociology, since the first ethnology *licence* (or university-level degree) was not established until 1968. Other benchmarks of legitimation such as the creation of a university chair occurred as late as 1943, when it was used to honor Marcel Griaule. By these criteria, ethnology (with perhaps the exception of general linguistics) thus stands "historically, as the last major disciplinary unit to enter into the university literary field in France."[81]

Mauss's 1933 assessment of ethnology indicates that by then the discipline had succeeded in declaring scientific independence from sociology. It also attained institutional visibility by means of courses and degree programs from the baccalaureate to the university. The author's tone is nonetheless overwhelmingly elegaic, a mournful reminder of the generation of brilliant young scholars lost to the ravages of the Great War. Among the sacrificed, André Durkheim was destined to succeed his father. Inconsolable, sociology's founder did not survive the massive devastation and the French school suffered an obvious decline with his passing. The survivors' homage was to continue the sweeping research program Durkheim had initiated by collecting data to fill any major lacunae. Mauss thus characterizes the postwar efforts as "less systematic and generalizing, somewhat dispersed and renouncing the terrain of ideas for that of facts."[82] Most demoralizing is his concession that by the 1930s the perception of the Durkheimian school was that it was primarily a conduit for republican ideology.

As the preeminent figure of French ethnology, Mauss distinguished his teachings by a brilliantly suggestive style coupled with vast erudition. Students recount following him from one lecture hall to another: "His courses were in fact essentially a questionnaire so that his auditors could find matter to reflect upon."[83] Most significantly, his influence is recalled as having furnished the ideas "that spiritually nourished an entire generation."[84] Moving among several institutions, he remained marginal to the university but was awarded a chair at the prestigious Collège de France (1931–42), where Durkheim had been denied the same honor. The major figures of the Collège de Sociologie discussed in this study—Georges Bataille, Michel Leiris, and Roger Caillois—all had some knowledge of Mauss's work, whether as students or through his publications.

All three reached their maturity in the interwar period. Too young to participate in any aspect of World War I, they did not share those formative experiences with many of the surrealists, including Breton. Bataille was trained at the prestigious Ecole des Chartes and until the late twenties appeared destined for a career as a numismatist. He never attended Mauss's lectures but was introduced to them by an ethnographer, Alfred Métraux, a close friend who dates Bataille's interest in ethnography from World War I. Responsible for Bataille's first "encounter with ethnographers" at the 1928 exhibit of pre-Colombian art, Métraux later claimed that Bataille's review of the event revealed him to be "the precursor to a school of ethnologists who sought to define the ethos or system of values which provides each civilization with its specificity."[85] With its sanguinary images of sun worship and Aztec sacrificial rituals, Bataille's commentary certainly prefigured the main elements of his theory of expenditure, subsequently enhanced by Mauss's erudite essay on the gift whose main points Métraux had transmitted to him.

A student of Mauss, Leiris joined one of the most important and extensive field expeditions of the period, spanning from Dakar to

Djibouti between 1931 and 1933. His was to prove the most sustained engagement with ethnography, leading to several specialized monographs arising from his investigations into the secret language of the Dogon of Sanga and possession ceremonies in Ethiopia.[86] Indeed, parallel to his acclaimed literary output, Leiris contributed essays on race and colonial relations under the auspices of the Musée de l'homme, where he maintained an office until the end of his life.

As the youngest of the major contributors to the Collège, Caillois was born in 1913 and therefore the most removed from the events of 1914–18. The influence he exerted during the early thirties among cohorts at the Parisian lycée Louis-le-Grand encouraged one friend and admirer, André Chastel, to view him as exemplar for the immediate prewar generation, otherwise "bereft of a legend: nor is it able to claim for itself a great novel. The narratives masked a sort of cultural mediocrity. The same can be said for art. The university dozed, and intellectuals sought an *engagement* which did not always succeed very well."[87] Caillois and his peers reacted to this desultory state of affairs by sarcastically commenting that a review entitled *Panique* would best translate the general ambiance. In their search for iconoclastic alternatives, they pursued paths opened by the Surrealists, with whom Caillois joined forces in 1932, to explore the margins of traditional culture. Similarly, they investigated anthropological references Chastel summarizes as esoteric to the authority and legitimacy determined by the positive sciences:

> To the extent it dominates minds, positivism, with its implacable and necessary power of elimination, relegates to the margins of superstition all sorts of speculations inherited from lost mythologies and cosmologies fallen into desuetude: herein lies the privileged terrain of childhood games, of fables, of collective passions disguised by naive or bellicose images, and of course, of all literature, whether good or bad.[88]

Caillois attended Mauss's courses at the Ecole pratique between 1933 and 1935 while enrolled at the Ecole normale supérieure.[89]

During the 1930s the primary area of contention for Mauss was no longer the border between sociology and ethnology but the place of psychology in relation to both. At stake was whether sociology was better qualified to address the nature of (collective) *représentations*. The findings of psychology were regarded as problematic because they could provide only extrapolations from the individual to the group without touching upon the distinctively collective—sui generis nature—of social facts. One of the abiding tenets held by Durkheim is that because social phenomena emanate from collective sources they are inherently superior to those generated by individuals. The existence of rules and laws exacting sacrifices from individuals confirms the sociological claim that it is by means of collective gatherings and rituals that individuals attain the higher level of social being traditionally equated with the sacred. Most disconcerting to reviewers of *Elementary Forms* was that Durkheim traced the origins of not only religion, but of virtually all major cultural forms, to effervescent gatherings whose model were the "wild" ceremonies of the Australian aborigines. Despite his disclaimers, the latter were likened by readers to the eruptions of crowd behavior haunting the fin-de-siècle conservative social imagination.[90] With its concentration upon archaic religious practices, Durkheim's *Elementary Forms* was also critiqued as the culmination of an intellectual and career trajectory in which politics received diminished importance within each succeeding phase. More damaging was that by the 1930s the National-Socialist and fascist mass movements appeared as horrific realizations of the sociological collective ideal.[91]

All of the preceding issues contextualize the formation of the Collège de Sociologie when, at the close of the "terrible thirties" (Caillois), the conjunction of sociology with the sacred appeared as a solution to the concerns of a generation caught between two hells, when the ambient sense of crisis apparently could not be adequately grasped by other, previously explored modes of intellectual and political activism. Conveners of the Collège recognized that fascism had tapped into latent desires for an alternative to capitalism but channeled such inclinations toward repressive ends. Their intellectual response was to initiate sociological studies of the affective basis for collective movements in the forces of attraction and repulsion they associated with the sacred. With its extension of the findings of the French school into a complex, ambivalent notion of the sacred derived from Hertz—encompassing both pure and impure, or right and left manifestations—coupled with investigations into the sacred's relevance to modern social phenomena, the Collège provided French social thought with a corrective to the bias that the category of the sacred should be reserved exclusively for the anthropological study of non-Western, nonindustrialized societies. In the chapters to follow we examine the consequences of these assumptions for politics, art, and eroticism.

Three

Politics and the Sacred in the Collège de Sociologie

Roger Caillois explained the impulse to create a group united by the notion of a sacred sociology by comparing it to the ferment that had fueled the surrealist project. Both he and Michel Leiris had actively pursued interactions with members of the avant-garde movement during their formative years, although conflicts with André Breton eventually led to a suspension of shared activity. Georges Bataille resisted formal identification with the surrealists and engaged in acerbic disputations with Breton in the late 1920s. That they subsequently collaborated on the 1936 *Contre-Attaque* antifascist declaration signals the complex relations arising from animosities as well as elective affinities within even this restricted cohort. By the time of the Collège, participants judged surrealism as a movement that had reached its apogee of influence a decade earlier. The closing years of the 1930s were haunted by a sense of war's inevitability, at odds with the pacifying official discourse. The urgency for a Collège forged from moral sentiments other than those to which scholars usually respond was exacerbated by the looming catastrophe. But the political pressures exerted by the debacle of parliamentary democracy coupled with a domestic as well as foreign fascist menace did not deter the Collège from an appreciation of the horror ahead in terms of the sentiments it provoked within.

Caillois points out that despite the unity fostered among the sur-realists through explorations of the unconscious—with its rich dream material and innovative forms of the "marvelous"—they remained in-effectual at translating esoteric experiments into cohesive political ac-tion. He imputes their failure to the discrepancy between intimate pre-occupations and collective causes, a gap better bridged by research in the social sciences effected for nearly a half century. Starting from the assumption that there exist certain "rare, fleeting, and violent mo-ments" upon which the individual places "extreme value,"[1] the prima-ry goal the Collegians set was to explore collective equivalents at the level of social formations, whether churches, armies, brotherhoods, or secret societies—groups whose etiology can be traced to the unifying movements of attraction and repulsion characterized as sacred.

Confirmation of the sacred nature of the group in archaic cultures reinforced what was already a basic premise of French sociology: that the group, rather than the individual, constitutes the basic unit of social analysis. The infusion of ethnographic data by Durkheim and Mauss nonetheless helped to deflect the conceptualization of modern social collectivities away from the reactionary politics of De Bonald and Maistre, whose opposition to the principles of 1789 advocated a total subordination of the individual to the collectivity reinvested with ab-solute authority. Whereas the latters' counterrevolutionary ideology could be dismissed as a scandalous aberration of little concrete politi-cal consequence, their social views were nonetheless judged as having provided the basis of a new science of society, sociology. Thus, even as Durkheim tried to reconcile the sociological primacy of the group with republican and democratic ideals, his extreme valorization of the collective placed sociology at odds with the dominant economic and political individualism of liberal theory. Because the history of free-dom has been written largely in terms of the individual, arguments for the preeminence of the group immediately went against liberalism's consecration of the heroic *conscience libre* standing for innovation and progress in the face of collective tyranny and oppression.[2]

By the end of the nineteenth century, French reflections on the group could be identified with two opposing tendencies: on one side, the positive endorsements of Léon Bourgeois's solidarism within the syndicalist and socialist movements; on the other, the crowd psycholo-gies of Tarde and LeBon, whose explicit political message was the denunciation of socialism as a manifestation of mass hysteria. This agenda was certainly a major contributing factor to the immense popularity of LeBon's *La psychologie des foules* (1895). Especially revealing of the author's political motives was his contention that the revolutions of nineteenth-century France could be dismissed as popular revolts that left fundamental institutions intact. Published in the heat of social unrest, rapid technological change and modernization, LeBon's treatise reassuringly argued that the changes crowds demand will never be implemented, since they are driven by "irreducibly conservative instincts, and like all primitives have a fetishistic respect for tradition, as well as an unconscious horror of innovations capable of modifying their real conditions of existence."[3] The historical significance of LeBon's treatise derives from its record of popular myths and phantasms regarding the crowd phenomenon. As heirs to the mid-century obsession with the expanding proletariat—*classes laborieuses, classes dangereuses*—the early crowd psychologies effectively discredited mass action at a time when workers were gaining access to legitimate parliamentary representation. Such texts elide the social origins of the post-Commune workers' movement in order to characterize it as an anonymous mass which, irrespective of its particular social composition, succumbs to predictable psychological laws. One explanation for LeBon's appeal outside the scientific community's general disdain resides in the fact that his contentions regarding the nefarious effects of crowd comportment—irrationality, lowered intellectual capacity of each individual, propensity to violence, the hypnotic influence of the leader over his followers—helped to justify the repression of political demonstrations vilified as mass gatherings. By documenting the primary source of violence in the forces of law and order, historical studies have provided an important corrective to the nineteenth-century equation of mass action with violent, irrational, hysterical, and easily manipulated, stereotypical crowd behavior.[4]

The academic exception to this trend within the social sciences was Durkheim, whose democratic allegiances were indisputable. From within the same social, historical, and epistemological framework that spawned the crowd psychologies, modern sociology emerged under his aegis. Friend of Jaurès, committed Dreyfusard and socialist, Durkheim was dedicated to resolving the problem of social solidarity and cohesion in terms consonant with his republicanism and moral individualism. His exceptionalism can be explained by the fact that his references to the *assemblée* or *rassemblement* preclude the group as a mob responsible, as he put it, for lynchings. Durkheim's dogmatic insistence that sociology expunge all vestiges of psychologism so that social facts be explained only by other social facts may have struck even his contemporaries as unduly rigid disciplinary protectionism. But it can also be appreciated as a necessary tactic to distinguish his theory of collective behavior from LeBon's crowd psychology, which reproduced widespread racist, classist, and sexist biases disguised as science.[5]

According to Durkheim, assemblies are intentional gatherings where individual minds are strengthened rather than weakened and where the sacred rather than evil prevails. But the strongest point of difference with LeBon resides in the value each ascribes to the outcome of collective behavior. Whereas LeBon cites the self-sacrificing enthusiasm of the revolutionary Conventionnels as evidence of the crowd's irrationality, for Durkheim the same reference instantiates his admiration for the collectivity's attainment of moral ideals. Similarly, Durkheim compares in laudatory terms the courage and surging energies accompanying collective life with the epitome of religious experience, while LeBon derides these effusions as dangerous outbursts of unbridled force.[6] Beyond respect for social ideals to assure survival of the group, Durkheim sought a more complex, affirmative representation of the social, one that would encompass its creative potential for regeneration and renewal. The outcome of the efforts Bataille characterizes as endemic to all of modernity was the lesson transmitted by archaic social organization, whose alternating pattern of dispersion and concentration was dictated by the opposition between the sacred and the profane as guarantor of social equilibrium.[7] Instead of calling for the revival of sacred values, especially those associated with the right sacred, Durkheim drew upon a radical representation of the sacred that did not recoil from the undecidable transformative effervescence associated with social and political innovations.

Sociology thus became an essential resource for the Collège's investigation of the interface between the social and the political as a key to understanding the nature of collective movements. But if Durkheim described how, under the effect of "some great collective shock," individuals gather more frequently, exchange ideas more intensely, and thus generate collective ideals and actions, the challenge to form a Collège was posed by the perception of a moral panic among the French populace confronting the threat of imminent war and possible

death. With its claim that death is the underlying catalyst for movements of attraction as well as repulsion, and that the need to mediate
encounters with it prompts the consecration of sacred places, persons,
or things, the Collège united under the banner of a *sacred sociology*.
Descriptions of collective effusion associated with sacred rites and festivals in *Les Formes élémentaires de la vie religieuse* (1912) provided a
common reference for the Collegians' ethnographic approach to the
sacred as well as a means for tracing its presence in modern society.
Conveners acknowledged their debt to the French school's basic premises that the social whole is greater than the sum of its parts, that the
collectivity induces transformations within its participants, and that
such transformation is accessible and sustainable only within a *mouvement d'ensemble*. For these reasons, the group was viewed as the privileged locus for explorations whose isolated pursuit could induce madness or suicide.

For the Collège, the group in question is ascribed the status of a
heterogeneous force of potential disruption—even destruction—within
the homogeneous whole. Correlatively, it is also conceived as the *foyer
d'énergie* or nucleus of what Bataille described as "violent silence"
responsible for transmuting the forces of the left sacred into those
of the right. Acknowledging his debt to Robertson Smith for the
added nuance between pure and impure sacred, Durkheim described
religious forces as both benevolent and malevolent, inspiring awe, respect, admiration, and recognition on the one hand, and fear and horror on the other. Like the sacred/profane antinomy, the opposition between right and left sacred is drastic and verges on antagonism: the
first category is forbidden to the second, and all contact between them
is viewed as profanation. Despite the distance separating the two
poles of religious life, there exists a strong filiation between them as
well: both maintain the same taboo relation to the profane and both
are removed from the normal circulation of objects and persons. Finally, both inspire ambivalent sentiments even though one is associated
with respect and the other with horror. As Durkheim reminds, "there
actually is a certain horror in religious respect, especially when it is
very intense."[8]

By affixing sacred to its general conceptualization of sociology,
the Collège underscored the active and dynamic characteristics of the
Durkheimian concept of the group. These transformations occur in
several ways: for the individual, it signals access to another "level of

being" (Levinas), which Durkheim equated with the sacred.[9] Its effects upon consciousness are significant, since it is when individuals gather together in moments of festivity or celebration that they are prone to open themselves to each other and their respective consciousness cedes to the presence of another. If this experience is qualified as moral, it is because individuals are projected *hors de soi,* beyond their immurement into a recognition of what Mauss admired as their "imbrication" with each other. This privileged moment is what Durkheim qualified as sacred because it occurs when the group becomes aware of itself as something other than a mere juxtaposition of individuals and as a result forges the bonds of solidarity. In a similar vein, Bataille concluded that the sacred was discerned in the communication it engenders and, by extension, in the formation of new psychic beings. The status of *person* is thus granted to individuals who initiate a rupture with their original social identity. Liberation from the unexamined life presupposes recognition of the deluded nature of primary modes of consciousness restricted to an individualized, internal sense of presence: "In any case, nothing allows us to content ourselves with the unique importance that the human consciousness of the lone individual assigns to itself." Bataille's deconstruction does not lead him to espouse the Durkheimian notion of a *conscience collective*—"Why not bluntly acknowledge that we are here in the most obscure domain of knowledge?"[10] What he asserts, and reiterates in subsequent works, is that a human being exists only within a social formation, and that the ties that render communication possible also effect some type of psychic modification. *Community* therefore designates the regrouping of individuals on a new plane, following the break with primary social affiliation.

In a postsacred society, sociological representations contribute to the *prise de conscience* by detecting survivals from the past capable of exerting the constitutive force that has always been a distinguishing feature of the sacred.[11] By examining groups formed through movements of attraction and repulsion, sacred sociology attempts to maintain the polarity of the two extremes. Bataille's schema of mediation offers an alternative to the recuperating effects of the dialectic by sustaining the possibility of a social nucleus through which forces otherwise inaccessible or intolerable to common states of consciousness must pass: "the fact [is] that union among humans is not immediate union, but is accomplished around a very strange reality, an incomparable and obsessive force; that if human relations stop passing through this middle term, this nucleus of violent silence, they are emptied of their human character." What emerges from these characterizations is that the basis for social formations is neither material survival, nor love, nor biological necessity, but a common repulsion, as evidenced in the center or sacred locus containing a taboo object or person. Occulted in daily life, repressed by the conscious mind, the repugnance and horror elicited by certain phenomena are brought to consciousness by the circuitous detours associated with the *prise de conscience:* "It is only to the extent that a mind has been led to recognize the fundamental identity between the taboo marking impure things and the purest forms of the sacred that it is able to become conscious of the violent repulsions constituting the specificity of the general movements that create human community."[12]

Distinguished from the *homo clausus* of Western philosophy or the Freudian subject torn between libidinal desires and the repressive exigencies of civilization, the sociological subject is determined by a group identity that passes through its conscience. Whether this awareness occurs by means of the structured cooperation of the division of social labor, or spontaneous moments of effervescence, it provides the basis for the consolidation of the group's existence:

> By themselves, individual consciousnesses are actually closed to one another, and they can communicate only by means of signs in which their inner states come to express themselves. For the communication that is opening up between them to end in a communion—that is, in a fusion of all the individual feelings into a common one—the signs that express those feelings must come together in a single resultant. The appearance of this resultant notifies individuals that they are in unison and brings home to them their moral unity.[13]

The research domains charted by the Collège—secret societies, religious orders, even the army, as well as political vanguard movements bypassed by most ethnography—were chosen because they illustrate a basic assumption: that the group provides what the individual cannot. These groups offer the means toward a collective end, but they also represent a modification, even satisfaction, of *the individual's sense of lack:* "We are whole only outside ourselves, in the human plenitude of an assembly, but we are only whole after having responded (through an assembly) to our most intimate demands."[14] Yet Bataille also concedes—as Durkheim warned—that moral mediocrity may lead one to believe that "a whole existence is no longer any more than a simple dream for us, a dream fed by historical descriptions and the secret gleam of our passions."[15] This is where the so-called contagious ethnographic representations play a crucial role in bringing to conscious awareness a possibility otherwise occulted within modernity.

When describing the nature of the groups they would study, Caillois and Bataille alluded to "secret" societies in order to connote a unifying basis in feelings and sentiments suppressed in most social settings rather than reference to a conspiratorial plot. *Secret* in this context is comparable to *myth*, since it touches upon a constitutive and seductive reality: "Myth is born in ritual acts concealed from the static vulgarity of a disintegrated society, but the violent dynamic belonging to it has no other object than the return to a lost totality."[16] *Totality* is understood as the palliative to the fragmentation of science and action, which require at least partial investment into a specialized activity. If this sounds like a rebuttal to the division of labor, we recall that Durkheim also assumed that workers would be "coordinated and subordinated to one another around a central organ which exercises a moderating action."[17] The totality in question here is distinguished from the "closed" system inherited from Hegel, incapable of accounting for the negativity or force that refuses, subverts, or explodes the recovering effects of the dialectic. As experienced by the Bataillian subject, negativity reveals an individual consciousness suffering the condition of an "open wound," in itself—so Bataille claims—a refutation of Hegel. Refusing the consolation of action defined as productivity, it seeks the possibility of completion in a sovereignty differentiated from Hegelian mastery. If Hegel recognized negativity either as destruction, or else sublimated into work, action, or a project, Bataille characterizes modern negativity as immobilized not from fear of action, but for lack of opportunities. One alternative is what Bataille deplores as the *ineffectual* negativity of a work of art where, as in the example of traditional religion, negativity is recouped as an object of contemplation, thus refusing it recognition "at the very moment it enters into the play of existence as a stimulus to major vital reactions."[18] Whereas institutionalized art and religion function to transmute the disruptive violence of negativity into socially sanctioned modes of expression, Bataille enlists the paradigm of conversion from the left to the right sacred in order to account for the movements of attraction and repulsion the Collège determined as its primary focus. Such an investigation falls under the purview of a sacred sociology since it points to a post-Durkheimian tracing of the subterranean movements of negativity prior to legitimation. Sacred sociology's alternative to the Hegelian equation of negativity with destruction draws upon the French school's bifurcation of the sacred to encompass a virulent, threatening, and powerful left sacred, as well as a right one associated with order and stability.

Following Hegel's recognition of the specifically human character of negativity, Bataille posited expenditure in the most extreme sense as the basis for social groups. Imputing to humans a need to move beyond themselves in order to participate in some broader social experience, he explained the origins of the sacred in sacrifice, in the ability to lose oneself as well as things, a sentiment traditionally sanctioned in an effervescent festival-like atmosphere of ritualized destruction. With this possible opening out onto other consciousnesses among individuals generally conditioned to resist such intrusions, communication occurs. What the sociological perspective argues is that the surge of energies expressed in religious sacrifices or in war, while ostensibly related to some function, possess an attraction "all their own." Historically, the rare expressions of such sentiments free of social censure were tragedy and religion. With their relative demise in the modern world it became necessary to consult the social sciences—especially the ethnographic representations derived from sociology's research into non-Western cultures—for intimations of what sacred experiences can reveal: "In this way science, to the extent that its object is human negativity— especially the sacred left—becomes the middle term of what is only a process of awareness."[19] From its inception, the Collège declared that participants must draw upon exotic representations derived from French ethnography without fear of their potentially "contagious" effects. Ethnographic representations would provide collective alternatives to the predominant categories restricted to the individual sense of self. Echoing Durkheim, the Collège texts point out, "Just as there exists a primitive, irreducible experience of self constituting the basic dynamic of anarchic individualism, the same sort of existential, inalienable basis of *collective* effort must be brought to light."[20] Myth, death rituals, and festivals may be marginalized in relation to the allegedly rational foundations of society, but these collective phenomena can provide insight into the (affective) basis of modern social structures.

The *prise de conscience* according to Bataille underscores the paradoxes of the sacred in relation to modernity. Durkheim circumvented the impasse of the sacred's marginalization as either superfluous or antithetical to action by redefining human *telos* in relation to *expendi-*

ture. Shortly prior to the appearance of *Elementary Forms,* he delivered a talk on values and judgments of reality, setting forth in no uncertain terms his own valorization of disinterested action. Arguing for recognition of the gratuitous precisely because it partakes of the same realm of morality motivating sacrifices (understood in the sense of an offering rather than renunciation), he provided a striking formulation of action as a mode of expenditure: "To live is above all things to act, to act without counting the cost and for the pleasure of acting. If the evidence demands that we do not discount economy, as man must amass in order to expend, nevertheless that *expenditure is his end, and to expend is to act.*"[21]

References to action in Collège texts, however, are fraught with paradox. The writers alternately deplore its mutilating effects or decry its impossibility in the modern world. We recall that the Collège de Sociologie was formed in response to the general ambience of paralysis and of doom experienced by the French populace. The Collegians attribute this reaction to a more pervasive condition of modernity: individuals are unable to act collectively in general, and even less so when specifically confronted with outward manifestations of internal fears and anxieties, especially those associated with their own mortality. Action is therefore perceived as contingent upon a *prise de conscience* that leads individuals (1) to discern the need for expenditure in the broad senses developed by both Durkheim and Bataille described above, and (2) to sustain negativity dissociated from an exclusively (Hegelian) connotation of destruction.

For Bataille, the paradoxical value of that awareness is to show that expenditure (or in its extreme version, *dépense*), which undermines accumulation and concentration, can also be recognized as the basis for social unification. Indeed, one of his central arguments is that the sources of social cohesion are not to be found in the rational contractual relations posited by Spencer, for instance, any more than those relations can account for the nature of political relations. In the same way that he had earlier enlisted Mauss's findings regarding the sources of the gift and gift-relations to present a view of social relations irreducible to pure exchange, so now Bataille envisions the sacred as a way to deconstruct assumptions regarding politics as a manifestation of those contractual relations within the realm of power. Both positions eschew Marxist economism or group psychology in favor of the contributions of French sociology that validate the allegedly irrational extreme expenditure Durkheim equated with the self-sacrificing morality of effervescent explosions leading to new forms of social organization and cohesion. By insisting upon recognition of mechanisms that militate against accumulation, the *prise de conscience* thus addresses the immediate demand for an analysis of fascism by demonstrating how it is that social, religio-sacred, military, and political forces became *concentrated* into a single figure or "head."

Assessments of the Collège de Sociologie as a group face the particular challenges posed by a sociohistorical phenomenon eccentric to standard disciplinary criteria. Some detractors have dismissed as puerile and/or impossible the very premise of surpassing conventional boundaries of intellectual exchange in order to generate political and social activity.[22] Another perspective holds that the deliberate provocation of such overflows of energy constitutes a flirtation with violence, a potentially dangerous swerve toward the impulses that feed fascism. While the Collège itself was exonerated from any overt collusion,[23] the belated French confrontation with the intellectual sources of anti-Semitism and racism in the thirties has encouraged postwar historians to place the entire period under suspicion. Especially targeted is the pervasive tendency among the "non-conformists of the 30's,"[24] disaffected from parliamentary politics, institutionalized religion, and university-based knowledge, to channel their discontent into the formation of elective groups. Even the Collège's recourse to ethnography, whether references to Dumézil or its allegedly "particular" enlistment of Durkheim, has singled it out for rebuke.[25] Thus, despite evidence to the contrary,[26] the history of the Collège has been ascribed an "exemplary" status, based on its allegedly shared fascination for National-Socialism with "vast sectors of the French intelligentsia."[27]

Durkheim's work suffered a somewhat similar fate, since by the mid-thirties the mass ceremonies in Germany made his emphasis upon collective representations and experiences increasingly problematic to evaluate. Mauss acknowledged the dangers of the French school's version of collective phenomena while defending his uncle against accusations that Durkheim's early endorsement of corporate associations may have served as a model for Mussolini's fasci. The following excerpt appeared in Mauss's response to his former student, Svend Ranulf:

> Durkheim, and after him the rest of us are, I believe, those who founded the theory of the authority of the collective representation. One

thing that, fundamentally, we never foresaw was how many large modern societies, that have more or less emerged from the Middle Ages in other respects, could be hypnotized like Australians are by their dances, and set in motion like a children's roundabout. This return to the primitive was not the object of our thoughts. We contented ourselves with several allusions to crowd situations, while it was a question of something quite different. We also contented ourselves with proving that it was in the collective mind *[dans l'esprit collectif]* that the individual could find the basis and sustenance for his liberty, his independence, his personality and his criticism *[critique]*. Basically, we never allowed for the extraordinary new possibilities.[28]

In another letter authorizing the publication of the foregoing passage, Mauss insisted upon the following addendum (May 8, 1938): "I believe that all of this is a real tragedy for us, too powerful a verification of things that we had indicated and proof that we should have expected this verification through evil rather than a verification through good."[29] Indeed, in one of his final lectures, this eminent representative of the French school—who had earlier claimed that an individual's ideas were the expression of the group—now felt compelled to endow each person with the ability to resist submission to a leader.

The defense of sociology provided by the rereading of *Elementary Forms* in chapter 1 offers an alternative to Mauss's position. We recall that Durkheim's demonstration of the paradox of the sacred as a propensity of the group to invest its collective energies into a symbol occulting its social source led him to appeal to collective representations in consolidating the individual's sense of identification with the social whole. In the absence of collective rites and rituals, the individual must attain an awareness of social dependence through other means. While critics who discern a progressive loss of reference to politics in Durkheim's work are literally correct, they also undervalue the shift to symbolic systems in his last phase, which is integral to the charge he imposed upon sociology if it is to influence the political life of the nation. By examining the crisis of representation described by Durkheim as early as 1893 in relation to the interwar period, it is possible to appreciate the connection between the sacred's centrality in *Elementary Forms* and the overall movement of a lifework committed to a moral vision based upon socialist principles.[30]

I therefore argue that it was precisely a political impetus that prompted Durkheim to denounce society's sacralization of certain individuals who, like the totemic gods, rob the group of its collective energies:

> If society should happen to become infatuated with a man, believing it has found in him its deepest aspirations as well as the means of fulfilling them, then that man will be put in a class by himself and virtually deified. Opinion will confer on him a grandeur that is similar in every way to the grandeur that protects the gods. This has happened to many sovereigns in whom their epochs had faith and who, if not deified outright, were looked upon as direct representatives of the godhead. . . . Moreover, the routine deference that men invested with high social positions receive is not qualitatively different from religious respect.[31]

With this demonstration of the parallel processes by means of which power is produced through the concentration of collective energies into social as well as religious figures, Durkheimian sociology provided Bataille with the theoretical perspective needed to substantiate one of the basic assumptions derived from Kierkegaard—that what passes for politics in the modern period often has a religious source.

The formation of the Collège was prompted by the perception of a generalized moral panic within a populace menaced by war. Characterized by "consternation, resignation and fear," the disarray of the French only reinforced the Collège's dismissal of available political positions and the failure of parliamentary democracy to foster a united front. That the Collège's politics elude definitive categorization in terms of traditional left/right distinctions can be traced to the group's refusal to support any specific party following its repudiation of the political sellout of the 1938 Munich accords. Instead, contributors diagnosed the international crisis as symptomatic of the modern fragmentation dictated by laws of the marketplace, whose rationalization of social life leads to specialization, isolation, and, ultimately, the sort of "emasculation" witnessed among men so fearful of death that it becomes the major impediment to spontaneous collective action. It is therefore significant that the Collège proposed an alternative to traditional sociology by studying only groups whose adherents had either initiated or selected them. Herein resides a crucial distinction between the orientation of the Collège and the fascistic celebration of the right side of the sacred, encompassing institutions sanctioned by official ideology and political hierarchy. With its attention to the left sacred (though a neat equation between politics and religion cannot be drawn, as Bataille noted), the Collège foregrounded areas otherwise dismissed as marginal but in fact capable of revealing how the prevailing homogeneous identity is forged. It is precisely the distinction between the fascist appeal to a *communauté de fait* (primary community)—whether the eternal *patrie* or *la vieille France* whose mythic solidarity often relies upon xenophobia and anti-Semitism—and the Collège goal of an intentional secondary community responsive to the historical context, that has been singled out as one of its distinguishing features.[32]

Because of fascism's broad social appeal, the Collège refused to place exclusive onus for its popularity upon a betrayal by the working class. By extending analyses to the movements responsible for social upheavals subsumed under the tension between the sacred and the profane, it sought to uncover the mechanisms—especially psychological—that account for the lure of fascism from within. In the sections to follow, I review the relevance of that point of view to the interim war period as well as to subsequent historical conjunctures.

Power and the Sacred

Within the context of the Collège, analyses of movements of attraction and repulsion responsible for the communifying movements deemed sacred represent the culmination of earlier efforts—most notably Bataille's—to explain the psychological appeal of fascism. Active in the Cercle communiste démocratique, which had been organized in the early 1930s by Boris Souvarine, a prominent leftist critic of the Stalinist turn of the Russian revolution, Bataille was also a substantial contributor to Souvarine's review, *La Critique sociale,* published between 1931 and 1934. In a two-part series entitled "The Psychological Structure of Fascism," he questioned how it was that the forces of discontent could be channeled toward repressive, that is, fascistic, rather than revolutionary/socialist ends. In Durkheim's accounts, the general effervescence characteristic of revolutionary or creative periods stimulates collective forces in search of dramatic expression whose outcome is unpredictable, leading to actions of "either superhuman heroism or bloody barbarism."[33] Given the labile, undecided nature of effervescent energies, the challenge presented by politics in the prewar period was to ascertain how certain groups were more adept in appropriating them for their own goals than others. As Bataille noted, the 1930s presented the virtually unique situation of simultaneous and parallel revolutionary movements: "An unprecedented situation resulted from the potential duality of effervescence. Within the same time period, the same society witnessed the concurrent formation of two revolutions hostile to each other as well as to the existing order."[34] Equally disconcerting was that both movements were distinguished from conventional social or political activity by effervescence. It is due to this common trait—and in this domain alone—that the left meets a nontraditional, fascistic right. But it was precisely the latter's appeal to diverse sectors of the political spectrum that accounts for Bataille's avowed interest in its methods.

Bataille's analytical framework for approaching fascism expands the basic profane/sacred duality to a *homogeneous* versus *heterogeneous* opposition. The homogeneous domain is identified through production and its criteria remain exclusively utilitarian. Homogeneity actively ejects all that threatens the foundation of its abstract equivalencies or commensurability. Exchanges are mediated by money and human relations assume an awareness of the identity of definite persons and situations, since, in principle, "all violence is excluded from an existence so defined."[35] Conversely, sacred or heterogeneous elements are recognized by their shock effect—allowing them to break the conventional barriers upon which homogeneity relies. Unable to define the sacred in positive terms, Durkheim nonetheless insisted upon its incommensurability with the nonsacred.[36] Bataille offers the insight that it is the profane, or what he calls homogeneity, that is ultimately dependent upon the heterogeneous for its identity. The distinction between a pure and impure sacred elaborated by Hertz justifies Bataille's inclusion of extreme elements within heterogeneity. He points out that they are subject to the same interdictions and evoke the same intense emotions as those associated with the pure sacred. The extension of the sacred to the cultural equivalent of Indian "untouchables," for instance, facilitates the elaboration of a point already made regarding the dependence of homogeneity upon heterogeneity:

> The inability of homogeneous society to find within itself a reason for being and acting leads to a dependency upon imperative forces. Similarly, the sadistic hostility of the sovereign toward *les misérables* propels them toward social formations that perpetuate the oppression of outcasts.[37]

Bataille then draws upon the ambiguous situation of workers to illustrate the dynamic whereby the homogeneous domain forges an identity through the creation of its heterogeneous antithesis. Economically constituted by the owners of the means of production—upper-class bourgeois as well as the middle classes—who derive personal profit from it, the homogeneous realm of production integrates the productive forces of workers while minimizing their acquisition of profit. Psychological homogeneity prevails within work relations. Outside the factory or workplace, however, a member of the proletariat is perceived as a stranger, or an individual of an irreducibly other nature. The proletariat thus constitutes the *social* domain of heterogeneity. As such, it stands along with other ejected phenomena—excrement, detritus, certain parts of the body, acts or words evocative of erotic affect, the unconscious processes of dreams or neuroses—heterogeneous elements resistant to social homogenization. These may also include crowds, warrior or aristocratic classes, *misérables,* violent persons, as well as those who reject rules—madmen, poets, or *meneurs.* The considerable variety of persons within heterogeneity can indeed be clustered into groupings that parallel the subdivision of the sacred into pure and impure categories, leading to a further distinction between those who constitute poles of *attraction* and those who inspire *repulsion.*

What the Bataillian schema demonstrates is that the sacred/profane social cycle of alternation has been disrupted. Instead of providing everyone with the respective experiences associated with each phase—certainly a requisite for collective well-being according to Durkheim—modern society instead sanctions one mode of behavior for certain sectors to the exclusion of others. Thus the social division of labor can now be correlated according to criteria that either permit or disallow for access to the sort of expenditure the sociologists equated with the sacred. For Bataille, social stratification in modern France is determined by the bourgeoisie, whose inability to define itself positively in relation to the nobility other than through the utilitarian values of production and accumulation led it to eject heterogeneous elements in two directions: above, toward the imperial mode of sovereignty historically monopolized by the nobility associated with orgiastic *dépense;* below, onto the social heterogeneity of workers thus marked by a distinct and persistent otherness. The psychological dimension of this social schema is also determined by the bourgeois expulsion of disruptive sexual forces from the homogeneous realm of productivity while projecting them upon the social heterogeneity of the workers. In contrast with the

traditional Don Juanism of aristocratic privilege, for instance, prole-
tarian sexuality evokes phantasms of repulsive genitalia.

The dynamism or *mouvement d'ensemble* animating these structures is explained by the fact that no one agent or thing can be totally
contained within a one-dimensional category. This means that the impossibility to provide clear-cut analytical distinctions between sacred/
profane or impure/pure sacred is explained by the two central notions
of *ambivalence* and *transformation*. We recall that no person, place,
or thing is inherently sacred, but is deemed as such as a result of the
projection of collective energies. Bataille elaborates in the same vein
by observing that the rule obtains in regard to the left/right or impure/
pure distinctions since most sacred phenomena are inherently unstable.
This undecidability is susceptible to a transformation from one pole to
another. Although most political conversions follow a left-to-right trajectory, the same cannot be asserted regarding social phenomena. The
example of *misérables* is a case in point. Initially consecrated as an
object of Christian charity and benefiting from that association with
the right sacred, the same group of paupers and outcasts came to be
assimilated to the mass or crowd that right-wing ideologues, such as
LeBon, stigmatized by claiming to be a source of potential political
and social instability. More typically, the left-to-right conversion is exemplified by no less than the Christ figure, moving from an initial heterogeneity, that is, association with outlaws, to a homogeneous deification purified of criminal content.

Ambivalence is inherent to heterogeneous phenomena. Violence,
excess, delirium, and madness partake of the heterogeneous domain to
varying degrees: when activated—either within persons or crowds—
they break the rules of social homogeneity. Even their reality is of a
different order from homogeneity since they are recognized by the force
or shock they transmit from one object to another. Symbols charged
with an affective value also play a fundamental role in stimulating heterogeneous forces. Thus, from a point of view diametrically opposed
to that of LeBon, Bataille enlisted a Durkheimian analysis that favors
the complementarity between sacred/profane, expenditure/production,
euphoria/dysphoria, concentration/dispersion, in order to bolster the
following argument: In the name of modernity, progress, and rationality, a triumphant bourgeois-capitalist mentality effectively devalued one
dimension to the detriment of the other. Most insidious, this led to the
consignment *of one side of the duality to specific social milieus*, result-

ing in the isolation, conflict, and *ressentiment* of the popular classes while also denying access to collective forms of heterogeneity to the bourgeoisie. These psychological repercussions subjectively reinforced the objective historical transformations responsible, Bataille argues, for the rise of militarism. The political manifestation of negativity or revolutionary effusion—"a destruction sparing nothing"—cannot exist in the modern period without leading to contradictions within the individual. With the exhaustion of the religious domain as well as of the revolutionary impetus, the ensuing vacuum facilitates a military takeover. In other words, the direct corollary to the great revolutionary upheavals in European history was the expansion of national military forces: "At this very instant, in the face of our impotent remonstrations, the military spirit alone dictates the fate of hypnotized masses, some overwrought, the others appalled."[38]

While Bataille notes with obvious sympathy the divergent reactions elicited by the spread of militarism, his reference to "hypnotized masses" requires further clarification since this conventional, even stereotypical, description of mass behavior stems from the tradition of crowd psychology. In contrast with the Cartesian cogito, the notion of the unconscious disseminated by LeBon is viewed as the repository of hereditary influences. While the majority of daily actions may be determined by "secret causes" emanating from the unconscious, their effect, he claims, is most potent and detrimental in crowd situations, when the controlling power of individual volition becomes subordinate to the suggestive influence of the "hypnotized" masses. In theory, according to Elisabeth Roudinesco, the "Freudian Revolution" proposes an alternative to the biases of LeBon by claiming as its object "neither the individual psyche nor the collective crowd."[39] Moreover, by evacuating the dominant notions of heredity, degeneration, organicism, race, or instinct characteristic of the French definition of the unconscious, the Freudian version emerged as a "field" in which drives, repressive forces, and transfers exert their respective influence. Freud, however, persisted in claiming that the most damning trait of a crowd is its active pursuit of a domineering leader: "A group is an obedient herd, which could never live without a master. It has such a thirst for obedience that it submits instinctively to anyone who appoints himself its master."[40]

The central point allowing us to differentiate these respective analyses is why and how the potential forces of disruption emanating from the heterogeneous realm—those Durkheim associated with the effervescence of a group—are ultimately concentrated within a leader who has subverted them to his own advantage. Within the paradigm provided by the hetero/homogeneous antinomy, Hitler and Mussolini— unlike democratic politicians—appear as incontrovertibly *other* and are likened to a force that shatters the tenuous foundations of the homogeneous. The illegality of fascism is only the most obvious sign of the transcendent, heterogeneous source of its appeal. Drawing upon Freud's analogy with hypnosis, Bataille attributes the link developed between the leader and his followers to an "affective flux" that flows in both directions. The *meneur* is united with followers as both become aware of the increasingly violent and excessive energies that he accumulates and to which he appears to have unlimited access.[41]

An outstanding feature of fascism's social program is contained within its etymological meaning of *reunion* which, unlike socialism, claims to bring together all sectors of society. By enlisting the military model, where the homogenizing process effectively reduces social distinctions as well as individual differences among recruits to the point of obliteration, fascism incorporates the exploited classes by denying their specificity. The explanation for why the latter embrace representations that efface rather than celebrate them, as does socialism, resides both in the social origin of the leader him- or herself and the modifications to which that leader, too, is subjected. Indeed, just as the social difference of the workers is occulted, so the original heterogeneous condition of the leader, who at some point experienced the exclusion and misery of the proletariat, is transmuted into its *opposite*. "This *affective value*," Bataille claims, "extends to the fascist chief as well as to his entourage, and is what—in its immeasurable impact— lends them the particular accent of violence without which fascism would not be possible."[42] Consistent with postwar historiography, Bataille's analysis underscores the distinctive traits of fascism—the fusion between nontraditional characteristics of political life, whether effervescent assemblies and a sovereign leader invested with transcendent qualities—in comparison with the traditional right-wing forces upon which it also depends. His conclusion is that "the unity of fascism is located in its specific psychological conditions and not in the economic circumstances that served as its basis."[43]

In a prefiguration of the Collège's formation, Bataille concluded his 1933 study of fascism with an exhortation to investigate the basis of social movements in the forces of attraction and repulsion. The change of circumstances in democratic societies render it possible to envisage alternative poles of attraction to those exerted by communism as well as fascism. Increased knowledge regarding the affective social reactions that traverse the superstructure can facilitate the ability to predict the nature of their future manifestations and perhaps even exert an influence upon them. To complete his methodological synthesis of German phenomenology, Freudian psychoanalysis, and French sociology, Bataille relied upon lived states or evidence derived from elective communities he could contrast with the hypnotized masses. Regarding Caillois's use of the term, he noted,

> I assume that the "elective community" or "secret society" is a form of secondary organization that possesses constant characteristics and to which recourse is always possible when the primary organization of society can no longer satisfy all the desires that arise.[44]

The lesson of archaic cultures is that the need for such secondary associations is not restricted to the inadequacies of modern society but arises in all types of social formations, however divergent their final goals.

Given the consolidation of fascistic governments that flagrantly exploited the popular appeal of symbols and sentiments evocative of the sacred, Bataille and Caillois proposed the following definition of power as it appears under fascism:

> Power in a society would be distinct from the production of a religious force, from a sacred force concentrated in one leader. Power would be the institutional merging of the sacred force and military strength in a single person who makes use of them for his own individual benefit and only in that way for the benefit of the institution.[45]

The critical challenge, then, would be to envisage a sacred force capable of sustaining the negativity of its otherness and of resisting the recuperative strategy that directs it toward conservation, accumulation, and profit.

The purpose of this section has been to situate the proposals by the Collège directed at countering the movement toward concentration of power—especially in one figure. Whether festivals or sacrifice, these examples of expenditure engage some type of collective action whose condition of possibility is the formation of the group itself. In his general response as to why and how the direction toward fascism prevailed, Bataille points out that a successfully subversive process must effect a double passage, so that the forces sweeping from bottom to top also return to their original source. The one-directionality of fascism is attributed to the "imperial" fascination exerted by a high, noble and nonutilitarian head that attracts a popular base as well:

> In these new conditions (in comparison with traditional revolutionary dissociations of monarchical societies) the inferior classes ceased to be exclusively attracted to socialist subversion, and a military organization began to draw them into its sovereign orbit. Similarly, the dissociated elements (belonging to middle classes or from the elite) also found a new outlet for their effervescence, and it is not surprising that given a choice between subversive or imperial solutions, they chose the latter.[46]

Bataille's understanding of the basis for fascism from within the psychological perspective of those upon whom it could exert an undeniable attraction thus addresses it from two angles: the unconscious dimension of culture associated with the sacred he expanded to the heterological, and a complementary inquiry into how the heterological enters consciousness, especially in a postsacred society. A 1933 article devoted to the problem of the state, for instance, carries an unequivocal condemnation of the triumph of concentrated power within all three major totalitarian regimes. His contribution to this predictable denunciation is to consider the subjective consequences of increased state hegemony upon the evolution of worker consciousness. More precisely, he claims that whereas during the nineteenth century, worker *conscience* evolved by dint of its antagonisms with the State and was buoyed by efforts to diminish its authority, in the modern period the exacerbated tendency toward authoritarianism produced a *conscience déchirée*. If optimism for revolution was kindled by signs of the dissolution of state power, what state of mind can develop in view of the unchecked domination of the major apparatuses for control and repression? The paralysis overcoming the workers' movement is induced by the vise squeezing them from the left as well as the right, since official communism at the time provided only an "abject optimism." The rare glimmer of hope discerned would emanate from the "liberating anguish" of the proletariat. Here is Bataille's cautious statement in regard to the potential of that force: "But the principles of democracy—discredited by liberal politics—can once again become a vital force only in relation to the anguish provoked within the working classes by the emergence of three all-powerful States."[47]

A possible counterbalance to Bataille's sense that only affective forces may incite workers to action when objective conditions foster pessimism is his insistence upon collective awareness, an alternative to the occultation of phenomena that fall under social and even individual censure. The blind spot within the individual mind develops from everyday practices dictated by the requirements of work or by the cultural norms of a society dedicated to its own reproduction. Bataille's most severe indictment of modernity stems not from the fact that it has robbed individuals of pleasure, but rather that it has denied them the very means to understand forbidden needs. The one-sided sublimation of energy into work and its complementary consumerism occults the fundamental duality structuring the totality of the individual already evidenced at the collective level: "Being is, in fact, continually drawn in two directions; one leads to the creation of lasting organizations and conquering forces, the other leads, through the intermediary of expenditure of force and increasing excess, to destruction and death."[48] The economic duality is essential to the project of the Collège and its subsequent impact because it parallels the Durkheimian opposition of the sacred to the profane. In this equation, the sustaining energies invested into work during periods of dispersion fill the profane phase antithetical to sacrificial festivities and banquets during which accumulated products are consumed. In one of his last lectures, Durkheim again wrestled with the nature of the sacred's specificity and concluded that it was radically incompatible with the idea of work. We recall that he then circumvented the impasse of the sacred's marginalization as superfluous or antithetical to action by redefining human *telos* in relation to expenditure. And for Bataille, no more crucial form of recognition exists than for human nature to acknowledge itself agitated by what it holds in greatest horror—the possibility for modes of expenditure so extreme that annihilation appears the only outcome.

The Collège text offers an extreme version of the notion of expenditure that Bataille first set forth in the 1933 essay, "La notion de dépense," published (with a disclaimer) by Souvarine in *La Critique sociale*. At that time, the revolutionary potential of workers was underscored by revising the standard analysis of class conflict. In place of a determination according to relation to the means of production, Bataille insisted upon the distinctions and animosities generated by the social history of expenditure in France. His schematized overview traces the displacement of aristocratic or ecclesiastical obligation to subsidize public festivals or spectacles by privatized, often guilt-ridden, bourgeois economism. Workers are restricted to expenditures relating to subsistence. Their social ostracism or heterogeneity is maintained through the signs of abject misery, a condition especially evident in the intractable poverty of the urban masses. By way of contrast, instances of vestigial archaic expenditure could still be observed in the French countryside until World War II, where peasants included the entire village in their celebrations.

Following the triumph of bourgeois rationality over feudal excess—at least in the public sphere—utilitarian criteria became the sole gauge of expenditure so that no one group was capable of experiencing the extreme, even violent *dépense* Bataille equated with sovereignty. Because feudal rank and privilege were symbolized through consumption patterns, Bataille never enlisted them as a viable model in his prescriptions to revive collective, nonproductive modes of *dépense*. Similarly, he viewed with ambivalence the archaic modes of gift exchange that retained a closer proximity to potlatch—one of the most extreme forms of destruction by which to acquire and maintain status—precisely because rank and power are the ultimate goal of "agonistic" competitions.[49] Archaic models are nonetheless valuable in demonstrating a structural means to undermine the accumulation of wealth by any one individual. Indeed, Bataille underscores the rules of a game which preclude the player's option to withdraw from the obligations of potlatch, including the head of a clan who must respond to the challenge of another. Not to be underestimated is the destructive dimension of potlatch Bataille considers its fundamental value in assuaging the need for *loss*. The obvious rebuttal to this position—that such expenditure is mandatory and therefore counter to the Bataillian imperative—is neutralized by Mauss's discussion of "obligatory" sentiments: Although dictated by social forms, such expressions of feeling are all the more intensely genuine for being collectively mandated. Possibly most contrary to the modern reader's expectations is that the emotions subject to formalized expression are those conventionally associated with some degree of release.[50]

With the institutionalization of exclusively productive modes of expenditure calculated with a view to some benefit, the possibility for expression of the will to loss is denied to all. The counterideal Bataille offers would be "a potlatch without return." The archaic open display of riches is preferable to the modern form of anonymous, hidden wealth, with its covert relations to power and influence. As subsequent analyses have demonstrated, power in many archaic societies is equated with giving so excessive it is tantamount to loss, the need for which, according to Bataille, "exists at the endemic state of every social group."[51] Dismissed as anthropological romanticism, this position has nonetheless been revalorized by a reading of Mauss informed by the Bataillian perspective.[52] Patterns of social exchanges based upon gifts that are distinguished from objects contributing to everyday economic subsistence do not dissemble or occult the "real" economy of production and accumulation.[53] Rather, Bruno Karsenti concludes, they serve to restrict the extreme expenditures constitutive of the basis of social life and organization. The archaic is not what has been superseded by modernity—with its alleged rationality based upon calculations—but what modernity has had to "forget" or repress in order to sustain its identity.[54]

Because a distinguishing feature of fascism's social revolution is its claim to encompass all sectors, it is relevant to reconsider the place and representation of workers within Bataille's social analysis of expenditure. Predictably, the bourgeoisie is historically identified as the group for whom the experience of glorious and sovereign spending is anathema. Lacking the dramatic, public displays enjoyed by the nobility, the bourgeoisie is perceived as distinguishing itself negatively, by means of an ascetic rejection of all that was excessive among the dominant aristocracy. Gone are the examples of generosity in public life. By extending the rationalized calculations of the marketplace to all domains of social and affective existence, the bourgeoisie is also seen as establishing its difference in relation to the workers by ejecting them socially as foreign and distinct, guilty in their own way of sexual excess.[55] So extreme is this social exclusion that "the *misérables* have no other means for reentering the circle of power than the revolutionary destruction of the classes which occupy it, that is to say, a bloody and unlimited social expenditure." Within the Bataillian schema, the revolutionary potential of the workers at the expense of the bourgeoisie is dependent upon the eruption of forces that are an integral feature of what Bataille touts as a new materialism, whose nonlogical difference is explicitly transgressive in its relation to the "restricted" economy of the universe, in the same way as "what crime represents to law."[56] Herein resides the subversive potential of expenditure, which may or may not result in the possibility for irreversible loss. As such, the revolutionary possibilities of extreme expenditure challenge the assumption that the only alternatives to utilitarianism are either aesthetic or modeled upon traditional forms of the sacred. Bataille's base materialism must also be distinguished from revisions to materialism that contributed to reactionary tendencies by proclaiming their antimaterialism.

That heterogeneous elements exert a power of attraction comparable to the forces associated with the sacred is the main argument relaying Bataille's early essay on *dépense* to his subsequent analyses of fascism. When describing radical modalities of expenditure, he insisted upon the possibility for *"new forms of the sacred so human that the traditional forms become intolerable."*[57] Indeed, the essay on fascism called for knowledge relating to the movements of attraction and repulsion that crystallize either in the radical imperial form or else in "profound subversion." It thus pointed to the need for more analysis in a direction subsequently undertaken within the framework of the Collège. The commonality to the two endeavors resides in their documentation of the ability of groups or collective movements to exert a counterforce to the diversion of social energies toward concentration in a single repository of power. That resistance was graphically emblematized by André Masson's headless figure for the "acéphalic" review and secret society Bataille convened parallel to the Collège. It was also the impetus for lectures to the Collège in which he enlists the natural sciences as potential models for esoteric conceptualizations of "composed beings" or the reorganization of state federalism as a structure of unity without a center or capital. Durkheim, we recall, countered earlier manifestations of right-wing nationalism with the example of medieval effervescence as a way to reimagine *foyers* of creative activity throughout a cosmopolitan Europe of loosely structured geopolitical units (see chapter 2). Further efforts to discredit the concentration of social energies into one chief or head of state extend to any orator. Rather than perceive this individual as manipulator of the crowd, Durkheim claimed him to be a projection of the group: "It is then no longer a mere individual who speaks but a group incarnated and personified."[58] In sum, these positions highlight significant distinctions between sociology and crowd psychology in two areas—the nature of the relation between a leader and a group, and the effect of collective assemblies upon the individual. Both areas compel us to reconsider the political consequences of effervescent transformations.

The Politics of Effervescence

The research domain charted by the Collège—secret societies, religious orders, or political vanguard groups—often passed over by conventional sociology, underscores the challenges contributors faced when attempting to conceptualize the nature of modern collectivities outside of the template imposed by the early crowd psychologies. Durkheim's enthusiasm for effervescent assemblies as both source of social creativity and harbinger of change has been downplayed in standard sociological scholarship. While the neglect of Durkheimian effervescence may in part be attributed to its resistance to conventional categories and methods of representation, from the very first reviews it also suffered from historical proximity to LeBon's sensationalism. Not to be underestimated is LeBon's *succès de prestige* within literary and philosophical circles even among readers who would reject his psychological current and its attendant racism, taken up during the Dreyfus Affair by the anti-Semites Drumont, Barrès, and Daudet. In his 1921 *Group Psychology and the Analysis of the Ego,* for instance, Freud refers to LeBon's "deservedly famous" study for his own views on collective behavior, whereas Durkheim's very different positions are not mentioned.

The difficulties inherent to an analysis of groups in relation to collective action were exacerbated by the stifling effects exerted by the early crowd psychologies upon subsequent research. In particular, the pseudo-scientific hypnotic model of suggestive influence has been singled out as effectively diverting attention away from the historical context of group gatherings and the social conditions prompting them. Confronted with dramatic historical transformations, crowd psychology updated a version of the theory of animal magnetism whose precedents can be traced to Paracelsus in the sixteenth century. The political impact of an anachronistic social model was to devalue mass action during a period of intense upheaval. From an academic standpoint, it also effectively discouraged inquiry into the social origins of collective behavior:

> Rather than being an attempt at scientifically grounding their social theory, their use of the analogy between mass behavior and hypnotic suggestion served instead as a powerful and well-diffused metaphor easily understandable by their nonscientist readers. But in making an association between the crowd psychology and the then-accepted psychiatric and psychopathological model for an *individual* behavior, this new theory would exclude a priori *political* and *social* aspects of the phenomena from the area of inquiry.[59]

Among the consequences of shifting attention away from social etiologies onto individual pathologies, the one most directly relevant to the projects of both Durkheim and the Collège is that

> the initial crowd psychologies and their disqualification of the masses represent another example of a "missed opportunity" of locating social psychological enquiry *explicitly at the crossroads of the sociopolitical and the individual levels.*[60]

Despite differences within their respective characterizations of collective assemblies and their effects, Durkheim and the crowd psychologists share a common esteem for the crowd's ability to foster a *moralization* of the individual, as expressed by LeBon in the following passage:

> [The crowd] is also capable of very lofty acts of devotion, sacrifice, and disinterestedness, of acts much loftier indeed than those of which the isolated individual is capable. Appeals to sentiments of glory, honour, and patriotism are particularly likely to influence the individual forming a part of a crowd, and often to the extent of obtaining from him the sacrifice of his life.[61]

They diverge, however, in assessments of the long-range and therefore political consequences of the new morality.

Bataille's acknowledgment that Freud was an essential contribution toward his understanding of fascism's appeal did not translate into an obvious debt to psychoanalysis by the time of his articles on the subject. One reason can be found in the fact that Freud's major contribution to group psychology—the model of identification with a powerful leader that replaced hypnotic suggestion—does not break with fundamental tenets of crowd psychology. Freud continued to characterize the individual as mesmerized by a charismatic *leader* as well as suffering identity loss, diminished reasoning capacity, relinquishment of willpower, and reduction to an automaton-like state. Effacement of the conscious personality is marked by a surge of "instincts" otherwise kept in check. LeBon similarly stressed the crowd's alleged propensity toward "impulsiveness, mobility, and irritability" and the potentially nefarious outcome of such effusions: "A crowd may be guilty of murder, incendiarism, and every kind of crime."[62] Isolation, though, allegedly encourages individual control.

If, as Freud contended, individual psychology in 1921 was still in the throes of self-definition, then one must consider how it compared with his presentation of group psychology. According to the Freudian evolutionary scheme, the individual leader is presented as independent and willful, however ignoble his methods, and the group becomes the locus for collective regression. In this sense, Freud perpetuates the popular phantasm of the crowd as instance of mass hysteria. Even his qualitative descriptions of identification are derived from comparisons with states of hypnosis and suggestion transported onto a mass scale. Certainly the contrast with Durkheim is most dramatic in the Freudian dismissal of religion as a neurotic disposition projected onto a socially sanctioned, collective "illusion":

> Even those who do not regret the disappearance of religious illusions from the civilized world of today will admit that so long as they were in force they offered those who were bound by them the most powerful protection against the danger of neurosis. Nor is it hard to discern that all the ties that bind people to mystico-religious or philosophic-religious sects and communities are expressions of crooked cures of all kinds of neuroses.[63]

Freud further reinforced the bias against the collectivity by means of an evolutionary schema. Drawing from the "anthropological" myth of the primal horde, he could claim that the individual emerges as a superior social agent from the undifferentiated group, whether family or clan. Initially, he had argued that just as primitive man survives potentially in every individual, so the primal horde may arise out of any random collection of individuals, and provisionally he concluded that "the psychology of the group precedes that of the individual, and the latter is, in fact, still in the process of distinguishing itself from that of the group."[64] In a reversal, he then asserted that the two psychologies must be coeval, but distinguished according to whether they apply to any individual, or to a father, chief, or leader. The horde myth illustrates the relationship between father and sons, since even in isolation the father acts in a "strong and independent" way. Requiring reinforcement from no one, loving no one but himself, he acknowledges the existence of others only to the extent they serve his needs. A successor to the father emerges from the group by manifesting the requisite psychological makeup for the leadership position, thereby effecting the shift from one psychological modality to another. In passing Freud notes that, appearances to the contrary, most group solidarity is grounded in fear, not love. One of the constant traits he emphasizes, especially in relation to artificial groups such as the church or army, is the intolerance exhibited toward nonmembers.

We recall that LeBon and Freud discredited the moral heroism induced by the crowd for being a transient phenomenon whose modifications within individuals as well as their institutional targets would not endure beyond the momentary exaltation. Nor, in their estimation, does the intellectual impact of the group fare much better: indeed, LeBon's "law" posits an inversion between affect and intellect. Similarly, Freud argued that if emotions in a collective context are heightened to the point of inspiring acts of great sacrifice and self-abnegation, the concomitant debasement of logical thought evokes comparisons with the "primitive mentality," the child's lack of cognitive sophistication, and/or the neurotic's subjugation to emotion. The latter trait is especially evident in Freud's characterization of religious faith as a sign of neurotic attachment to a regressive maternal "oceanic" feeling. The individual's subordination to the group causes him to share with these other categories a tolerance for contradictory notions, a devaluation of truth as final goal, and a logic dominated by images. Certainly the notion of rationality is implicit throughout all these discussions, serving to reinforce the dividing line between behavior that is sanctioned or censored. It also reminds us that criteria for rationality subtend any discussion of collective behavior, including, as we shall see, its moral component. In light of the rationality/irrationality polemic informing Durkheim's position on the group, Nisbet's comparison with the Freudian contribution is especially pertinent: "Durkheim shares a large part of the responsibility for turning contemporary social thought from the classic rationalist categories of volition, will, and individual consciousness to aspects which are, in a strict sense, non-volitional and non-rational."[65] That this distinction eschews the criteria of psychology and returns to those of classical social theory is argued this way:

> Freud's has been the more widely recognized influence. But there is every reason to regard Durkheim's reaction to individualistic rationalism as more fundamental and encompassing than Freud's. Freud, after all, never doubted the primacy of the individual and intra-individual forces when he analyzed human behavior. Non-rational influences proceed, in Freud's interpretation, from an unconscious mind and within the individual, even though it is related genetically to a social past. The individual, in short, remains the solid reality in Freud's thought. In Durkheim, however, it is community that has prior reality, and it is from community that the essential elements of reason flow.[66]

The semantic slippage from group or society to "crowd" and "mass" becomes an effective means for identifying modes of social activity which, according to their alleged level of violence, will incur repression or not. The issue is not only whether certain social formations are transient or permanent but whether they are constituted by or through the masses, more exactly, elements of the working class. LeBon's crowd is a code word for the latter, whereas Freud's group is equated with artificial entities, such as the army or religious orders, whose characteristics are nonetheless extended to all units beyond one individual.

Durkheim's earliest reflections upon solidarity correlated the state of society with the nature of the moral type it tends to foster. When tradition prevails and rules and order predominate during periods of stability, one encounters individuals of "solid reason and robust willpower."[67] A "cold" physiognomy also mirrors inner rigidity and successful self-containment. Periods of transition, however, such as fin-de-siècle France, require the formation of open and generous citizens capable of spontaneous élans or sacrifices preferred with joyous abandon. Lectures gathered under the title *Education morale* argued that the goal of a moral education is precisely to demonstrate the double-sidedness of the social, so that one can appreciate how it encompasses a "legal imperative" or realm of duty requiring curtailment of individual inclinations that is nonetheless amply compensated by a much richer reality than any accessible to the individual—"and to which one cannot be attached without experiencing an enhancement of one's being." These two dimensions of the individual's representation of social morality are encountered to varying degrees within the conscious mind without one ever dominating the other entirely. In their extreme incarnations, they reflect temperamental archetypes: The first possess self-mastery developed through the practice of duty, whereas the second are characterized by the creative energy that flows from a continual communion with the source of moral ideals—society.[68] At the time of the lectures on moral education, which predate the *Elementary Forms* by a decade, the distinction between the two types was then accompanied by the exhortation to socialize citizens toward behavior characteristic of the expansive morality viewed as essential to the revitalization of European society.

Durkheim's typology of ideal personalities yields yet another revealing contrast with crowd psychology since it parallels the distinction LeBon made between *individual* and *crowd* behavior:

> Taking the word "morality" to mean constant respect for certain social conventions, and the permanent repression of selfish impulses, it

is quite evident that crowds are too impulsive and too mobile to be moral. If, however, we include in the term morality the transitory display of certain qualities such as abnegation, self-sacrifice, disinterestedness, devotion, and the need of equity, we may say, on the contrary, that crowds may exhibit at times a very lofty morality.[69]

Citing the two notable historical instances of collective action also favored by Durkheim—the Crusades and 1789—LeBon argued that since individual morality is guided by self-interest, "[c]ollectivities alone are capable of great disinterestedness and great devotion." He therefore concludes that one must not totally discourage such behavior, since it is responsible for the achievements of civilization:

> We should not complain too much that crowds are more especially guided by unconscious considerations and are not given to reasoning. Had they, in certain cases, reasoned and consulted their immediate interests, it is possible that no civilization would have grown up on our planet, and humanity would have had no history.[70]

The impasse in LeBon's thinking stems from his attribution of opposing tendencies of crowd behavior to a common imperviousness to reason. Socialism's appeal, for instance, is especially widespread among those who *"stand to lose most from it"* (LeBon) and is explained by the impact of crowd mentality upon individuals who have lost sight of their own self-interest. Collective morality is irrational, leaving reason as the only guarantor against the crowd's allegedly destructive potential. While this valuation would serve LeBon's immediate antisocialist motives, its broader implications persist among subsequent followers of group psychology, including Freud. By dictating what is deemed rational or not, LeBon's positions are of immeasurable political consequence. As a result of labeling a collectivity the crowd and its morality a crowd psychology, he provided *a model for social containment of group action by circumscribing it within a particular space and milieu.* In this way, LeBon's segregation confirms the Bataillian reading of the social landscape presented above. There, the opposition between homogeneity and heterogeneity reconfigured the traditional terms of class conflict and distinctions, since heterogeneous sovereignty—associated with disinterested expenditure and sacrifice—was split between the imperial (right) and abject (left).

LeBon sought not to rescue the masses, but rather to instruct future leaders in the art of manipulating them. He overtly affirmed his sympathies with fascism to the point of praising Mussolini, who in turn claimed that his political practice was an implementation of crowd psychology's central theses. LeBon's death in 1933 was met with generalized silence and extended the academic ostracism that had always contrasted with his work's popular appeal. This was also the moment when Bataille undertook his own investigation into the sources of fascism's psychological structures. It is significant that he did so within an intellectual space detached from the university and research institutions where Durkheimian sociology's endorsement of collective effervescence would incur such sharp rebuke that Mauss felt obligated to repudiate that dimension of the sociological legacy. Following the left-wing demonstrations during the "days of February, 1934" Bataille had described in his journal as moving in an arc from collective feverish anxiety to an effervescent outburst, Boris Souvarine deplored the inability of the socialist party to assimilate the "new elements" of youth in search of innovative outlets for its profound discontent. Only a tabula rasa of existing political forms and myths could bring about the innovations required by the crisis. Short of a willingness within the socialist party to engage untried ideas, tendencies, and alliances, he argued, the new forces would have recourse to "the internal contradictions of effervescence—*rightly or wrongly said to be fascist.*"[71]

Effervescence has indeed been recognized as one of the features to distinguish fascism from traditional forms of right-wing politics. It is also a characteristic shared by what has been termed a "left-wing" fascism that exhibits all the same characteristics—cult of virility, hierarchy, and violence—of its right-wing counterpart. Far from advocating war as the only solution to the need for expenditure in the modern world (even though he would eventually analyze it in those terms),[72] Bataille was concerned that his definition of *dépense* be distinguished from the manipulation of expenditure and sacrifice by those in power. Consequently, he strained to clarify distinctions among notions of force, "puissance" and power ("pouvoir"), with the critical criterion being whether the net outcome results in material or symbolic gain. As witnesses to the Nuremburg feasts, Collège participants insisted upon discriminating their celebration of the sacred by means of the festival, for instance, from gatherings that serve either as safety valves for pent-up forces normally kept in check, or else whose purpose is to incite feelings of animosity in one group contributing to the exclusion and destruction of targeted others.

Thus far, we have examined speculations regarding the various ways in which effervescence was directed most effectively toward right-wing domination. Conversely, we also reviewed those social mechanisms activated to resist its concentration into a single group, milieu, institution, or person—whether head or chief. Initially, it would appear that the resolution to the undecidability of effervescence resides in sustaining devices that direct collective energies exclusively to the left pole of the sacred. Therefore, alongside his concern with the perversion of sovereign expenditure toward profit and power, Bataille explored the more complex process by which the negativity of the left sacred was transformed into the right. Or, as Durkheim pointed out, how it was that collective states could metamorphose from one identity into another:

> In summary, the two poles of religious life correspond to the two opposite states through which all social life passes. There is the same contrast between the lucky and unlucky sacred [*sacré faste et néfaste*] as between the states of collective euphoria and dysphoria. But because both are equally collective, the mythological constructions that symbolize them are in their very essence closely related. While the feelings placed in common vary from extreme dejection to extreme highspiritedness, from painful anger to ecstatic enthusiasm, the result in all cases is communion among individual consciousnesses and mutual calming. While the fundamental process is always the same, different circumstances color it differently. In the end, then, it is the unity and diversity of social life that creates at the same time the unity and the diversity of sacred beings and things.[73]

Following Durkheim's ethnographic detour, Bataille's most developed illustration of the sacred as a transformative process leads to the antipodes of the exotic, since he refers the reader to the cemetery behind the church located at the heart of every typical French village. The entire complex, comprised of building and burial ground, forms the essential "kernel" necessary for the transformation of the negative forces unleashed by the proximity of death into the sacred right of religious order and consecration. The process is symbolically represented by the passage from the church to the underground crypts and vaults preserving the purified bones of saints and holy persons now denuded of putrefying flesh. However devoid of traditionally religious sentiments one may be, claims Bataille, it is possible to recognize that the sacred locus is shrouded in the aura of violent silence respected as a necessary mediation in the face of death and destruction. Tears and laughter, common reactions to such forces, may add depth to communication but cannot impart the same humanizing dimension as the sacred nucleus—"the structure of the sacred center that is necessary to collective human emotion."[74]

It is precisely within this rarefied experience that the movement traversing the group can be transmuted from one emotive extreme to another. Bataille's position is indisputably sociological in that it requires social forms to render possible what would otherwise be dissipated in random acts of violence or terror: a mediating "silence laden with tragic horror weighs down on life to make it profoundly human."[75] The church mediates the repulsion elicited by the proximity of the graveyard with its associations of putrefying flesh, in contrast with the purified skeletal remains of saints within the church itself, which have passed to the right side of religious respect to the point of becoming objects worthy of emulation. If Bataille insists upon the need for nuclei whose active effect or "denaturation" allows access to the forbidden and forbidding attraction of the horrible and repugnant, it is because he believes that "nothing is more important for us than that we recognize that we are bound and sworn to that which horrifies us most, that which provokes our most intense disgust."[76]

In contrast with LeBon's containment of effervescence, it is now possible to appreciate how the ethnographic detour demonstrates that social forms circumscribe the potential contagion of the sacred in order to provide conditions of possibility for access to it. This paradox illustrates why the right/left distinction within the sacred must not be abused by assuming that it implies an absolute correlation with left/right in politics, any more than an exclusive attention to the left side provides a guarantee against recuperation. Any approach to the divine, supernatural, or heterological incurs danger and requires mediation, including those spatial correlatives to the inner sense of fear and trepidation—as well as excitement—evoked by death's proximity:

> Supernatural forces are not all of the same order; some exert their power in consonance with the nature of things, possess a regular and august character which inspire veneration and confidence; the others, to the contrary, violate and trouble the universal order, and the respect they impose is especially one of aversion and fear. All of these energies offer the common trait of being opposed to the profane; for latter, they are all equally dangerous and forbidden.[77]

The need to mediate contact with death through the transformation of the left into the right sacred explains Bataille's advocacy of institutional support—in this case, that of the church—easily misconstrued, he acknowledges, as an apologia for Christianity.

The main thrust of the assessment of the Collège thus far has been to examine its formation of a sacred sociology that demonstrates the unique contributions of the social. Recognition of those possibilities and the desire to mobilize the energies liberated by such a recognition promote the development of sociology as a psychoanalysis of the social. By this is meant sociology's ability to discern the ways in which a society stimulates, represses, and channels the negativity of social energies toward specific goals and meanings or whether it allows for their free play in a variety of cultural forms. Rather than follow the Freudian extrapolation from the individual to the collective, Durkheimian sociology envisions the social as a field of *mouvements d'ensemble,* energies that emerge in moments of effervescence, consolidate into groups, and effect transformations upon the psyche of social subjects. The unmarked nature of effervescent forces provisionally shields them from being socially or politically overdetermined as is the case in both the crowd psychologies and psychoanalysis. Indeed, Marthe Robert has pointed out that the Freudian topology of the conscious/unconscious is not immune from sociological correlatives. Predictably, the unconscious is associated with the lower classes responsible for violent and irrational outbursts.[78] As early as 1927 Bataille had deconstructed the sexual and scatological projections upon the working class encountered in the moral judgments rendered in the social imaginary and challenged those biases by calling attention to the subterranean associations between the architecture of the human body and its attendant taboos:

> Those in whom the forces of eruption accumulate are necessarily located below. The communist workers appear to the bourgeoisie as ugly and as dirty as the hairy or base sexual parts: sooner or later this will lead to a scandalous eruption in the course of which the noble and asexual heads of the bourgeois will be severed.[79]

In this section, we examined contributions by Bataille to the Collège's stated goal to devise a model for collective behavior located at the intersection between the individual and the social. At stake was the possibility to develop an alternative understanding of group dynamics to the one propounded by the early crowd psychologies with which Freudian *Massenpsychologie* remained closely aligned. More exactly, we explored the political implications of the sociological perspective informed by the sacred/profane duality that structures the possibility for effervescent assemblies without circumscribing them within a specific social milieu. The remaining section of this chapter returns to the other dimension of the sacred/profane duality that has directed our reading thus far: the nature of the inner transformations it effects. To do so, the roles of Caillois and Leiris in the Collège's ongoing polemics regarding the impact of socialization are presented. Indeed, the various positions taken in regard to these issues prefigure the final eruptions of dissonance within the Collège itself.

Politics and Politeness

A central contribution of the sociological approach emphasizes the transformations effected within general social and political movements. For both Durkheim and Bataille, the nature of that experience is described as a *prise de conscience,* connoting a heightened awareness within the conscious mind inseparable from the ideals also credited to the group's moralizing impact. Sociology functions as a scientific safeguard against misrepresentations of the social origins of those forces and their resultant channeling into "false" religions or political movements. The sacred sociologist seeks out the infra level of forces that account for the very formation of groups—however ephemeral—but with greater emphasis on the nature of the attraction and even repulsion that would account for their unifying impetus. Both models of collective action, however, are contingent upon modification of the participants' psychic configuration. Not surprisingly, Durkheim derived the example for the transformative experience from ceremonies marking access to the sacred: "This is why, for a long time, the initiation into sacred things was at the same time the operation by means of which the socialization of the individual was accomplished. Man, when entering religious life, also acquired a new nature, became a different person."[80]

According to the reading of *Elementary Forms* proposed in chapter I, the inner transformation resulted from the effervescence generated in the course of gatherings during the sacred phase of social life. The sacred/profane duality as a social alternation between concentration and dispersion replaced an earlier evolutionary model that envisioned social progress in terms of a move from mechanical to organic solidarity. It is now possible to appreciate how that basic pattern also correlates with the two moral types posited by Durkheim described above, so that they are no longer perceived in terms of one superseding the other. Rather, both are necessary to the social equilibrium and can be fostered by social forms, especially those that allow for the expression of altruism. For instance, in keeping with the sociological dictum that refuses psychological explanations for social phenomena, Durkheim regards the quest for food monopolizing psychic as well as physical energies during the profane phase of social life in purely social and collective terms. Even in the relatively dispersed state characteristic of the profane, individuals are never totally free from communal obligations. Yet their moral ideals are fully realized only when work ceases and expenditure prevails during the sacred moments of social life.

In his study of the morphological contrast between the opposing social phases, Mauss demonstrated that their alternation was irreducible to a seasonal causality. When autochthones were displaced to geographical locales where climatic conditions no longer marked seasonal shifts as dramatically as in the Pacific Northwest, social patterns nonetheless continued to reproduce the same opposition between production and consumption. The religious framework was no more a condition of necessity for the realization of this basic structure than the seasonal contrast itself. Contrary to expectations, as Durkheim pointed out, the actual time devoted in archaic societies to sacred activities is not necessarily as considerable as in more modern ones. The critical distinction between cultures resides in the social forms that enable the alternation/distinction to occur, even though Durkheim succumbed to stereotypes by claiming that the natives described by Spencer and Gillen exhibited the ability to shift emotional states more rapidly than was feasible among "civilized" men.[81] The possible tension latent to the contradictory commitments dictating behavior during the sacred versus profane phases is resolved by the inner transformations induced by and within the group experience. But whereas Durkheim uncritically celebrated the advantages of the concentration of individuals associated with the winter months of extreme fusion, Mauss qualified his enthusiasm by citing the need for withdrawal expressed both by an indigenous tale and by the ethnographer reporting from the field who seconded its sentiments. These differences between the masters of sociological thought find their parallels in the work of their disciples within the Collège, most notably in regard to the transformative effect of the group, described by Caillois, for instance, as a *sur* or supersocialization.

In the "Wind of Winter"—certainly the most unambiguous expression of elitism offered by any of the major Collège figures—Caillois warned against social forces directed at breaking down individual will, so that individuals must constitute their resistance through a community of their own. The values uniting such a group, although emanating from a marginal position, ought to be viewed as eventually viable for the center by effecting the migration from a Satanic to a Luciferian example. The transformation is described as a move from profanation to sacralization. Rather than braving the forces of convention in the name of greater liberation, however, Caillois's hero meets an ideal that is consistent with the sociological premise that prohibitions are not gratuitous but necessary. With his internalization of taboos, the hero demonstrates his superiority by wrestling with his own demons before conquering those that threaten the social order: "There is nothing to hope for from those who have nothing to suppress within themselves."[82]

This statement appears in the subsection of Caillois's address devoted to the ethical basis for a "closed community." Besides the ability to attain self-mastery, the new hero must exhibit "contempt, love of power, and courtesy."[83] Most revealing, Caillois closes with a Baudelairean description of *courtesy,* despite the fact that the poet in many ways epitomized the individualism of the nineteenth century otherwise repudiated by the Collège's collective commitments. It is indeed noteworthy that the Dandy was representative of a new elite to which one gained access by dint of highly developed internal discipline:[84]

> Precise and meticulous as court etiquette, courtesy, which ritualizes human beings' mutual relationships in their secondary aspects, for that very reason, relieves the mind and increases its ease accordingly. Moreover, it contributes to maintaining a certain internal tension that would be hard to preserve if simple manners were neglected. In a closed type of association, destined to aggravate separations, courtesy is part of the ethic and becomes almost an institution. Codifying the relations of the initiates, its esoteric and conventional character finds itself reinforced because it must serve to differentiate them even further from the uninitiated. The discourteous person, in fact, is not so much one who neglects customs as one who is ignorant of them or practices those of another group. Therefore, courtesy, a way to recognize each other and to recognize intruders, becomes a practical

means of standing aloof. In fact, when one must demonstrate one's hostility or one's contempt for someone, all that is necessary, as we all know, is to affect an extreme courtesy which makes the other as uncomfortable as a reprimand would and immediately excludes any familiarity. In this regard, we should never forget the manner in which certain important individualists, such as Baudelaire, sensed how implacable a weapon perfect correctness concealed, and made dandyism the privileged form of modern heroism.[85]

What Caillois derived from the Baudelairean version of dandyism is the possibility for men to bond through imitation of a traditional heroic ideal recast for modernity. Identifiable by his adherence to a synthesis of inner restraint, emotional impassivity, impeccable manners, and sober elegance, the modern dandy is distinguished from his bourgeois counterpart by a supreme disdain for work. Paradoxically, immersion in the "bain de foule" tests the new hero's mettle by his ability to maintain social distance while enduring the physical proximity of the "people." But whereas the evolution of politesse was associated with the politics of absolutism by reinforcing strict obeisance to rank, modern dandyism attracts an elite or secondary group, which—in theory at least—disregards class origins.

Denis Hollier attributes Caillois's seemingly aberrant positions to Marcel Granet's study of exclusively male, virile, and virulent Chinese groups whose winter rituals were devised to match the climate's harsh conditions. Alternatively, I will argue that the work of both Durkheim and Mauss raise comparable issues. Among the controversies associated with Durkheimian effervescence, the nature of the social bonds it may foster continues to divide scholars. Contrary to the general view that Durkheim was primarily focused upon the sources of social disintegration, Mark Traugott has argued that the centrality of effervescence confirms the sociologist's commitment to the consolidation of social bonds. In a similar vein, Hans Jons revitalized Durkheim's appreciation of collective life by inscribing it under the rubric of "social creativity."[86] It is therefore important to recognize that beyond the shift in dualities from mechanical/organic to sacred/profane, the Durkheimian social vision is informed by a yet more fundamental movement between dispersion and concentration responsible for the modification of social relations and the distribution of social forces. The intensification of bonds arises from a concentration of collective energies and presupposes changes in the psychic economy of individuals otherwise conditioned by a rationalized calculus dictating their *habitus*. Mauss, who abandoned the category of the sacred (but explored the effect of ritual chants and movements upon the body) for the *total social fact,* explains that he initially enlisted the Latin term *habitus* because its connotations are more complex than the French *habitude* and encompass the interaction between mind, body, and milieu. *Habitus* retains traces of "exis" (acquisition), as well as "faculty," both connotations intended by Aristotle, who Mauss argues must be recognized as a psychologist.[87] Mauss is responsible for extending the sociological gaze into areas his uncle would have resisted as taboo, so that the notion of *habitus* could indeed claim to an awareness of the totality of the individual's socialization by including minute details of bodily training and development. But Mauss also reasserts the value of the civilizing process as a means to instill the self-control and *conscience* characteristic of men of the elite, but rarely encountered in the less disciplined ranks of society.[88] The object of sociological analysis, he states, will never be the exceptional individual, but rather the average man, product of a statistical mean. And this is what the Maussian notion of a "complete" or "total" individual signifies—one not yet subject to the demands of consciousness that cause him to become divided, so that one stratum of being enters into conflict with another:

> It is in fact only the civilized man of higher castes within our own civilization and a small number of others, whether preceding ones, or oriental, or of the past, who know how to control the different spheres of his *conscience*. He differs from other men. He is specialized, often hereditarily differentiated by the division of social labor. But, especially, he is yet again divided within his own *conscience*, he is a conscious being. He therefore knows how to resist instinct; thanks to his *éducation,* to his concepts, to his deliberate choices, he knows how to exert some control over each of his acts. The man of the elite is not simply homo duplex, he is more than double within his inner being; he is also, if you will allow me the expression, "divided": his intelligence, his will power, the deliberation he places on the expression of his emotions, the way he controls them, his criticism— often excessive—stop him from ever totally abandoning his entire *conscience* to momentary, violent impulses.[89]

This is not to deny that even the most ordinary individual is endowed with a sense of dual being, of possessing a soul or seat of conscience. The crucial distinction, however, resides in the capacity for self-control of violent impulses—precisely the civilizing trait necessary for the modulation of the feudal warrior into an *honnête homme*. The political significance of this elitism and its compatibility with Mauss's socialism can be found in the ideal of depersonalization of the individual evidenced in Mauss's personal subordination to the group by means of a "voluntary anonymity."[90] Conversely, the immediate context of authoritarian mass movements compelled Mauss—as well as Caillois—to reassert the capacity of individuals to resist the direction of prevailing winds.

The political ramifications of manners, affect control, and their impact upon the psychic economy of the individual so critical in the prerevolutionary period also permeate the models of comportment devised by succeeding generations of artists since the last century. These behavioral signs are tantamount to declarations of moral positioning in relation to the bourgeoisie, which, as the new social majority, exerted their power as cultural arbiters as well. For these reasons, the social personae cultivated by the bohemians of the nineteenth century were inseparable from their aesthetic positions. Conflicting interpretations regarding the nature of the transformative effects of the group according to the model of concentration and dispersion therefore touch the core of the fractious polemics within the Collège and are responsible for the apparent contradictions between its political stance and social analyses—a tension that demonstrates why assessments of the group must consider the latter irreducible to strict alignments along the left/right (political) axis.

In contrast with Bataille's uncompromising and subversive exhortations to an expenditure without reserve, Leiris conceded his own attraction to the "pure" side of the sacred: "For to achieve a certain pitch of impurity one must expend too much energy. And I am fundamentally lazy." More willfully, Baudelaire posited the need for concentration, a centripetal counter to the "vaporisation" of God-the-prostitute. His model is the Dandy, walled off from the crowd—inscrutable, impassive, impersonal. Leiris obliquely invokes Baudelaire's exemplary figure of modernity by concluding *Manhood* with a dream in which he explains to a female friend "how necessary it is to construct a wall around oneself by means of clothing."[91] The Dandy, like the Bohemian, was a new figure to emerge from post-'89 society, whose bourgeois sons did not renounce their class so much as try to sustain and extend its revolutionary legacy.[92] Baudelaire incarnated the contradictory impulses of the bohemian rebel; Leiris the poet described his own sentiments as vacillating between disgust and nostalgia—a rebellion ultimately turned against himself by invoking examples of Prometheus and Icarus, both of whom incur some form of punishment, including symbolic castration. Generating their own mythologies, the romantic realists of the last century set the pattern of ambivalence characterizing most attempts to revise relations to the dominant class and ideology well into the modern period.

The divisiveness of these issues can be traced to Bataille's early polemic with Breton, prompted by the surrealist model of revolutionary ideology and practice repudiated by Bataille for repeating the transmutation of left heterogeneous elements into an idealized version manifested in earlier patterns of revolt as well. In the effort to dissociate from his origins, the bourgeois attempts to establish solidarity with the "lower" classes by aligning himself with marginal, potentially subversive, and heterogeneous forces—whether dreams, eroticism, the irrational, or the workers themselves. With a move toward legitimation, however, the rebellion aligns itself with superior values, such as the surreal, spirit, or absolute, even if it means spiritualizing material phenomena. Most blatantly, the idealist deviation appropriates traditional symbols such as the eagle, to the point of creating a mythological *sur*eagle for itself. When the goals of class warfare are occulted, bourgeois rebels are misled into an idealistic, Icarian version of revolutionary illumination. Bataille cites the case of the political icon of the eagle entering into an alliance with the sun and castrating any figure that attempts to undermine its authority, including Icarus, Prometheus, and the Mithraic bull. Significantly, Bataille does not condemn the recuperation since he recognizes—to some degree—its inevitability. In reference to Nietzsche's precedent, he acknowledges that

> The only means of emancipation from his class for a bourgeois individual derives from the action prompted by an Icarian complex. It is impossible to betray one's class out of solidarity for the proletariat, but only out of the desire to steal the "fire from the sky," in keeping with a properly Nietzschean terminology; and even this is accomplished by means of simple subversion and because of the pleasure to transgress supposedly intangible laws.[93]

Bataille's concession is made in recognition of the fact that most bourgeois are attracted to rebellion the way moths flit to the light, inevitably bringing about their own destruction. His main target—the surrealist claim to seek a point transcending the "old" antinomies (Breton)—is used to illustrate the modern version of the archaic deviation whereby heterogeneous phenomena are appropriated and then sublimated into higher, immaterial ones. Bataille's last word on the matter is consistent with his generally extreme positions during the prewar period, when he asserts that the only viable negativity is a base materialism in rupture with any vestiges of a dialectic of recognition. The bourgeois must agitate in concert with other groups and cannot establish himself as representative of another class. With considerable acuity, he points out that the impulses leading toward lower as well as higher values are at work in every milieu, but the political reality is that the bourgeoisie can claim the realm of ideas as its own, and for the most part, that group monopolizes the production of representations.

When Bataille organized the Collège de Sociologie in 1937 with Caillois, they declared their intention to explore "the *points of coincidence* between the fundamental obsessive tendencies of individual psychology and the principal structures governing social organization and in command of its revolutions."[94] The modification of surrealist terminology apparent in the notion of a "point of coincidence" rather than point of encounter in the surreal would not be lost on Collège participants and readers of its own version of a manifesto. As dissident surrealists, they cautiously avoided positing a privileged "sur" position while projecting the possibility of a new topos:[95] a sacred sociology where the traditional dualities opposing the social and the political, the individual and the collective, contemplation and activism, could be radically revised. For the Collège, the encounter would mean exploration of the psyche in terms irreducible to individual pathologies and entail turning the tools of ethnographic investigation upon oneself, identified as a member of a group in search of collective modes of action. Underlying these investigations was the critical question to which neither LeBon nor Freud could provide the response: what did it mean to advocate—even militate—for modes of behavior at odds with the very socialization, or what Mauss called the *habitus*, of which the investigators themselves were, to varying degrees, the products? Whether Durkheim's call for the renewal of festivals or collective assemblies that generated effervescence, Bataille's push for extreme *dépense* and ritualized transgressions, Leiris's aspiration to an eroticism tinged with the aura of the sacred without its paralyzing effects, or the Collège's own projection of a collective alternative to the prevailing panic—all required radical modification of the nature of social relations to which they were accustomed, and forms of action and engagement to which they were not. The spectacle of fascist rallies confirmed LeBon's and Freud's cynical predictions: is it any wonder that their success would exert some degree of fascination upon Bataille, who conceded as much? Bataille's sociological claim to seek nothing less than the revision of human relations leads to the unsettling notion of a sacred sociology, a heterodoxical approach to the social sources of behavior that transpose into collective forms those ephemeral instants individuals value most because in them they intuit the secret motives for transformations identified with the sacred.

The realm of the sacred is characterized as one of communication or indefinite fusion. To grasp its totality entails a comprehensive view resistant to the specialization required by science and leads to the subjective understanding derived from the lived states Leiris described. The consequence of this reasoning can also lead to the implementation of such experiences. Already at the time of the Collège, its parallel secret society known through the brief publication, *Acéphale,* contemplated stagings or reenactments of (in)famous crimes, especially a sacrificial celebration of the king's beheading. One could argue, however, that this literal resuscitation of the tragic spirit was ultimately less significant than the praise Bataille lavished upon the representation of the "community of the heart" depicted in the revival of *Numance* in 1937, a Cervantès tragedy with obvious resonances for the Spanish Civil War. Bataille refuses the local interpretation for precisely the reasons elaborated in his final address to the Collège: *Numance*'s significance is irreducible to an exhortation for support of the Republican cause. More generally, it offers the possibility of representing a community united through its confrontation with death—the only viable counter to fascism according to Collège declarations. The acephalic community would be linked by a tragedy marking the decapitation or death of the chief himself. Most daunting would be a representation of death as a modality of expenditure and thus the communal basis for society. Only the community or secondary society described in this study as the sacred group according to the sacrificial model provides the requisite resistance to the accumulation of forces bolstering a nationalistic figure or movement. The exemplarity of *Numance* also points to the missing term in Wahl's recap of the

Collegians' common history—literature—subsumed within Durkheimian sociology by collective representations.

Displaced by the contagious ethnographic representations, the role of literature in effecting moral and spiritual transformations nonetheless continues to inform the meditations of the three authors considered here. Moreover, they are united in their indictment of the act of writing for being anything less than an expression of expenditure comparable to sacrifice and therefore capable of inducing sacred communication. Bataille would subsequently address this paradox in the preface accompanying *La Part maudite (The Accursed Share)* (1949), his most sustained meditation upon the possibility for a general economy based upon expenditure rather than production. By preparing a manuscript and the effort it entails, was he not adding to the accumulation of energies and products he believed needed to be expended? What his own conclusions taught is that production must be regarded as but one phase within the total economic cycle, so that "accumulation was only a deferment, a retreat in the face of the inevitable, when accumulated riches would acquire value within the instant of their expenditure."[96] Leiris's effort to resolve the paradox of writing led to comparisons with the bullfight—literature envisioned as a tauromachia—despite his own reservations at elevating a simulacrum of the risk of death to such an exalted status. Perhaps the most apposite rethinking of the nature of writing under the sign of the sacred must recall the transgression of utilitarian criteria Bataille subsumed under the notion of a sovereign expenditure. In the same way that social forms must be appreciated as a response to the solicitation for expenditure as well as for production, so writing must be seen as an occasion to satisfy the urgency for a projection *hors de soi,* which in the new economy without reserve, the ethno-scriptor transgresses with the left hand what the right one has inscribed. Within the context of the Collège, Caillois also concluded that however enlisted—whether through elective affinities or other means—a group formation is imperative, because writers and artists can fully deploy their creative potential only within a collective situation. Because even art is not immune to the diversion of sacred energies toward perverse ends, the nature of representations became as pressing for contributors to the Collège as it had been for Durkheim. In the next and last chapter devoted to sacred communication, we therefore examine how they modeled their approach to art and eroticism according to sacrifice.

Four

Sacrifice in Art and Eroticism

Rather than the inventory of the Collège's activities Bataille intended, his last lectures provided a defensive finale. Leiris, for instance, felt that undue emphasis upon the sacred had betrayed the Maussian *total social fact*,[1] and Bataille's response was to argue for a subjective approach to the sacred despite the malaise it may engender.[2] Given the particular resistance the sacred poses to representation—especially its "vital animation"—he favored images that venture to the extremes of sacrifice and crime and credits psychoanalysis for his as well as Leiris's ability to confront such taboo areas of experience. More influential, Bataille claims, were Leiris's descriptions of contact with the sacred during the famous 1931–33 expedition across French equatorial Africa, which the fledgling ethnographer joined following studies with Mauss. As official secretary to the interdisciplinary team headed by Marcel Griaule, Leiris kept a diary where, with scrupulous "documentary" detachment, he recounted the pillaging exploits of the French hunters and gatherers for ethnographically significant objects and information. Published under the title *l'Afrique fantôme* in 1934—Griaule's objections notwithstanding—it remains a brutally honest testimony of the encounter between Europeans and colonized peoples.

In the wake of seventy pages of desultory details for the expedition's first five months, the entry for August 31, 1931, marked a dramatic high point. At the village of Nkourala, Leiris and his colleagues observed a sacrificial offering involving the use of a fetish described as follows:

> It is an amorphous mass which, as the four men lift it with great care from its niche, turns out to be a sack of coarse, patched canvas, covered with a sort of pitch made of congealed blood, stuffed with what one guesses to be an assortment of dusty things, with a protuberance at one end and a small bell at the other.[3]

Unexpectedly, given the author's lamented inability to engage in most scenes he witnessed, Leiris joined the natives in recognition of the fact that

> [a] great religious effusion is brought on by this simple, dirty object whose abjection is a fantastic force, because men have condensed into it their own sense of the absolute, and because they have imprinted their own power in it, as when a child playing with clay rolls between his fingers a little ball of earth.[4]

Later, at Gondar, Leiris seems to fulfill the goals of the official mission as well as overcome his personal inhibitions by immersing himself in the experience of the *zar* or spirits of possession. One noteworthy reflection ensued from a sacrifice, when the author's head was anointed with butter in the traditional fashion: "Alone on the bench I feel very separate, very saintly, even chosen. I remember my first communion, if it had been as solemn, perhaps I would have remained a true believer; but true religion begins with blood."[5]

Such high drama contrasts with the domesticated version of the sacred Leiris subsequently depicted in the 1938 address to the Collège de Sociologie entitled "Le sacré dans la vie quotidienne." Jean Jamin has duly noted the modifications to the Durkheimian model the latter representation offers:[6] rather than the eminently social and collective phenomenon celebrated in *Elementary Forms,* Leiris's sacred appears to be individualized (if not individual), the outcome of childhood experiences and games shared with friends and siblings. Using Bataille's extreme version as foil, Jamin contrasted the notion of *dépense,* where expenditure, loss, sacrifice, eroticism, and violence provide the basis for communication, with Leiris's "left" sacred, in the sense of gauche, awkward, or discomfited. In Jamin's presentation, Leiris did not actively transgress the rules of conduct and bourgeois respectability so much as he tripped over the subtle lines of acceptability. Firmly anchored in a quotidian punctuated by ephemeral breakthroughs, this version of the sacred rapidly shifts focus onto the "open sesame" power of language through a poetics of linguistic perversions, deviations, and demi-entendres.

However endearing, this portrait of the artist as young clod bypasses the more tumultuous representation of the sacred found in *l'Age d'homme*, an innovative autobiographical narrative published in 1939 but outlined concurrently with *l'Afrique fantôme*. By dissociating Leiris's representation of the sacred within daily life from the violently disruptive and transgressive forces associated with the left sacred, the latter's crucial proximity to death has been effectively kept at bay. Yet "tears of eros"[7] are shed throughout his memoirs as a sort of ritual ablution of unconsummated sexuality, when the exaltation associated with eroticism is experienced as an uncontrolled *chavirement* or unsettling of the illusory stability of bourgeois order. The terror evoked by the loved one is so intense that the usually garrulous author is reduced to silence. In *Manhood*'s introduction, the bullfight is invoked as the standard by which other simulated and less admired rituals of *mise à mort* are gauged. Leiris is certainly closest to his friend Bataille when he perceives the powerful emotions elicited by any rapprochement with death as providing the affective substrate of the erotic experience. Both derive their model for eroticism from the sacred, whose distinct advantage over other analytical categories resides in its tolerance for antithetical notions. Love—and the profound attraction associated with it—according to Leiris elicits a sacred horror, a permutation of the superstitious terror that accompanies all possibilities for carnal contact.

Reference to the sacred also encompasses sacrifice, so the act of love is compared to the corrida, where the ceremonial protocol confers a religious aura and obviates the initial impression of sadism surrounding the bull's death. The bullfight ceremony derives prestige from its archaic religious sources in contrast with devalued modern equivalents that remain purely symbolic. But whereas Bataille always strained a rhetorical muscle to maintain his discourse at the level of death, Leiris explores the downside of the *jouissance* cycle as well. Fearful that his love is diminishing, he recounts scratching his entire body with scissors "with a kind of furious and voluptuous determination."[8] The powerful scene is evocative of the photograph of Chinese torture which holds a privileged place within Bataillian iconography.

Leiris's illustration of the encounter of opposites in a sacred violence erupting within daily life introduces a section of his autobiography where images of wounds, painful penetration, and mutilation are associated with sacrificial scarification and a pathological reaction to female genitalia.

Traces of the ethnographic detour in Leiris's representation of the sacred are not limited to the powerful charge they provide his erotic experiences. Indeed, the prevailing theme of the spectacle throughout *Manhood*—reflected even in the formal "staging" of the dramatic episodes that organize the autobiography—must be read in terms evocative of sacred ritual. Just as writing itself that pushes self-revelation to the extreme garners some of the tension associated with the matador's temptation of destruction, so other realms of daily life acquire an added drama by their reinvestment with sacred associations. Areas of experience that have lost the sacred aura either because of social evolution or economic profanation, or because they are allegedly superseded by the increased rationality and decreased violence of everyday life, take on a revised significance. Dancing, for instance, is compared to possession. Clearly influenced by his African experience, Leiris asserts that possession provides the best way to impart meaning to the social gatherings that claim so much of his time. One can perceive in them a religious dimension, since communion occurs through the eroticism of dance. In reference to writing and poetry, the "lyric state" is equated with a trance. At another point, he recounts the intensity—even exaltation—attained by means of conversation with a close (male) friend that must be compared to the violation of a taboo or sacrilege.

But the strongest continuity with Leiris's African experience is manifested in *Manhood*'s description of a form of communication that defies Western categories. He recalls observing the Ethiopian woman Emawayish during the ritual that precedes the onset of possession trance: after killing the ram, she begins to imitate the sounds of the animal and to drink its blood. The contact established by means of the sacrifice, Leiris reminisces, is indeed more intimate than any carnal encounter. With this anecdote, the timorous Leiris offers readers a privileged insight into the workings of sacrifice as a mediating mechanism with the otherness of the sacred. Communication with the forces of life as well as death, which Hubert and Mauss proclaimed to be the source of sacrifice's attraction, is echoed in his interpretation of the bullfight when it encourages a union between the bull and toreador—

"just as in sacrificial ceremonies, there is 'fusion' between all those officiating, and the beast who will serve as their ambassador to the forces of the beyond."[9] Fusion is the outcome of a minutely regulated ritual whose rules may transgress the injunction against killing but also redeem the cosmological and social drama of sacrificial murder from degenerating into slaughter.

These flashes of sacred intensity lend their special color to the otherwise bland daily life of a bourgeois Parisian intellectual, for whom the sacred superimposes a map upon conventional domestic or social space so that new polarities are created and reinforced by means of dividing lines marking interdictions as well as their infractions. Like all social forms, these invisible demarcations provide access to or mediate contact with the unknown or unfamiliar. The potential titillation provided by a brothel, for instance, is experienced at the *threshold* of entry, rather than within.[10] The particular feelings associated with the sacred do not enter the bourgeois domestic space so much as they erupt within the imaginary configuration inhabited by the ethnographer of the quotidian. One incident from *Manhood* will illustrate this point: reaching out to take her younger son in her arms, the author's mother slips, falls, and gashes her head. Leiris makes no further comment upon the scene but inserted it within a chapter entitled "wounds, etc." The sight of maternal blood recalls the African experience Leiris recounted above, when he equated religion with a sacrificial offering. What would otherwise be reduced to a regrettable accident incurred in the service of domestic duty now acquires the aura of maternal sacrifice. Devoid of moralizing, the incident's power resides in its intimation of mortality—a fissure within bourgeois domesticity's insulation from death and passionate extremes. Pressed to conclude his presentation to the Collège, Leiris characterized the sacred as prestigious, dangerous, ambiguous, forbidden, breathtaking, and, in the final analysis, supernatural. Without directly citing Durkheim's query as to why every society colors some things sacred, Leiris's final statement nonetheless reminds us of the epistemological claims made for the study of archaic religious experiences:

> If one of the most "sacred" aims that man can set for himself is to acquire as exact and intense an understanding of himself as possible, it seems desirable that each one, scrutinizing his memories with the greatest possible honesty, should examine whether he can discover

there some sign permitting him to discern the color for him of the very notion of the sacred.[11]

By equating the search for self-knowledge with the sacred, Leiris returns us to Wahl's question as to why sociology came to be viewed as the endpoint of a trajectory that abandoned surrealism, revolutionary politics, and psychoanalysis in its wake. *Manhood* offers at least one response. The author expresses considerable ambivalence toward psychoanalysis, despite the possible analytical insights it might provide into the origins of the "intimate mythology" he has fabricated through dreams, erotic fantasies, and legendary icons. Although the torment of internal distress had compelled him to undergo psychotherapy, he rejects its therapeutic *telos*—"my repugnance for anything claiming to cure ills other than those of the body."[12] Indeed, despite considerable floundering in the inexplicable confusion of terror and pity, he aggressively declares

> When modern investigators invoke the unconscious, refer to Oedipus, castrations, guilt and narcissism, I do not think this advances us greatly as to the essentials of the problem (which remains, I believe, linked to the problem of death, to the apprehension of nothingness, and therefore concerns metaphysics).[13]

The repudiation of psychoanalytic reductionism is related to the constellation of figures derived from classical and biblical antiquity through which the author expresses some of his most complex emotional states. Describing his attachment to the diptych of female figures, Judith and Lucretia, Leiris points out that the particular mixture of sacred terror and pity they evoke is tinged with a sense of remorse due to his own cowardice as well as cruelty. These sentiments in turn prompt "the superstitious fear of punishment," but Leiris is absolved of any guilt because he also places himself in the position of victim.[14]

In his quest for evasion from his own obsessions and milieu Leiris experimented with the alternatives that had become the common legacy from Baudelaire to succeeding generations of avant-garde artists and rebels. Preeminent among them is love, now envisioned in terms antithetical to the domesticated sentimentality of bourgeois marriage and, therefore, as sacred, erotic, and an integral part of the general movement *hors de soi*. But Leiris also discovers the contradiction inherent in trying to sustain extreme sensations over time:

> Love—the only possibility of a coincidence between subject and object, the only means of acceding to the sacred, as represented by the

desired object in so far as it is exterior and alien to us—implies its own negation because to possess the sacred is at the same time to profane and finally to destroy it by gradually robbing it of its alien character.[15]

Bataille's response to Leiris's methodological critique was that he had in fact resituated sociology within the serious perspective it deserved. Paradoxically, his object—erotic activity—is a domain that is at "the greatest possible departure from our union with the social group."[16] We recall that one of Bataille's inaugural lectures to the Collège rejected love as a possible model for community because it isolated the couple from the larger group. Thus, to Durkheim's capacious definition of religion as the basis of virtually all social forms[17] and to Mauss's expansion of the socialization process to the most intimate details of bodily techniques,[18] sacred sociology contributes yet another dimension: the erotic. Product of the interplay between interdiction and transgression, at the antipodes to any spontaneous outburst of libido, and irreducible to biological sexuality, eroticism is a social phenomenon. Under the rubric of the sacred, it can be explored in terms commensurate with its powerful evocations, whether the ambivalence described by Leiris or the antithetical tears of eros that fascinated Bataille.

The latter's view of eroticism draws upon a dramatic conception of human interaction in which two persons produce a new entity by opening onto each other in a way that is compared to a wound, and the binding convulsion it requires so intense it elicits tears of eros. Love itself arises from the need for sacrifice, for that desire to be *hors de soi* Mauss attributed to the source and development of the earliest social rituals.[19] But we recall that he also insisted upon two dimensions of the ritual, one that allowed for contact or communication with the otherness of the sacred—including its threatening potential for destruction—and the second, complementary part that returns the sacrificer to the profane realm of everyday objects and things. In contrast, Bataille's experience of the limits of the self—to the point where the initial will to loss in another entails a violent rending of the conventional boundaries of self and other—is an extreme relinquishment that stimulates a yet more aggressive movement "that finds that the only limit to its excessive actions is fear, and more, which uses this fear it provokes to make itself even more ardent, even more frenzied."[20]

Bataille's high-toned rhetoric aside, the relation between eroticism and sacred communication could nonetheless be evidenced in the "sacred group" that evolved among Bataille, Leiris, and Colette Peignot.[21]

"Laure," as Peignot was known, was raised in Paris according to the rigid codes typical of her affluent, bourgeois, Catholic background. Her childhood was marked by the World War I tragedy that took the lives of her father and his three brothers. Rebellion against this milieu was asserted by the late twenties, when she became the companion of Boris Souvarine, born of Russian parents and editor of the review *La Critique sociale,* which she helped to edit and publish through her inheritance. Active in left-wing intellectual circles organized by Souvarine, Peignot also accompanied him to the Soviet Union, where direct observation reinforced Souvarine's denunciations of the betrayed revolution. By the late thirties, her involvement with Bataille is detectable in writings informed by a preoccupation with the sacred. The moment of "coincidence," according to Bataille, occurs when, shortly after Laure's premature death in 1938 (she was mourned by Leiris as well), he discovers writings in which she describes the "color of the very notion of the sacred": It is that "infinitely rare moment" when the "eternal part" of each being is revealed and projected into a universal movement.[22] The menace of death transports individuals to intoxication, but the sacred is inseparable from the communication it induces with and among others who share it. However extreme this communication— comparable to a violation of the self—it remains an eminently social phenomenon.

Bataille claims to be overwhelmed by the convergence with his own shift away from any substantive definition of the sacred to privileged instants responsible for the strong form of connection he compared to the experience of sacrifice: the sacred is communication and as such responsible for the formation of "new beings."[23] Only such rare moments are capable of providing the violent representation called for by the "profoundly ambiguous, dangerous, and mortal" nature of the sacred. Like Laure, he continues to view even this version of the sacred as social, since it is "that which arises as most elusive among individuals, [the sacred] being only a privileged moment of communal unity, a moment of convulsive communication of that which is ordinarily stultified."[24] With the death of God and thus the primary limit or constraint upon human will to extremes lifted, modernity can now envisage the possibility for a new field *(champ)* of experience: the sacred instant of expenditure.[25]

As final homage to Laure, Bataille and Leiris published her writings in 1939, contemporaneous with Bataille's own article, "Le Sacré," which appeared in *Cahiers d'Art*. Notes published posthumously indicate the importance he granted to this brief text, from which he projected a future book devoted to the sacred. In them, he also comments upon the question posed by the sacred in relation to the temporality of love and refers to the passage from Leiris cited above. The sociological progression Bataille must effect from the dyadic relation of the lovers to that of the larger community does not impede him from projecting a similarly extreme vision of the community's *telos*. Thus, "communities formed by deep emotional bonds recall the passionate union of lovers; and there is no lack of forms that have in common with erotic perversities that the loss of self in a vaster being occasions the loss of self in a chaotic universe and in death." So powerful is Bataille's conviction that the will to loss illuminates the most obscure forms of behavior, it carries his theory of expenditure to the point where cause and effect are inverted. Indeed, just as earlier speculations upon the role of *dépense* in the foundation of community concluded that the community becomes the "alibi" for expenditure, so the same reversal is effected in his appreciation of both eroticism and the festival. Men gather for sacrifice and festivals to satisfy the rending opening onto others that is ultimately "a liberating tear."[26] In such situations, the individual is at minimum vaguely aware that the desire propelling the movement outward beyond the self is responsible for the formation of the community. But the man attracted to a woman, especially if she is beautiful, is convinced that it is the object that stimulates eroticism, so that it is indeed much more difficult to arrive at a clear-cut judgment and decide

> whether he makes love because he is attracted by this woman, or if he uses that woman out of a need to make love. By the same token, it is hard to know to what extent the community is only the propitious occasion for the festival and sacrifice or if the festival and sacrifice are proof of love given to the community.[27]

In the conclusion to *Manhood*, Leiris credits psychoanalysis with taming his most destructive obsessions, but a gnawing sense of void remains. To which cause worthy of total sacrifice can he commit himself? The question cannot be dismissed as youthful posturing since it will haunt the sexagenarian as well. Similarly, in exergue to Bataille's final lecture, the absent Caillois's letter to the group queried,

> Is it possible to find any reason for fighting and dying other than country or class, any reason for fighting that would not be based

upon material interests? Is it possible for the concern with human greatness that is shouldered by a few to constitute alone a sufficient reason for existence? But what, exactly, does one mean in speaking of greatness?[28]

Sociological evidence, or more exactly the Bataillian point of view, suggests that both questions have reversed the terms of the proposition to favor the goal rather than the cause, so that, when conventionally posed (as in the example of Caillois), the query remains unanswerable. Movement beyond the self is impelled by the desire to break certain confines and possibly even to experience a sense of loss irreducible to personal idiosyncrasy or the psychological aberration of a subset of individuals.[29] Social recognition of that need is reflected in the very existence of social forms that structure the moment of transgression for which—as Mauss quipped—prohibitions exist. Only the possibilities rendered accessible through collective moments of infraction, such as the transformative instant when a new level of being is attained, are worthy of the designation sacred.

The potential for misrecognition of what exactly constitutes the sacred is also acknowledged, given the equally powerful solicitation motivating individuals and societies to produce, conserve, and accumulate. The blind spot of modern society and culture is that the extremes marking the opposition between the two tendencies have virtually disappeared. As Leiris eloquently noted, only in sexual transactions do they reemerge, in part due to the contrast between the intensity of initial passion and its erosion over time. Bataille's formulation is equally devastating: "The vacant horror of steady conjugality has already enclosed them." The erotic alternative is an outlet of turbulent passion, high drama, and the ineluctable horizon of death. For Bataille, the two directions or economies do not seek out the homeostasis of social alternation provided either through seasonal shifts (Mauss) or the sacred/profane dualism (Durkheim). Rather, one exists to enable the other, so that even in relations that unite lovers, "[t]heir need to lose exceeds their need to find each other."[30]

The subversion of the profane in favor of what Bataille associates with the sacred is now complete: "Beyond the common being met in their embrace, they seek infinite annihilation in a violent expenditure where the possession of a new object, a new woman or new man, is only the pretext for an even more annihilating expenditure." Moreover, the extreme nonpositive affirmation—as Foucault phrased it—is not restricted to eroticism alone, but extends as well to religious figures in whom sacrificial devotion to the community is pushed to the point where the desire to challenge all limits causes individuals "to no longer live for the community, they live only for the sacrifice." In defiance of all restrictions, Bataille concludes that the contagion that was always a characteristic of the sacred disseminates the sacrificial frenzy: "In the same way that eroticism slips easily into orgy, sacrifice that becomes an end in itself lays claim, beyond the narrowness of the community, to a universal value."[31] The universal equivalent to the community must be found in the form of a figure capable of extending the sacrificial orgy beyond limits indefinitely. Formerly, gods served individuals who sought some return from their flirtation with death. But what about those who like St. Teresa of Avila "desire only to be lost without being found"?—those who challenge the very notion of composite being according to some alternative model of Totality?

The sacred continued to provide a central organizing principle for Caillois's thought well into the final years of the decade and culminated in the 1939 publication of *l'Homme et le sacré*, a Durkheimian reinterpretation of the festival's regenerative capacities. The particular color of the sacred for Caillois was also influenced by his other ethnographic mentors—Dumézil, Granet, and Mauss. Though often absent from the actual meetings, he entrusted Bataille to deliver his presentations. At the time of the Collège, Caillois's ongoing struggle with the nature of literature in relation to the sacred led him to devise several striking formulations. Because the latent energies associated with the sacred are rarely discerned by other modes of thought and inquiry, sociology's double mission would be to detect signs of movement prior to their realization in forms that may undermine their unifying potential. The two-dimensional process is best exemplified in his appreciation of literature's effect on the individual as he or she accedes to the magic circle of a community of readers:

> One can only call religious the subterranean impatience which the novel expresses under so many guises. It marks the moment when these invisible and new forces still remain dispersed, unknown to each other, though linked by a secret element, precisely like the readers of a book. But they are already attracting each other, as so many fine magnetic needles, and risk suddenly revealing themselves soldered and inseparable, manifesting their existence through an unexpected blaze which, only too late, will be perceived as inextinguishable.[32]

Bataille remained more skeptical regarding art's ability to penetrate its "secret" and attain the limits of representation in pursuit of the sacred instant.[33] The discussion of aesthetics and eroticism is therefore continued below more explicitly in terms of the model of sacrifice influenced by the French school of sociology.

Art's Secret

The secret of art, proclaimed Bataille, resides in the following proposition: like sacrifice in relation to the victim, it removes its object from the realm of things. But it is no secret that herein resides the motor force of the Bataillian opus—to demonstrate that an essential part of human nature seeks to extricate itself from an exclusive subordination to work, production, and accumulation. Irrespective of a culture's level of material riches, humanity in all times and places has manifested the desire to expend its energies and resources as well as direct them toward constructive goals. It is possible to argue that the need for loss is as powerful as the drive to accumulate and reflects the realization that extreme expenditure can provide pleasure of a violent sort. The widespread appeal of these Bataillian premises testifies to the discontent wrought by modernity and the challenge to cultural theory it poses—that an increase in material wealth has exacerbated servility to rather than emancipation from utilitarian imperatives.

The Bataillian alternative experience of sovereignty has little to do with material objects—laughter, eroticism, and effervescence explore collective modes of expenditure that simulate the effects of sacrifice through a radical modification of the *subject*. Isolated in a world according to things, where the horrors of death and destruction are occulted, individuals seek to transmute their anguish into the ecstasy of the sovereign instant. Eschewing the feudal model of sovereignty in which expenditure ultimately reinforced class privilege, the idealism for which he rebuked the Surrealists, or the aestheticizing solution of art for art's sake, the perspective of Bataille's self-described Copernican revolution considers forms of giving that seek no return. In its most systematized expression, the theory of a general economy posits a menacing, cursed reserve destined for destruction at the center of a point of view of human activity so capacious it claims as much relevance to artists as economists.

Art, however, does not provide privileged reference points within the labyrinth of Bataillian writings. Few artists are discussed in any sustained way other than Edouard Manet, the subject of a study commissioned in the mid-1950s. The problematic status of art was indeed set forth early, when Bataille aggressively argued that even if individual artists offer local examples of rebellion, the place of art in Western culture is more accurately assessed by the pervasive role fulfilled by architecture in monumentalizing the principles of domination and authority. His global indictment encompasses all manifestations of *construction*— whether evidenced in physiognomy, dress, music, or painting—as testaments to the moral straightjacket of idealism. Materialism presented the dilemma of how to conceptualize something other than "dead" matter—a passive derivative from idealism. Bataille's *base* materialism is therefore defined as an actively creative force, historically comparable to that of the early Gnostics and encompassing a scatological predilection for the filth, waste, and detritus shunned by metaphysics.

Art's uneasy place within the Bataillian corpus is symptomatic of the dramatic revisions in the act of seeing required for expenditure to emerge from its occultation by utilitarian criteria. The instant of sacred communication resists representation, just as the impulse to communicate through the dismantling of individual boundaries and overcome the "suffocation" of imposed thingness in the world of homogeneous relations defies the conventions of a discursively determined reality. Both requirements lead to a characteristic innovation of Bataille's early writing practice: his "operation" upon certain privileged metaphors, notably the sun. The need for expenditure is paradoxically obscured by the light of reason, a rationality whose economy of energies are primarily—if not exclusively—directed toward production. Within the dominant ocularcentric paradigm—to borrow Martin Jay's apt description—aesthetics privileges sight over the other senses and facilitates the appropriation of its objects. By redefining the sun in terms of its task or *besogne*—as Bataille argued all words should be understood—to generate combustion and noxious gases as well as boundless energy, a second sun appears whose blinding force provides the requisite insight into expenditure as it approaches annihilating destruction. This re-vision of the privileged metaphors of Western metaphysics entails a reinscription of the disembodied senses, but in the shocking form of a "pineal" eye (*pine* being the slang word for "penis" in French) jutting from the head, or the automutilations inflicted by a dazzled Vincent van Gogh. The exorbitant sun of the general economy circulates within an alternative paradigm determined by visual as well as linguistic homologies—especially with the eye and egg—relayed by their obscene status in relation to the conscious mind. By staging enactments of transgression involving their migration to the body's orifices, Bataille's narrative traces unconscious associations that provide an erotic jolt at the limits of sexuality. Unlike conventional pornography, his texts play with images derived from the archetypes of classical myths, especially Prometheus, Icarus, and the Minotaur. Sacred horror, not titillation, is the desired effect. Admittedly religious in its inspiration, the Bataillian sensibility seeks contact with the divine forces of death and destruction.

One of Bataille's earliest published texts—an account of the 1928 exhibition of pre-Columbian art in Paris—suggests the connection between art and sacrifice that would remain a constant throughout his career. This introduction to Aztec society reinforced his understanding of sacrifice at odds with the utilitarian assumption that it entails an initial relinquishment made with a view toward some ultimate recompense. Rather, the Bataillian claim is that the fascination exerted by sacrifice resides in its function as ritualized drama, where the group is collectively projected into the realm of the divine. The role of the sacrificial victim is to mediate the collectivity's encounter with the menacing forces segregated by religion as sacred. The review essay dating from 1949, in which the opening analogy between sacrifice and art cited at the outset to this section appears, further explains that the sacred's demise in the modern world is not the inevitable consequence of heightened rationality but signals a pandemic fear of confrontation with suppressed horrors. In sacrifice, violence is liberated, and the discontinuity separating individuals momentarily obliterated, so that the intimacy of continuity may be recaptured in the sacred instant. The crucial context here is not provided by religion in the traditional sense, but by the notion of the *divine* explained as follows:

> The divine is not in and of itself opposed to horror: it excludes neither evil nor ugliness. In truth, it is distinguished only from the vulgar necessities of life, those which order a world of things and, within this world, individuals who are treated like *things* and reduced to a use value or function. The divine, then, is contrary to the *thing*, whose form and meaning can only be external, and find meaning in its servitude.[34]

Bataille's writing practice was therefore distinguished by the intuition that sovereignty is approached on condition that the subject submit to the same dramatic transformations—strained to the limit of destruction—as the object it is willing to immolate. The experience of extreme expenditure is never an endpoint but an interminable process. As with the sacred, it is impossible to predict when sovereignty will erupt or can be identified within a work of art. Manet's exploration of the possibility for an annulment of the subject within painting is described as an "impersonal subversion." More exactly, the pervasive term equivalent to sacrifice in the case of Manet is "indifference." Yet Bataille also acknowledged the paradox of the author or artist who contributes to the accumulation of things through the investment of energy into the production of works. Though logically insuperable, this tension reappears when devising safeguards against the perversion of sovereignty identifiable in the abuse of power through acts ultimately directed toward acquisition or profit rather than loss, or, as Jean-Luc Nancy's meditation upon "painting in the grotto" via Bataille elaborates,

> But this sovereignty is not exercised over anything; it is not domination. It is not exercised; in truth, it is exceeded: its whole exercise is to exceed itself, not being anything but the absolute detachment or distancing of what has no foundation in the property of a presence, immanent or transcendent, and of what is thus in itself the lack, the failing of a presence that shows itself as a stranger to self, in itself a stranger to self, sovereignly alienated.[35]

The attempt to eliminate such exploitation also explains Bataille's insistence upon a certain congruence between writer and text, or artist and work, that may otherwise appear as a retrograde facet of his art criticism.

In its parallel function to sociology as a psychoanalysis of the social, painting provides a concrete index of those areas critical to the development of the unconscious within the evolution of civilization up to and including modernity. From the trans- or de-formation of classical figures admired in the painting of Joan Miró and Pablo Picasso, for instance, emerges the history of art as revelation of what Rosalind Krauss termed the "optical unconscious." Bataille's idiosyncratic survey focuses on "figures" whose appearance within a particular historical juncture serves as marker for the nature of the relation of the general economy of expenditure to the restricted one; namely, how the repressed need for extreme *dépense* inhabits and subverts the strictures dictated by the equally powerful solicitation for production and accumulation. Among those featured in his prewar atheological pantheon, an Aztec priest kneels at the base of a temple dedicated to sacrifice and raises a still-beating heart to the blinding sun; van Gogh expresses the supreme gesture of sovereign "freedom" or movement *hors de soi* by hurling a sacrificed ear in the face of bourgeois convention; the acephalic figure designed by André Masson has a head reappear as a skull in the place of genitals, the right hand holding a flaming heart, the left a sword, and the abdomen exposing the intestines in the form of a labyrinth; and the photos of Chinese torture reveal the "ecstatic" smile of the lacerated victim. Similarly, the study of the Lascaux caves claims that they witnessed the birth of art, and that their paintings testify to the emergence of a new being, albeit not actually represented, but the imagined artistic *homo ludens* responsible for the drawings. Manet's canvases usher in artistic modernism (also credited to some facets of Goya's work), while his maieutic brings forth a seductive creature whose movements remain indifferent to the demands of conventional beauty. In both inaugural moments, innovation is attributed to transgression.

In the beginning—or nearly so—there was art, since art coincides with the festival, when the worker that he first was *homo sapiens* threw down the tools by which he transformed nature. In so doing, he demonstrated the capacity to break the very rules or prohibitions he had imposed upon himself and through which he sought protection from the disorder of death and sexuality. Transgression marks the moment when necessity is transformed into abundance and the products of human labor are sacrificed. In this, Bataille follows Durkheim on the close relation of art to religion, and the recreative vitality of religious rituals and festivals as essential antidote to the exigencies of work:

> Thus, religion would not be religion if there was no place in it for free combinations of thought and action, for games, for art, for all that refreshes a spirit worn down by all that is overburdening in day-to-day labor. That which made art exist makes it a necessity. It is not merely an outward adornment that the cult can be thought of as dressing up in, in order to hide what may be too austere and harsh about it; the cult itself is aesthetic in some way.[36]

Conversely, all festivals, even those devoid of religious affiliations, ultimately acquire a religious nature by dint of the effervescence—even delirium, so close to a religious state—they foment. The distinguishing feature of the gathering is that the individual is transported beyond the self and thus effects a rupture with the quotidian. In the atmosphere of generalized transgression characteristic of the festival, sexuality's proximity with death is replaced with erotic pleasure that knows no end other than its own, and play prevails over purposeful activity. To conflate the birth of art with the transgression of the festival, Blanchot noted, leads to the paradox of sacrificial art: namely, that art does not coincide with the festival in order to celebrate human labor and its products, but rather marks a refusal of the reduction of humans to a level of thingness, when the outcome of travails are relinquished—the glorious moment of gratuitousness equated with sovereignty.

The correlative to the sacrificial dimension of art is that aspect of Bataillian anthropology that envisions prohibitions as part of the total cycle entailing their transgression, thereby providing a *structure,* so that

> transgression exists only from the moment when art itself is manifested, and that more or less, the birth of art coincides . . . with the tumultuousness of play and the festival, which is announced in the depths of the caverns where figures explode with life, where transgression supersedes and completes itself in the play between death and birth.[37]

Art emerges when the thingness of an object is sacrificed, its utilitarian significance annulled, and communication in the strong sense of sovereignty is realized.[38] Sacrifice is a crime at odds with the common morality that prohibits killing and destruction. By attributing to art the status of a transgressive act, Bataille lauds its instantiation of a hypermorality beyond good and evil or beauty and ugliness.

Within the history of aesthetics since Kant and Nietzsche that situates art at the antipodes to utility and morality within the realm of taste, Bataille also figures as heir to the ethical imperative promoted by the Surrealists that art be produced by all, not one. In the absence of ritualized sacrifice, he followed Durkheim in seeking the sacred in moments of collective effervescence the sociologist credited with the production of major cultural and religious forms. Bataille's numerous collective endeavors reflect his conviction that aesthetic, moral, and political transformations occur within a larger network or community. By the time of the postwar writings on Lascaux and Manet, the possibility for community was translated into the affinity experienced for certain artworks or artists and this connection was placed under the sign of friendship. It encompasses intimate collaborations with the artists André Masson and Jean Fautrier, for instance, or is enlisted to describe the sovereign "presence" of the figure that emerges from the work's sacrificial operation. In Lascaux, the viewer is moved by the lone representation of a human—a paltry stick figure in erection discovered at the base of a shaft hidden deep within the cave's recesses— because its sacrifice releases the elation of the artist who, through the negation of unmediated animal sexuality and of his own death-fearing self, attains the sovereign majesty of the magnificent creatures depicted. The daily intensity of the friendship between Manet and the poet Stéphane Mallarmé consecrated their shared aesthetics of indifference to the bourgeois subjugation of art to social ends.

In his praise for Bataille's review of the 1928 pre-Columbian exhibit, the respected ethnologist Alfred Métraux nonetheless expressed reticence in regard to his friend's rapprochement between sacrifice and the sacred, especially the argument that a society creates the sacred by removing certain persons or objects or even events from the realm of things by means of sacrificial rituals. Yet Bataille never desisted from his conviction that sacrifice constitutes *the* decisive enigma of human activity. Moreover, he devoted considerable effort to exploring how modern art displaced traditional rituals, especially those entailing a dimension he qualified as cruel.

A postwar meditation upon the connections between cruelty and art exposes what Bataille calls the dual trap or lure, which inheres in the very experience he seeks to explicate. In order to remain antithetical to utility, art must induce within the viewer an instant of recognition of that which is held in greatest horror. However, once an object (represented) is destroyed, nothing is left but emptiness. This conventional view presupposes that sacrifice's goal is to satisfy the fascination with death (and one's own simulated mortality) through destruction of the victim. The sacrificed object is then consecrated in a ceremony that ultimately celebrates the basis for social unity through the ambivalent status of the sacrificial thing or person, which is both reviled and sacralized. In contrast, Bataille argues that the effect of cruelty and destruction redounds upon the subject. Indeed, the goal of the trap exerted by death and transmuted into art is to destroy the viewer's status as object. Human objectification results from servitude to a particular utilitarian function and leads to the condition hauntingly described as an *enigmatic isolation*.[39] Sacrifice within the Bataillian lexicon signals the

breakdown of the economy of the subject in the concentrated autonomous and "closed" state necessary for its survival in a restricted economy based upon work and production. Only with a modification or
inner transformation can the passage *hors de soi* take place. What
Bataille retains from Mauss and Hubert's (1899) essay on sacrifice is
precisely the need for a movement beyond the self that their sociological perspective discerned within the sacrificial ritual.[40] And this movement is what Bataille describes as sovereign, since it entails the painful
transmutation of a certain construct—or more accurately, economy—
of the self. The reward for depersonalization is contact with the divine
forces that elude the isolated individual, since their potential for destruction requires mediation by means of either a sacrificial ritual or the
sacred nucleus (see chapter 3). When such contact occurs, the sovereign
instant of expenditure leads to communication. Sacrifice is therefore
no longer understood as the endpoint of the sacred so much as its *condition of possibility:* the sacred is the instantiation of communication
among individuals who have overcome their enigmatic isolation for a
moment of glorious exaltation. Philosophy thus encounters sociology
as well as aesthetics in the forging of a new model of the subject and
subjectivity.

This convergence returns us to the question: why art? We have already acknowledged Bataille's ambivalence toward writing, leading to
the possibility of a writing practice dedicated to transcribing the annulment of the writing subject in an impersonal subversion. If the study of
Lascaux complemented and enhanced the insights derived from the
French school of sociology characteristic of Bataille's early essays, then
the Manet opus firmly resituates his aesthetic meditations within the
history of social relations determined by what Elias referred to as the
ethos of expenditure, first set forth in Bataille's 1933 essay on expenditure (see chapter 3). Bataille's own predilection is to reappropriate
the criteria of the feudal aristocracy, when self-sacrifice was the ultimate validation of the warrior mentality. In both Manet's *Olympia*
and representation of Maximilian's execution, Bataille finds that this
royalty does not belong to any one image, but "to the passion of
the one who has realized in the self 'silent sovereignty.'" "Indeed," he
continues,

> modern painting offers the sole response to the medieval cathedral,
> since the essence of the cathedral is secret: The sacred today cannot

be proclaimed. . . . [O]ur world knows only an "inner transfigura-
tion," . . . silent, somewhat negative. . . . [I]t is impossible for me to
speak of it, except as a definitive silence.[41]

Sovereignty in painting is approximated by means of images liberated from the *lourdeur* or oppressiveness that signals bourgeois subordination to a criterion for beauty equated with the classical cachet.
Manet's vaporization of the ponderous bourgeois can be compared
to Bataille's Lascaux experience, where the conventional image of Ne-
anderthal as a plodding hirsute figure is metamorphosed into *homo
ludens*—a speculative turn inspired by the immediate affinity between
the viewer and the magnificent mammoths who seduce through their
glorious indifference to death. The solemnity of bourgeois rectitude is
transmuted into the poetic elegance of modern man, incarnated by
Manet himself and depicted in his portrait of the spirited poetic genius
Mallarmé.

Sovereignty thus explodes historical and social specificity to find
expression in a series of figures—whether acephalic or icthyphallic—
that emerge from the Bataillian corpus irrespective of conventional
aesthetic criteria or association with any particular artist or movement. The silence of these self-effacing figures (whose secretive nature
Blanchot contrasted with the overwhelming presence of the animals
drawn)[42] bears within them art's secret—its ability to effect a rupture
with thingness and accede to the sacred by resisting narrative recuperation. Indeed, the most consistent sign of the sacred is its power to impose silence. The dual meanings of *interdit* in French as both "reduced
to silence" and a "prohibition" are therefore inextricably tied to art's
ability to instill terror and the necessary respect for death, if one is to
have contact with the divine forces with which it is associated.

Possibly the most powerful instantiation of the moment of sacred
communication occurs when Bataille sees the recently discovered cave
paintings for the first time: temporal as well as spatial distances are
eradicated and the extraordinary force of the inscriptions imposes upon
the viewer a sense of presence. Bataille identifies the immediacy he experiences with all great art, and the sentiment it evokes with "friendship" *(amitié)*: "Is friendship not passion, the always already posed
question to which beauty is the sole response?"[43] The study of paleolithic art also allows him to elaborate an anthropological perspective
regarding the origins of the sacred. With an explicit repudiation of the

tendency among sociologists and historians of religion to view prohibitions in isolation, he asserts outright that human life cannot exist without them, that they must be examined as constituting a systemic whole. Most striking is the moment he envisions from within—the point at which the interdiction becomes a necessity in order for the group to survive. United by a shared acknowledgment of forces beyond their control responsible for the destruction of life and continuity, paleolithic society acknowledged the presence of death within human life by concretely and temporally circumscribing contact with its manifestations. Physical as well as psychological boundaries were drawn around the dead body by delineating enclaves and impeding individuals from succumbing to the undeniable fascination exerted by a corpse. Because the isolation of certain objects was motivated by a sentiment of terror and deemed sacred, a new value was created. Thus evolved a fundamental classification between those things, persons, and places to which one has unlimited access, and those restricted through prohibitions. The first constitute the realm of the profane, the second the sacred.

Injunctions were also imposed upon another class of phenomena—those relating to sexuality. For similar reasons, sexuality, like death, inspires awe, fascination, and terror, due to its disruptive nature, and is therefore placed under prohibitions that distinguish between the sacred and the mundane realities of work and everyday life. In one of his last efforts to circumscribe the sacred's specificity, Durkheim underscored its radical incompatibility with work.[44] Taking up the qualification provided by Durkheim, Bataille contrasts the shared nature of death and sexuality as sacred phenomena because they are *tout autre*—entirely other in the way that heterogeneity is to the homogeneity of the profane:

> Entirely other than work and the regulated repetition of distinct relations that it imposes between men and things, and among the diversity of humans. When one examines the ensemble of prohibitions which generally determine the reactions of paralysis and anguish when faced with what suddenly appears as entirely other, the totality of historical and ethnographic information reveals to us a humanity very much like ourselves on this point: for all of known humanity, the realm of work is opposed to that of death and sexuality.[45]

Confirmation of the sacred's otherness is that one remains silent or, more accurately, is reduced to silence in its presence. The tradition of respectful silence is only the extension of the encounter with the otherness that cannot be translated into discourse, and in turn produces a sense of "something other" than what is usually associated with discursive reality. Coextensive with the foundations of civilization and society, the opposition between the sacred and the profane laid the groundwork for all subsequent organizations of time and space. Prohibitions are the mark of that founding moment, a *prise de conscience* that emanates from within and is irreducible to any externally imposed injunction. The sacred emerges with the recognition that forces exist that are disruptive to any order of things, and that they must be held as distinct, apart, and, when necessary, qualified as nefarious and dangerous.

Thus far, we have correlated new ideal types with theoretical transformations within sacred sociology—Durkheim's alter ego among the Australian aborigines was announced as early as the study of moral education, when he called for an alternative to the regnant model of self-restraint, whose disciplined control could be read in the distortions imposed upon the individual countenance. Alternatively, he envisioned a moral exemplar whose willingness to expend would contribute to the effervescent innovations required by the period of transition French society was experiencing at the turn of the century. Bataille confessed that in his own case extreme expenditure and the will for loss could lead to the worse deviations, especially under the influence of fascism. With the publication of his study of the cave paintings at Lascaux, inspired by his discovery of the immediacy of paleolithic civilization, he forged a different incarnation of expenditure. Borrowing from Johan Huizinga, he counters the conventional representation of early *homo sapiens* as heavy, lumbering, and slowly deliberate with the *homo ludens* revealed through the extraordinary quality of paleolithic art—a sovereign, laughing, seductive prototype: "Only with play, and while playing, and with the ability to impart to play the permanent and marvelous dimension of the work of art, did the human being acquire the physical aspect to which his pride remained attached." And in one of the most striking formulations of the transformation that occurs among individuals liberated from desultory necessity, he extols the recognition through art of the inner impulse toward expenditure—"that marvelous outburst of riches for which each of us feels born."[46]

Bataille's extrapolations from the paintings to their imaginary artist required a perilous leap from the vital and dynamic animal representations to the sole humans outlined at Lascaux—a rudimentary stick figure at the bottom of one panel and, in another, an inverted "hangman" at the end of a secret shaft virtually inaccessible except by crawling. The affinity evoked by the paintings resides in their extraordinary élan, irreducible to utilitarian motives, whether sympathetic magic to ensure a successful hunt or protection from some spirit against the animals' greater force. But while Lascaux places the viewer in contact with the terror evoked by the possibility of death, its art also communicates a distinctly social phenomenon: the moment when that fear is overcome through transgression and produces the sui generis reality of the sacred.

In an uncanny prefiguration of the Lascaux paintings, which were not discovered until the 1950s, Bataille had already flirted with the connections between sacrifice and the erotic in representations of the bullfight found in his underground text, *Story of the Eye* (1929).[47] The privileged ritual of bullfighting as revelation of the sacred similarly inspired Leiris's magnificent 1937 piece—"The Bullfight as Mirror"—in which the analogy between eroticism, the bullfight, and sacrifice is also traced to the Mauss/Hubert essay. Bataille describes the center of social space where sacrifices occur as a nucleus of violent silence, where the sacred concentration of destructive forces is delineated through the increasingly profane concentric circles drawn around it. Leiris, however, depicts the ability to face death through the figure of a tangent, a curved line that approaches, without ever completely intersecting, another line or point of encounter—"two slopes of the curve, one ascending, one descending . . . probably the symbol that comes the closest to communicating what lies at the real heart of our emotional life." In the bullfight, this figure is represented by the position of the toreador on one side and the bull on the other. "Suavely," as Leiris puts it, the man seduces the bull into the cape of the muleta, and as the bull passes as close as possible, he must twist his body to the left and then straighten into a line as free from curves as possible. All the while, the crowd has been urging him to swerve farther and farther left, to tempt the bull and his own fate. The beauty of the corrida, as in love, is conferred by the twisted element providing the necessary transgression in relation to some ideal limit, since "no pleasure would be possible according to this aesthetic without there being a violation, a transgression, some excess or sin with respect to an ideal order representing the rule;

absolute license, however, like absolute order, could never be more than an insipid abstraction bereft of significance." The sacred spark is lit by the "presence of the twisted element whose junction with the straight ignites—and this is the burn of the ultimate trance—the feeling of the sacred."[48] Most instructive is that despite the bullfight's appearance of an impeccably structured ritual that exploits the left/right opposition, it can nonetheless veer from one extreme to the other in a way that demonstrates the fundamentally ambiguous nature of the sacred:

> It appears, then, in the final analysis, that everything related to sin, corruption, dissonance, obsession—everything that to some degree signals evil and, more generally, misfortune—intervenes necessarily in the apprehension of the sacred, inasmuch as thereby the presence of a left face is manifest next to a right face, and this ambiguity marked—this ambiguity of which the sacred (springing up at the precise instant when each of the two elements topples over into the opposite) could well be simply the most intense, diamond-studded expression.[49]

The place of eroticism within Bataillian anthropology was also announced in the Lascaux study, where he explains why it is that the initial prohibition in relation to death would be extended to sexuality. That he again draws upon sacrifice to capture the specificity of eroticism is examined next.

Eroticism and Communication

Central to Bataille's analysis of eroticism is a concept of the self as closed being, whose awareness of death as irrevocable separation becomes the founding moment for the sacred: "The principle of the entire erotic undertaking is the destruction of the *closed being* which is the normal state of the partner so engaged."[50] Religion attempts to respond to that realization by invoking a cosmic dimension in order to palliate the horror of the void between self and world. As such, it provides an explanation for the force responsible for death, and possibly some consolation for its devastating effects as each person confronts individual as well as collective mortality. Anthropology addresses the cultural consequences of the *prise de conscience* of death in human terms by comparing the varieties of its treatment within the spectrum of societies. Bataillian anthropology describes the realization that a fundamental abyss exists between and among humans as a condition of discontinuity—"we try to communicate, but there is no communication capable of overcoming a fundamental difference. If you die, it is not I who dies. You and I are discontinuous beings."[51] Paradoxically, continuity is associated with death, including its simulacrum in the little death of eroticism. The possibility for communication as well as knowledge of one's fundamental discontinuity can occur only obliquely and through detours, in the same way that contact with continuity must be mediated. We recall the earlier discussion of the foyer of energy or violent silence Bataille described as providing such mediation. In relation to eroticism, the detour provides the path to its secret—the violence of death that tears beings away from the desire for duration or discontinuous being. Eroticism, as a specifically human phenomenon distinct from animal sexuality, represents one manifestation of the equally powerful impetus toward a mode of communication that would overcome the state of discontinuity.

Indeed, the general model for communication within eroticism is patterned after the one between the sacred and the profane resulting from the destruction of a sacrificial object. In an analogous fashion, the female functions as sacrificial object and the male as sacrificer, so that both may then lose themselves in the continuity created during sexual consummation. Bataille justifies his provocative reinforcement of the stereotypical view of the female as the partner who offers—"To give of oneself is the fundamental feminine attitude"—by adding that sacrifice is never an end in itself. Rather, erotic desire seeks, and can only reach, its goal when continuity is experienced. The postwar meditations reiterate the proviso found in the essays relating to expenditure: that *dépense* is sovereign only so long as it eludes recuperation toward a specific goal. Especially reprehensible would be the betrayal of sovereignty toward some form of profit and/or power, including the violence exerted by one partner over the other. Eroticism is therefore qualified as sacred according to the criterion of *continuity*: "The sacred is precisely the continuity of being revealed to those who, in the course of a solemn ritual, fix their attention upon the destruction of a discontinuous being."[52] We recall that in the very early essay on pre-Columbian cultures, Bataille defined the sacred as the production of objects for sacrifice. Whether he is convinced that the female possesses an innate disposition toward self-sacrifice is not clear, but he does clarify that from the masculine point of view, the dissolution of the "passive" other has only one goal—to prepare both partners to attain the same point of dissolution. To preempt further distortion he adds that the biological death of one of the partners would not enhance the quality of the experience.

The overarching issue here is the relationship between taboo and transgression. With the imposition of an initial negation upon death and sexuality, human societies established the possibility for a separate realm restricted to work, the conscious awareness of death, and limited sexuality. Bataille recognizes that his view from within regarding the necessity for the prohibition goes against the grain of challenges emanating from psychoanalysis to the effect that interdictions are pathological manifestations of neurosis. Nor does he share the view that prohibitions can be reduced to external mechanisms imposed for social control that a more enlightened society would abolish. His argument therefore proceeds as follows:

The prohibition creates the fascination for the object or force placed under restricted contact. This is the inverse of the Freudian contention that a taboo exists as a protective barrier against excessive desires directed toward specific things. Moreover, the purported rationality science enlists to justify its condemnation of archaic taboos as part of a so-called primitive mentality is made possible by the very same *conscience* that imposed the prohibition in the first place. The ramifications of this *prise de conscience* are most directly felt in the social construct of prohibitions that are complemented and completed by a lifting of the interdiction. The result is a distinctly new sensation and different sense of self than the initial state that inspired the prohibition. Social rituals marking the alternation between prohibitions and transgressions are therefore perceived as the outward translation of an inner experience, one that intuits the need for mediations to deal with the anguish surrounding death. Science, like the profane, is antithetical to the religious sensibility that "ties desire to terror and intense pleasure to anguish." The distinguishing element of religion is that it retains an awareness of the anguish responsible for the taboo, as well as of the complementary desire to break it. Thus, an understanding of the taboo is meaningless without an appreciation of the complementary transgression, defined as follows: "Transgression is not the negation of the interdiction, but surpasses and completes it."[53] Correlatively, the negation of the negation surpasses itself without returning to the original condition or state it had negated. Something "other" is produced in the transgressive moment of the second negation that Durkheim and Bataille associate with the sacred.

The silence surrounding eroticism and the paucity of explanations from within social anthropology can be attributed to the nature of the phenomenon itself. Bataille claims that his interpretation thus elucidates Mauss's apparently absurd contention that taboos exist to be transgressed. The prohibition on murder never stopped war, for instance—that distinctively human and social phenomenon—but actually rendered it possible. Bataille's predilection is to locate the erotic within the same social space reserved for phenomena that are violent in the sense of intense or breaking barriers rather than harmful or exploitative of the other. Resistant to representation or scientific modes of discourse, eroticism therefore effectively precludes access to it through conventional modes of communication. Herein resides Bataille's indebtedness to Mauss for providing a scholarly explanation of eroticism's singular origin within the social structure produced by the tension between prohibition and transgression.

By means of the category of the sacred, Bataille, Leiris, and Caillois revised the limits of the literary experience as understood by their contemporaries. Although Durkheim addressed the creative consequences of religious effervescence in very general terms, Bataille takes up a discussion of the sources of literature in religion with more precision:

> Literature can be situated in the wake of religion, whose legacy it inherits. Sacrifice is a novel, a short story, illustrated with bloody images. Or rather, at the elementary stages, it is a theatrical representation, a drama reduced to a final episode, where the animal or human victim plays alone, but plays unto death.[54]

Nowhere is the literary representation of erotic violence played out to greater extremes than in the writings of de Sade. Indeed, they exemplify Bataille's insistence that eroticism is the sexual activity of a "conscious" being. Because violence challenges logocentrism, de Sade's perversity provides a detour for the individual *conscience* to confront suppressed horrors. Reversing the traditional subject-object relation to explain the lure of sadism, Bataille argues that the characteristic cruelty associated with the sadistic personality indicates a negation of the self carried to the point where it is transformed into an explosive destruction. Moreover, in its seemingly unlimited depersonalization, the experience of limits exceeds individual *jouissance* in its quest for uncompromised sovereignty. De Sade's sovereign man becomes his own victim, propelled by the requirements of an impersonal movement that puts individual considerations into play. This imposition of will and particular sense of self can only be paradoxically described as an "impersonal" sort of egoism. While reminiscent of Bataille's description of the extremes to which the need for a movement beyond the self will carry persons individually and collectively, the depiction of Sadian man also reminds us that the alternative to the closed being cannot be restricted to an ideal model. From paleolithic *homo ludens* to the Sadian protagonist, explorations of the open being offer certain constants, but no one prototype.

The discussion of Sade in the study of eroticism illustrates the convoluted byways through which any attempt to circumscribe the sacred must pass. With the acknowledgment that for the modern world work must appear a considerably more urgent matter for consideration, Bataille nonetheless exhorts his readers to sustain their interest in a phenomenon capable of eliciting contradictory sentiments:

> Under the rubrics of "sacred" and "divine" men of all times have recognized a sort of internal, secret animation, an essential frenzy, a violence that appropriates an object, consumes it like a fire, and draws it to its ruin. This animation was held to be contagious, and, passing from one object to another, brought a deathly miasma to its host. There is no greater peril, and if the victim is the object of a cult, whose goal is to offer it up as an object of veneration, it must also be obvious that this cult is ambiguous. Religion strives to glorify the sacred object and to render a principle of ruin the essence of power and of all value, but it also seeks to reduce its effect to a restricted circle, so that an insuperable barrier separates it from the normal or profane world.[55]

More than three decades have elapsed since Bataille's death in 1962, when Malraux banned his posthumous last book, *The Tears of Eros*. Its collection of images—spanning from prehistoric statues with visual sexual puns to the photo of Chinese torture—serves as visual support for Bataille's final epiphany: death and sexuality meet, just as the most beautiful and horrific find their encounter in art. Indeed, his reward for having probed the impulses informing a sacred sociology is the understanding that religion is based upon sacrifice, so that there exists an identity between divine ecstasy and its opposite, extreme horror:

But only an interminable detour allows us to reach that instant where the contraries seem visibly conjoined, where the religious horror disclosed in sacrifice becomes linked to the abyss of eroticism, to the last shuddering tears that eroticism alone can illuminate.[56]

Though the *coincidentia oppositorum*, like the *mysterium tremendum*, constitute staples among the mystics with which Bataille was familiar, he nonetheless credits his personal experience—with its idiosyncratic refashioning of those inherited notions—to the conjunction between two events: first, the gift by the psychoanalyst Dr. Borel of the photo of Chinese torture: "This photo had a decisive role in my life." In it, one finds a young man subjected to death by systematic laceration of his skin and limbs, but who appears to have a smile upon his face that defies any readymade description. Bataille qualifies his look as ecstatic. The second critical intervention is attributed to the practice of yoga and leads to a reassessment of an earlier condemnation of the image's inadequacy to capture the sacred instant. Now, however, he discovers its infinite capacity for reversal:

Through this violence—even today I cannot imagine a more insane, more shocking form—I was so stunned that I reached the point of ecstasy. My purpose was to illustrate a fundamental connection between religious ecstasy and eroticism—and in particular, sadism. From the most unspeakable to the most elevated.[57]

While exploring the relation of art to cruelty, previous essays had warned against the aestheticization of areas intended to provoke a sense of sacred terror. In reference to Manet, for instance, Bataille sums up originality as an operation that foils the conventions of aesthetic expectation. Willing to sacrifice the subject, Manet also subordinated his ongoing desire for public recognition to the more insistent painterly imperative of presenting that which is: an Olympia, for instance, so denuded of convention that she elicits sacred horror. Eradication of social signs—precisely those identifying traits accumulated and inherited from the civilizing process by means of which the bourgeoisie as well as aristocracy could claim recognition among themselves as well as from others—demonstrates the possibility for sovereignty within a revised semiotics of master/slave relations. In a movement within esthetics comparable to the philosophical and social upset he had earlier theorized, Bataille posits the extreme version of an expenditure without reserve as challenge to the Hegelian dialectic. In their refusal to appeal to the viewer other than in their own terms, Manet's sacrificial subjects hearken to the description of heroism conceived by the Dandy taken up by Caillois while avoiding his disdainful elitism. Conversely, Bataille credits Proust with describing the deflation that accompanies too readily met expectations—even transgressive ones. Not surprisingly, Proust's celebration of the instant of involuntary memory also elicits Bataille's admiration as an exemplar of the alternative economy of *dépense*. The interplay between expectation and innovation discloses the secret of art according to the sacrificial analogy: this aesthetic proves most effective when providing new representations that transfigure, while skirting the extremes of abjection or sublimation.

The stated goal of *Tears of Eros* is to expand consciousness to domains repellent to reason without aspiring to emancipation from their obsessive effects. Rather than aesthetic criteria, the basis for inclusion within the heterological repertoire compares with the typology proposed for literary texts at the time of writing *The Blue of Noon* (1935)—those to which their authors had been *constrained*. Bataille's recurrent illustration is the phenomenon of sexual arousal at the sight of a dead body, including his own mother's. Intimately related to the *prise de conscience*, then, is the need for representations, especially those that are "extremely charged with emotive value (such as physical destruction or erotic obscenity, an object of laughter, of physical excitation, of fear and tears)."[58] The shock quotient of the Bataillian aesthetic is thus intensified by its willingness—as well as ability—to depict states of being that may escape individual volition, but to which the subject bears witness.

In their role as psychoanalytic gauge of social limits, representations reveal the arbitrary but also necessary nature of interdictions. The incursion of the sociological perspective into areas deemed individual and private is most pronounced in the Maussian essay regarding the obligatory expression of sentiments. As the following passage illustrates, one of sociology's fundamental premises is that emotions can serve as markers within a grid of cultural taboos, mapping the range of social forms of expression, including sentiments not only acceptable but even required:

> laughter, tears, funeral lamentations, ritual ejaculations, are as much physiological reactions as they are obligatory signs and gestures, obligatory or necessary feelings, either suggested or employed by

collectivities with a precise goal, in order to allow for a sort of moral and physical release of its expectations, since they, too, are of a physiological and moral nature.[59]

In a similar vein, some of the most dramatic illustrations of effervescent ceremonies recounted in *Elementary Forms* derive from piacular rites that mediate the group's encounter with death and demonstrate that mourning is far from being a spontaneous expression of individual emotion. What is most striking about these rites is the nature of the transformation of feelings involved, all of which are imposed by the various stages of the ritual. As such, they bolster several fundamental precepts of the sociological approach to sentiment: the need for organizing forms to mediate contact with powerful, often virulent, events that reflect upon the group's existence rather than individual feeling; that the emotions expressed by and among individuals within a group are obligatory but certainly no less intense for being so; that the significance ascribed to the effervescence so induced is determined by the social goals designated for it.

These reflections return us to the question of effervescence and its unmarked nature, explored in the preceding chapter in terms of Bataille's emphasis upon the dual phenomena of ambivalence and transformation, of belonging both to the left and right sacred, in an attempt to explain how social energies are socially channeled toward political ends. Earlier discussions by Durkheim primarily associated effervescent energies with the joyous exuberance of festivals or ceremonies celebrating social renewal often promoting the efflorescence of new ideas and social relations. We have also noted that their esthetic dimension expresses the need for communal revitalization antithetical to the exigencies of daily tasks. The analysis of mourning rituals demonstrates Durkheim's willingness to explore ritualized violence, yet another domain of religious life that would appeal to the Bataillian sensibility. The nature of this violence abides by the criteria detected within the sacrificial representations of the authors discussed thus far: Indeed, within the wild, angry gesticulation and self-inflicted and often mortal wounds incurred by a grieving widow or relative, Durkheim discerns the precise etiquette of a familiar ritual. The intensity of energies reflects the impact of communal symbolic expression rather than the emotions of any one person. Cries, destruction, and flowing blood, while painful, attain a high level of vitality. Most revealing is that the effervescence generated impedes one from interpreting the group's emotions as exclusively depressing:

> That this excitation has arisen from a sad event matters little, for it is no less real and not specifically different from the one observed in joyful feasts. As a matter of fact, it sometimes manifests itself through movements of the same kind. The same frenzy takes hold of the faithful, along with the same inclination to sexual debauchery— a sure sign of great nervous overexcitement.[60]

In the same way that Bataille liked to cite the more familiar example of the Irish wake, Durkheim notes that in its most dramatic transformation the labile effervescence arising from a funeral service will conclude the mourning observance with an explosion of gaiety and celebration.

Durkheim's explanation remains within the parameters of the sociological rules since the sensation of collective life and energies imparted to all participants cancels the frightening and potentially demoralizing intrusion of death that had destabilized the social order. Whether experienced in the form of pained irritation or joyous excitement, the life force neutralizes the redoubtable power of *thanatos*. As for the suffering—including cuttings—that mourners endure, Durkheim concludes that they can be considered a means to conjure evil and a way to heal from illness. Only later would more utilitarian explanations see them as a way to appease angry gods. In their frenzied self-lacerations, the grieving aborigines bear comparison to the scene in which a despondent Leiris described "curing" himself of a miserable love affair through scissor slashes.

It is also now possible to appreciate the political significance of the obligatory expression of sentiments and their place in an evaluation of (collective) representations. At the outset to the discussion of Durkheim's views on French literary culture, we argued that *Elementary Forms* does not enlist ethnography as a juggernaut against religion in the name of the social, because the social domain is subject to the same mystifications and abuses traditionally associated with religion. This is why we concluded that his analysis of religion is ultimately political, in that it demonstrates how the *simplisme* that projects social forces onto external figures or causes is exploited for the benefit of those in power. The ideological ramifications of Durkheim's position are further evidenced in his discussion of evil. When a society passes through periods of stress and crisis, it obliges its members to express their anxiety, fear, or anger through actions or manifestations of

emotions—even those inflicting pain—because "these collective manifestations, and the moral communion which they show and strengthen,
restore to the group the energy which circumstances threaten to take
away from it."[61] And, as Bataille contends, the same diversionary tactic is exerted by political figures or artistic representations that do not
abide by the "sacrificial" criterion. Social forces are often interpreted
as maleficent beings, when in fact they are the objectification of collective states. The benefit of the social ritual is accomplished when the
group recoups its social energies rather than projecting them against
an alleged external source or an internal scapegoat.[62]

A decade earlier than the Collège, Bataille and Leiris had contributed to *Documents,* the eclectic review Bataille edited between
1929 and 1931, which leveled an iconoclastic, innovative, and subtly
scandalous assault on the hierarchy within the arts in Western society.
Joined by fellow excommunicants from surrealism—Michel Leiris and
Jacques Baron—as well as the ethnomusicologist André Schaeffner,
the art critic Carl Einstein, and the ethnographer Marcel Griaule,
among others, Bataille contributed texts whose impact was bolstered
by their symbiosis with the surrealistic photographs of Eli Lotar and
Boiffard. *Documents,* as Michel Leiris noted, was an "impossible"
undertaking—a glossy journal of commentary upon modern art in the
minds of its backers, at odds with Bataille's determination to explore
the impossible underside of bourgeois civilization. Yet the results undoubtedly stand among the outstanding contributions to cultural criticism in the twentieth century. Bataille was responsible for a critical dictionary whose entries applied scholarly references to seemingly banal
or everyday objects, which, when isolated and then juxtaposed with
esoteric figures, created an effect the critic Briony Fer compared to the
sensation of the uncanny or, for its defamiliarization, James Clifford
would describe as ethnographic surrealism. Roland Barthes admired
Bataille's ability to reinterpret icons of industrial civilization and even
the body—one thinks of the big toe as well as the factory chimney—
in affective terms that resisted both the psychoanalytic "police" and
the temptation to aestheticize. Instead, the Hegelian *Aufhebung* was
revised so that the opposition between material objects and their ideal
models were not superseded by means of a higher synthesis. Idealization is occluded by the introduction of a third term, whose transgressive function is to disrupt the very foundation upon which hierarchical

dualisms are based, as well as to pose an alternative to the usual inversions that would leave their theological underpinnings intact.

The first entry to the a-cephalic dictionary—*abattoir* (slaughterhouse)—introduced the theme of the loss of sacred status in the modern world, a recurrent lament throughout Bataille's more mature essays as well. Here it is explained as a consequence of the abattoir's separation from religious temples, where slaughter was integrated into the ritual sacrifice of animals. Similarly, the split between religion and eroticism in Christianity precipitated the demise of religious prostitution. The diremption of these original "coincidences" is also noted by Leiris in *Manhood*, when his surprise at finding an empty brothel on a religious holiday is greeted by a prostitute's sententious declaration: "Religious holidays are not cause for celebration in the brothel."[63] Conversely, he offers a rapprochement between brothels and museums that exemplifies the coincidence contributors to *Documents* and the Collège would use to provocatively highlight traces of the sacred within modernity.

Bataille enlisted the sacred to gauge the demise of collective experience in the modern world in his search for social forms capable of mediating the individual's confrontation with the absolute separation represented by death. Leiris perceived a personal deficiency in his reticence to move beyond the confines of individual activity in order to partake of a collective effort that would affect the course of history. Beyond their close friendship, they met on the common ground of the Collège, where sacred sociology held out the possibility to reconsider the intersections of the individual with the collective, the social with the political. Their *écriture* (Barthes) exemplifies a general economy that never allows it to conclude. The absence of all hypostasis in Bataille's concept of an "inoperative community" *(communauté désoeuvrée)* is responsible for Nancy's remark, "Incompleteness is its principle."[64] The disruptive effects of a sacrificial aesthetic reasserting the necessity for prohibitions—rather than their lifting—must be situated within a model of sacrifice conceived as a process that commits art to the interminable task of rescuing its object from the forces of appropriation while subjecting it—as the eloquent formula inspired by Manet's painting insists—to "a ravishment without repose."

Bataille never completed his announced work on the sacred, but the issues it entails are clearly central to the three major works published prior to his death in 1962: *Lascaux ou la naissance de l'art*

(1955), *l'Erotisme* (1957), and *Les Larmes d'Eros* (1971). With these final works he may have indeed reached the ultimate synthesis of his sociological vision. He also appears to have left academic discourse irretrievably behind. Yet the studies united under the title *Eroticism* contain a detailed review of Lévi-Strauss's *Elementary Structures of Kinship* (1949) that underscores the cultural centrality of gift exchange in terms consonant with his own notion of expenditure.[65] The coincidence is not entirely surprising, given the common source for both in Mauss's essay on the gift, whose continuity and overlap with the earlier article on sacrifice are significant.

Although Mauss's early essays were devoted to sacrifice and prayer, and despite the fact that he was eventually elected head of the section of religious studies at the Ecole Pratique des Hautes Etudes, one historian concluded that overall, his work "owes little debt to Durkheim's social philosophy, especially regarding the primacy of the sacred in collective life."[66] Indeed, we recall that moving away from any preconceived equation between sacrifice and personal denial or self-abnegation, the study of sacrifice concentrated upon the social context from which it derives meaning as well as symbolic power. Consistent with Durkheim, the authors concluded that the objects or persons designated as sacred do not manifest distinctive traits and the many examples cited confirm Mauss's primary dictum regarding the nature of all social phenomena—their arbitrariness. Nothing inheres in the phenomena separated, segregated, and placed under interdiction to warrant such treatment, other than the social necessity to do so. Like Durkheim, Mauss never denies the force accrued as a result of the energies concentrated into the sacrificial object. In their final response as to the nature of the sacred, the authors move beyond the standard explanation in terms of the sacred's social function to underscore its role in reminding individuals of their social identity: "In our opinion, the sacred is conceived as that which, for the group and its members, qualifies society." Grounding his explanation in the concrete social process that ordains some object, place, or thing sacred, Mauss observed the enduring social relevance of the movement of consecration: "If each god in his turn leaves the temple and becomes profane, we in turn see human, but social, things—the nation, property, work, the human person—reentering one by one."[67] By examining the permutations of an ostensibly religious phenomenon in social terms, Hubert and Mauss provided the generation of Collège scholars with a model of the French school's analytical relevance for modern formations.

The theme of social debt is echoed in Mauss's later (1923–24) essay on the gift, where the dramatic exchanges of virtually every aspect of social life solders subgroups into an "indissoluble" bond, and whose ultimate function is to communicate in concrete terms their mutual interdependence:

> In fact, this symbol of social life—the permanent influence of things exchanged—directly translates the manner in which sub-groups of segmental societies of an archaic type are constantly imbricated with one another, and feel that they owe everything to each other.[68]

We recall that Lévi-Strauss's central argument is that the conventional wisdom positing incest as a prohibition upon sexual relations with blood relatives must be inverted, since kinship relations reinforce the injunction that men within a group are obligated to share their sisters and daughters with others. Women are regarded as gifts, albeit a special category within the ensemble of generalized gift-exchanges Mauss understood as constitutive of the symbolic order. With his reassertion of the primacy of taboos in founding the very basis for culture and communication, Lévi-Strauss validates Bataille's contention that their apparent arbitrariness by no means undermines their necessity, a position unequivocally restated in *Eroticism: "Above all, I wish to reassert to what extent I find useless those banal affirmations, according to which the prohibition on sexuality is a prejudice, and that it is high time to rid ourselves of it."*[69]

Indeed, what was viewed as progress in the form of liberation from constraint is rejected because it banalizes the danger involved in contact with the sacred, discredits the intensity of feelings it engages, and individualizes the energies that are in fact collective. Moreover, Durkheim often pointed out that the actual size of a group did not necessarily correlate with the impact of effervescence, as witnessed in his expansion of the consequences of medieval effervescence to geopolitical concentrations that overflowed regional and national boundaries. The study of kinship also facilitates access to the "inner experience" of eroticism by returning to the prohibition in terms of its complement—transgression. Thus, the renunciation of animal sexuality imposed by the taboo is what renders the gift of women possible at the same time that it enhances their desirability. The prohibition does not change the violence of sexual activity but, claims Bataille, opens to "disciplined men" the door of transgression through which animality could not enter. In terms of the psychological or inner consequences of the social structure, the sentiments of individuals are not so much focused on their renunciation as they are invested in the gesture of giving, in the act of generosity toward the collectivity with which they are engaged in an endless cycle of reciprocal relations.

A very different conclusion, however, appears in the final passages of *The Elementary Structures of Kinship,* inspired by indigenous myths the anthropologist claims function to resolve the inner conflicts created by the rules governing kinship relations:

> To this very day mankind has always dreamed of seizing and fixing that fleeting moment when it was permissible to believe that the law of exchange could be evaded, that one could gain without losing, enjoy without sharing. At either end of the earth and at both extremes of time, the Sumerian myth of the golden age and the Andaman myth of the future life correspond, the former placing the end of primitive happiness at a time when the confusion of languages made words into common property, the latter describing the bliss of the hereafter as a heaven where women will no longer be exchanged, i.e., removing to an equally unattainable past or future the joys, eternally denied to social man, of a world in which one might keep to oneself.[70]

Conflicting interpretations of sacrifice also prolonged the dissensions manifested among Collegians well into the postwar period. Bataille's damning review of Caillois's book on the sacred in 1950 repudiates an approach whose claim to objectivity undermines the most urgent reason for focusing on the sacred—its relevance to modernity. By framing the discussion of sacrifice in terms of that which the individual is willing to relinquish, Caillois, according to Bataille, banalized the sacred's inherent power by reducing it to relative values subject to personal considerations—"where profane interest dominates, one can abandon tranquillity and perhaps even risk all, without necessarily moving beyond a sordid calculus of advantages and inconvenience."[71] Equally damaging was Caillois's view expressed in his Collège address on the festival (in essence, a reading of what would become the second chapter of *l'Homme et le sacré*). In opening paragraphs that virtually paraphrase the passages from *Elementary Forms* cited at the outset to this study, he pessimistically dismissed the viability of the sacred/profane opposition for the modern world. The moment of social transgression represented by the festival, signaled by sexual license and material pillage, is also characterized by a mythological dimension. For it is in periods of suspended profane activity that the social group's revitalization draws upon a mythic *urzeit,* prior to the fall into work, temporality, and libidinal control. However, the need for transient dream-states and their dramatic demarcation from the quotidian no longer appears as imperative within modern social formations:

> But it seems that societies, in the course of their evolution, tend to lose their differentiation, moving in the direction of uniformity, leveling, and relaxation of tensions. As it becomes more pronounced the complexity of the social organism is less tolerant of the interruption of the ordinary course of life. . . . The opposition between vacation and working days seems really to have taken over from the old alternation between feasting and work, ecstasy and self-control, that annually revived order out of chaos, wealth from prodigality, and stability from frenzy.[72]

The two former Collegians converge in their assessment of the modern world's inability to present temptations capable of inspiring unconditional giving. Nietzsche understood that the rigors of asceticism and saintliness no longer seduce, leaving only war and revolution as sufficiently exalting alternatives. Curiously, the devastation of the actual war experience appears to have had little impact upon the respective positions espoused by both prior to the holocaust. Caillois continues to represent war as the evacuation of the social waste and detritus he claimed all social formations must foresee, so that his 1950 revision to the final sentence quoted above appends frenzy to read

> has been replaced by an alternation of a completely different order, and yet the only thing offering the modern world a nature and intensity comparable. This is the alternation between peace and war, prosperity and destruction of the results of prosperity, stable tranquility, and compulsory violence.[73]

Bataille's 1949 *La Part maudite* expanded upon earlier statements to the effect that war was not the ideal of expenditure he envisioned as a deterrent to accumulation. By pursuing the implications of the sacred from a subjective point of view, he would counter Caillois's more detached presentation and reassert the unshakable conviction enunciated at various points in his career: that neither respect for ancient traditions of a prestigious past nor the alleged remoteness of primitives should obviate recognition of the immediacy of the sacred within the contemporary world as an eminently social phenomenon responsible for the major upheavals and disruptions by means of which groups enter upon the stage of history.[74] Indeed, so long as discussions of effervescence or the sacred remain within the confines of an anthropological perspective restricted to non-Western, traditionalist cultures, their repercussions are tolerated. But when enlisted by sociology to analyze the dynamic of modern, industrialized societies, such notions are met with skepticism. As considered in the concluding section, the consequences of this bias are most evident in the fate of the sacred/profane distinction within postwar social thought.

Effervescence from May '68 to the Present

> *This discussion may appear external to sociology, but in fact it touches on an essential dimension of all human societies: the relation between the sacred and the profane.*
>
> Edward Tiryakian

The point of departure for this study was to respond to Jean Wahl's query as to why sociology exerted a unifying effect upon iconoclastic members of the interwar generation previously identified with surrealism, revolution, and psychoanalysis. The answer proposed is that the explicit qualification of sociology by the sacred signaled what was innovative to the Collège de Sociologie's project, and that it is in the conjunction of the two terms that its current significance should be assessed. The historical and epistemological framework reconstructs the significance of sacred sociology through immediate reference to Emile Durkheim's *Elementary Forms of Religious Life* (1912), in which he claimed to address an issue relevant to the modern period according to the example derived from the ritual assemblies of Australian aborigines, described as one of the most primitive peoples on ethnographic record.

Durkheim's midlife shift exemplified a renewal in the twentieth century of the long-standing French specificity of anthropological thinking emanating from the sixteenth, when discovery of the New World prompted moral and social philosophers to develop a self-reflexive discourse about the nature and quality of European civilization. The ethnographic detour into alternative cultural practices, moral codes, and social relations provided the conditions of possibility to broach topics otherwise subject to official, social, academic, or personal/psychological censorship. Montaigne's essay on cannibalism set the standard by drawing upon the sensationalism surrounding the consumption of human flesh as a screen to address contemporary manifestations of barbaric behavior that went unchallenged.

A guiding hypothesis of this reading was, therefore, that the reappearance of the ethnographic detour was symptomatic of equally stringent—though perhaps less evident—constraints acting upon as well as within the modern discipline of sociology. By enhancing the comparative, self-reflexive perspective with a desedimentation of the qualitative dimension of social forms, sociology effects a psychoanalysis of the social for the collective life of contemporary society. The ethnographic detour enables sociology to arrive at prescriptions for the future based upon archaeological conclusions derived from excavations within our own societies: "Perhaps through a study of [these] obscure aspects of social life we will illuminate the path our nations, their morality, and economy should pursue."[1] By opening the path to the future, Mauss provided a resolution to the crisis we discerned within Durkheim's thinking regarding the limits of sociology to act prescriptively, even though the sociological revolution effected by *Elementary Forms* encouraged the rereading of his entire work as the realization of such a goal.

The specific focus for the present study was determined by the centrality of effervescence to an understanding of the sacred according to Durkheim. The elusive quality of effervescence, the nature of the transformations it induces, and their consequences for a host of issues, especially sociopolitical movements, designate the basic parameters of the problematic addressed here. Indeed, it is to the potentially revolutionary explosiveness of effervescence that the Collège referred when distancing itself from predecessors in the French school of sociology, wary of the "contagious" nature of ethnographic representations they had nonetheless been responsible for introducing into Western thought. Mauss's fear that in the modern period ethnographically inspired collective representations and experiences would sanction regressive behavior and be diverted toward horrific ends were echoed in the subsequent critiques by Jürgen Habermas. Focusing on the decentered subject and emancipation from the criterion of usefulness, he accused Bataille of promoting an "antimodernism" (albeit couched in modernist attitudes). More pointedly, Habermas reproaches Bataillian epigones—notably Foucault and Derrida—for taking a step outside the modern world since

> They remove into the sphere of the far away and the archaic the spontaneous powers of imagination, of self-experience and of emotionality. To instrumental reason, they juxtapose, in Manichean fashion a principle only accessible through evocation, be it the will to power or sovereignty, Being or the dionysiac force of the poetical.[2]

Yet the formulation of a sacred sociology was intended as a counter to the reductionism of an exclusively aesthetic consciousness, a legacy of the romantic revolt. As Caillois lectured to the Collegians, the artist of the twentieth century must redefine his or her role in relation to society in order to overcome the outdated model of predecessors a hundred years ago. A sign of the modern, the outlawed hero engaged in a general denunciation of the family, state, nation, morality, religion, and, on occasion, even reason and science. But the effect of profaning the (right) sacred was "illusory," enacted by verbal blasphemy and sarcasm against institutions capitalism was already undermining through pandemic commodification.

Because traces of the sacred can be detected within the Parisian abattoir (slaughterhouse) and Aztec sacrifices, the fervor of Dreyfusards and the effervescence of Australian aborigines, brothels and bullfights, the ethnographic detour provided the conditions of possibility for the formation of a new space of modernity irreducible to an esthetic escape from the long history of the civilizing process writ large upon the social body as well as inscribed within the most intimate details of the individual's *habitus*. This willingness to apply to one's own society the same criteria and objectifying process imposed upon others continues to inform the current definition of sociology in France, even if, as Bourdieu and Passeron have argued, comparison with foreign social practices is not explicit. Indeed, the radical implications of such a methodological reversal are not easily assimilated into current practice:

> For proof of this, one has only to observe the furor aroused by the anthropological approach when, in keeping with the Durkheimian

tradition, which made no distinction between ethnology and sociology, it is rigorously applied to familiar behavior and institutions, whether with reference to the functions of a university or to attitudes to works of art.[3]

The authors distinguish between the revival of this tradition among younger sociologists and the example of Lévi-Strauss, whose recourse to cultural or social anthropology, they claim, skirts the reflexive examination of institutions central to the Durkheimian project.[4] In another context, Bourdieu also argued, "The distinction between ethnology and sociology is a typically false frontier. . . . [I]t is the pure product of history (colonial), which has no logical justification."[5]

In his 1945 assessment of French sociology, Lévi-Strauss expressed reservations regarding the primacy of the collective over the individual in the Durkheimian tradition, yet exhorted future anthropologists to sustain the critical tradition illustrated by the fruitful symbiosis between sociology and ethnography found in *Elementary Forms*. Ironically, the domination of the structuralist approach in anthropology Lévi-Strauss developed was subsequently perceived as the strongest deterrent to research on effervescence during the postwar period. Georges Gurvitch, for one, advocated a general revival of Durkheimianism and touted effervescent phenomena for their global impact since "everything that had previously been proposed as given, stabilized, or crystallized in social reality appears before them as an obstacle to be conquered." He also urged sociology to take up Durkheim's example by demonstrating how certain ideas can be tested, seized, or affirmed only through collective acts. By so doing, he argued, sociology could once again realize its enormous potential as "a negative and critical contribution to philosophy and the works of civilization."[6] Despite a passing critique of the discipline's exaggerated focus on structure, however, Gurvitch did not pursue a broader discussion of the general devaluation of Durkheimianism in the postwar period nor why, beyond the influence of structuralism, the issue of effervescence disappeared from the topics slated for sociological investigation. Durkheim's commentators have speculated upon the experiential sources of his notion of effervescence—whether Bastille Day celebrations, the ferment of the Dreyfus Affair, or the socialist ideas exchanged at the Ecole normale supérieure mentioned in his writings—without arriving at any definitive conclusions. By the time of Mauss's influential essay on the gift (1923–24), effervescence captures the "atmosphere" of gift exchanges, whereas the sacred is subsumed by the totality of that social "fact." With the exception of Jean Duvignaud and his followers, the phenomenon of effervescence received scant attention within the French postwar sociological tradition. By contrast, effervescence reentered the discourse on society under the guise of the festival, where it refers to the transformative potential of collective energies emanating from the social periphery capable of effecting changes throughout.

More pointedly, by 1969 Victor Turner decried the virtual censorship exerted by anthropology's "grooved dependence" on structure as the sole sociological dimension. His own study of the ritual process (subtitled "Structure and Anti-structure") describes transitional states of liminality or *communitas*, when a group transgresses institutional norms and is temporarily stripped of its structural, defining attributes. In contrast with the norm-governed, abstract, institutional nature of homogeneous society, *communitas* is associated with the spontaneous, immediate, and concrete social relations generated between only whole or "total" persons. By its very marginality such experience is thought to be dangerous—though sacred—and menacing to the extent it induces "unprecedented potency." To skeptics who would reduce *communitas* to the upsurge of biological drives momentarily released from cultural constraints (crowd psychology), Turner responds, "Rather, it is the product of peculiarly human faculties, which include rationality, volition, and memory, and which develop with experience of life in society."[7] As for effecting change, liminality, marginality, and structural inferiority are credited with forging the templates for new cultural forms. More than a periodic reclassification, this salutary leveling process also incites individuals to action. By claiming cross-cultural and transtemporal relevance for liminality and *communitas*, Turner was rebuked for violating the boundaries of his own discipline. Turner's position, like that of Durkheim and the Collège, refuses to restrict *communitas* to archaic, preliterate, and traditionalist cultures, so that the collective dimension of such upheavals can be found at all stages and levels of culture and society. The strongest argument forwarded by Turner asserts that the dialectical relationship between structure and *communitas* is so fundamental that society cannot survive without it.

One purpose of introducing Turner's contribution is to reexamine the ideological and political consequences of the suppression of effervescence in relation to modernity as a by-product of the disciplinary territoriality that separates anthropology from sociology. More tendentiously, it has been argued that while absent from sociology, effervescence has been effectively displaced onto anthropology, with the consequence, I would reply, of neutralizing its critical potential in regard to the West. If British and American anthropology's concentration upon tribal societies did not automatically preclude the enlistment of anthropology as cultural critique, its practice nonetheless eclipsed the reflexive dimension we have come to associate with the French sociological revolution dating from the sixteenth century. With the notable exception of Margaret Mead, the only historical precedent for the self-reflexive approach that could be cited in a recent prolegomenon for a revitalization of anthropology is that of the French school. Marcus and Fischer, for instance, in *Anthropology as Cultural Critique* restrict their examples to Maussian sociology of the interim war period.

Virtually inaccessible as a collection until the 1970s, the contributions to the Collège de Sociologie expand the social analysis provided by *Elementary Forms* in ways that meet Edward Tiryakian's appeal for a dynamic view of the sacred/profane relation: "In fact, what shakes society in its foundations is the conflict between the sacred and the profane and, correlatively, between the process of secularization and sacralization." Moreover, Tiryakian perceived the reintegration of the sacred/profane categories into contemporary sociology as providing a renewal of the study of society from the point of view of its elementary forms, since "[o]ne of their important aspects is that they constitute the essential structures of social existence, and that without them social order would not be possible. In their capacity as general frames, their function consists in introducing form and meaning where there would otherwise be only ambiguity and social chaos." The social structures so produced are not neutral, and express tensions formulated in moral terms that elude quantitative assessments yet provide insight into the most fundamental meanings and representations by which individuals and groups direct their thoughts and actions. Because in contemporary society the sacred is associated with religion, its broad social relevance is easily misconstrued as a regressive force. Yet it is precisely the dialectical interaction between the sacred and the profane and the need for periodic shifts in their distribution that motivate major upheavals in social history: "This explosive force of the sacred, when it enters into contact with the basest or the most profound levels of global society, appears as one of its most important properties.

When it is manifested directly, which is very rare, it can unsettle all intermediary social structures and put into question their very legitimacy."[8] To appreciate the power exerted by symbols and representations, Tiryakian introduced the contributions of existential philosophy of the prewar period (more German than Sartrean), in order to renew his own discipline and provide the basis for an existential sociology.

The program outlined for an existential sociology resonates with the aspirations expressed by the texts of the Collège de Sociologie among contributors formed by the thinking of Durkheim and Mauss. What interests us now, however, is not so much the programmatic convergence between these various historical strata as the specificity imparted by recourse to the sacred/profane dualism in order to gain access to the *total individual* and the *social whole*. Central to such an investigation is the revised version of the sacred into both the divine and the demonic or, as Hertz demonstrated, into left as well as right. Durkheim initiated this perspective when he insisted upon the global nature of religion to encompass evil as well as good. Both Granet and Hertz also provided elaborate accounts of the pure/impure sacred in all their consequences for social life. What social thought in their wake can do, for instance, is examine the impact of the long-standing conditioning of the left/right opposition upon a host of internalized perceptions, including—and perhaps most significantly—the political positions correlated with them. As Robert Hertz pointed out in his study of the social basis for the preeminence of the right hand, one of the signs of a well-mannered child is the virtual inability of the left one to function independently because it is subjected to a "veritable mutilation," a deformity traced to its sources in the broader cosmology imposed by the religious polarity between sacred and profane.[9] And as Bataille often reiterated, the etymological "coincidence" between sinister and *sinistra* (left) reveals the long social and cultural history inscribed within the hierarchy of bodily *habitus*. This was the approach adopted by Bataille in his early *Document* essays, as well as in the analysis of the proletariat cited in chapter 3. By introducing the added correlation of sexual phantasms he appropriated the contributions of psychoanalysis for radical social criticism. But the nagging question that persists is how the opposition between the sacred and the profane—the central dualism constitutive of the symbolic order of all cultures—came to be viewed as some exotic phenomenon with little or no relevance to complex Western industrialized societies.

For a Socio-logic of Effervescence

Several basic premises had to be revised in order for ethnography to provide a viable basis for cultural criticism: one, that ethnographic examples enlisted no longer be treated as at a different stage of development. Indeed, this is a common critique leveled at Durkheim's continuity/development model since it appears to relegate other societies to the status of "primitive" in that evolutionary sense.[10] Conversely, the primitive or archaic example should not be the object of nostalgic projections or inverted ethnocentrism, as Caillois reproached Lévi-Strauss and the basis for his postwar repudiation of the "ethnographic revolution."[11] Furthermore, it was crucial that comparisons not be effected between what appeared to be two relatively homogeneous social formations or cultures at completed levels of development, thereby applying or importing the example of one for the purpose of imitation into another.[12] With these modifications, the sacred/profane duality could be investigated as an opposition that is active within all social formations.

Among the conclusions gleaned from rereading Durkheim according to the socio-logic of effervescence was that the sacred/profane duality structures moments of exceptional intensity that result in a heightened awareness of the social's ubiquity. The otherness induced through collective effervescence also demonstrates the sui generis nature of the social generally occulted in modern societies. By way of contrast, spontaneous representations consistent with an ideology of individualism reinforce a predominantly exigent sense of the social. They rarely accentuate the social's beneficient contributions toward the individual's completion within the social totality. Durkheim's lectures on pedagogy similarly pointed out how the secular state socializes citizens according to moral criteria consonant with anachronistic literary representations. His insistence that sociology intervene in the socialization process necessitated a review of the possible agencies he envisioned as providing alternative collective representations. Whether corporations, the division of labor, the state, the religio-sacred, or the new literary history, each was examined according to its potential to induce a sense of the individual's relation to the totality and thus implement the lessons of the ethnographic detour through a demonstration of their mobilizing effects.

Rereading *Elementary Forms* also led to the conclusion that the most neglected dimension of the sacred/profane opposition associated with effervescence is the inner transformation effected in the course of collective assemblies. When addressing the point of intersection between sociology and psychology, Tiryakian provided a succinct formulation of the process of socialization as a dual movement that appropriates and interiorizes the exterior while effecting an exteriorization or outward manifestation of the social. Most relevant is that he describes socialization as "a process of social *becoming* at the level of the person, in the same way that global society and all the intermediary social structures (family, class, political party) are comprehended within the dynamic of the totality."[13] The concept of global society is indebted to the sociology of Georges Gurvitch. Combined with Mauss's *total social fact,* both notions justify sociology's claim to a comprehensive synthesis. Here we can also recognize the elaborate theoretical efforts of Pierre Bourdieu to reconcile the social determinism of the French school, based upon documentation of the effects of centuries of the civilizing process, with a model of agency that provides for a dialectical account of the interactive effects of both internal and external forces upon individual action. François Héran has pointed out that the centrality of the notion of *habitus* to Bourdieu's lexicon reflects his efforts to resolve "a certain number of false alternatives encumbering sociological thought, such as individual and social, liberty and determinism, subjectivity and objectivity, qualitative and quantitative, micro and macro, and so on."[14]

The ethnographic detour strikes a challenge as well to the nature of the inner transformation effected within moments of effervescence according to the paradigm dictated by the early crowd psychologies. The changes wrought by the effects of such moments of intensified sociality are viewed as irreducible to the rationality/irrationality dichotomy that subtends economic and liberal political theories. Rather, the transformation in question exhibits the sui generis logic of the social that sociology sought to demonstrate: that the (social) whole is greater than the sum of its parts and therefore provides possibilities inaccessible to the isolated individual, whether in the form of creative effervescence leading to the great works of civilization or through mediated access to those states of being so dangerous to individuals they would otherwise risk annihilation. Transformations incur a depersonalization of the individual comparable to the effects of sacrifice, in which the psychic construct required for survival in the profane realm of homogeneous relations is momentarily placed in abeyance and modified by the moral élan motivating the group. Individuals are projected beyond themselves and the "closed" being is opened onto modes of communication qualified as sacred. The motivation for this sacrificial logic refuses a psychoanalytic explanation in terms of unconscious self-hatred, either on the part of bourgeois defectors from their own milieu or among workers victimized by representations ultimately dominated by the long-standing hegemony of aristocratic values in the social sphere. By undermining accumulation in one group or person, the paradox of the *socio-logic* is that the need for expenditure of a violent sort, Bataille argues, reconstitutes the qualitative basis of social relations.

If LeBon feared this transformation as undermining the individual's self-interest, then one must recognize the viability of an alternative notion of interest irreducible to economism and capable of encompassing as political criteria "the good and pleasure," as Mauss argued at the conclusion to the gift essay.[15] Herein resides the morality of the collectivity that justifies the claim for a political reading of *Elementary Forms,* since the inner transformation must be appreciated as the precondition for the return of the group's collective energies in order to direct them toward innovative social and political movements. A strong point of continuity between Durkheim and Bataille is that the individual's metamorphosis stimulates an awareness of the social sources of being. For the Collegians, these volatile effusions demonstrate the tumultuous underpinnings of political life, including the fear, violence, and repulsion informing erotic as well as social relations. The sacred/profane dualism is therefore appreciated as a (if not *the*) primary structure of the symbolic order, and the slash indicative of the relation between them as one of interdiction and transgression. The question of the sacred is impossible without this tension; otherwise, its dynamism is stymied and mobilizing potential reduced to respect for the status quo of all that has been consecrated on the right side of the sacred. Effervescent assemblies foster solidarity that contrasts with the socialization modeled according to outdated notions of civility, especially those correlated with the literary-based general culture. Durkheim's history of French pedagogical practices cited another example of effervescence—medieval scholasticism. It is the screen utilized in this particular work to advocate the rupture with traditional

class, social, and national formations incited by the regenerative movements he characterized as sacred.

The problematic nature of the socio-logic derives from the fact
that the most dramatic manifestation of the social group's potential is
the effervescence generated by collective assemblies. Although Durkheim acknowledges that its transformative effects may be undecidable
at the individual level, his critique is directed at the moment of the diversion of the group's energies away from collective goals to individual advantage or profit, including the sacralization of persons whose
social prestige mimes the reverence generally reserved for religious figures. All the thinkers examined here meet in their conviction that the
group exerts a moralizing effect upon individual motivation and self-
interest. What distinguishes LeBon as well as Freud from the sociologists is that they discredit that effect by dismissing it as temporary and
devoid of lasting consequence. When confronted with historical tur-
moil, LeBon's reflex was to discredit worker and popular collective
movements through association with the masses and to devise psychologically based forms of control and manipulation. Alternatively,
Bataillian theory argues that effervescent eruptions must not be circumscribed to a specific social group, political movement, or psychological model.

The socio-logic of effervescence posed specific methodological
problems set forth in the earliest essays of the Collège regarding the
status of the sociologist in relation to the movement he hoped to insti-
gate. Whether to be regarded as scientist or sorcerer—Bataille poses
that question again in the introduction to his postwar theory of a
"general economy" encompassing the movement of natural, energetic
forces from within a global perspective. Indeed, the ambiguous position of the objectifying subject in relation to his "boiling point" abuts
on the most intimate obstacle—his own effervescence: "To the extent I
could envisage the object of my study, I could not personally refuse to
myself the effervescence in which I discovered the inevitable goal and
value of the cold and calculated analysis."[16] For Habermas, this aporia
can at best lead to a to-and-fro, or science from within, since there is
no possibility for a theory "that reaches beyond the horizon of what is
accessible to reason and thematizes, let alone analyzes, the interaction
of reason with a transcendent source of power."[17] By demonstrating
that the "source of power" resides within the social energies of the
collectivity occulted within profane social and economic contractual

relations, the ethnographic detour circumvents the preceding objections by revitalizing the sociological revolution, which allows us to appreciate the archaic—sacred—basis of modernity. Unlike readers (viz. Habermas) who perceive the archaic as a distant point from which to gauge progress to the present, or would consider effervescence an exotic alternative to the civilizing process, sociology demonstrates it to be a permanent feature of social and political life that informs current social practices.

Finally, the socio-logic revalorized by means of the ethnographic detour puts into question the very basis for the opposition between conscious mind and unconscious reproduced by Freud's group psychology. It highlights the French school's contribution to a psychology that insists upon the "logic" of feelings and emotions that Gregory Bateson pushed as far back as Pascal's contention that the heart has reasons that reason itself does not understand, and which Karsenti relates to the influence of Ribot's "logic of sentiments" upon the French school.[18] Recognition of this socio-logic can be subsumed under the most significant consequence of the methodological turn to ethnography, which facilitates sociology's function as a psychoanalysis of the social.

Following the example of Mauss, Karsenti has pointed out that sociology's first methodological step toward arriving at archaeological conclusions is to enlist the ethnographic detour in order to dispel those false histories or genealogies inherited by the discipline. For instance, a common critique of Durkheim's call for the revival of feasts and banquets as the basis for future solidarity is that it is unworkable. Legislated festivals simply do not elicit the same fervor—as Durkheim himself noted—when he made a similar reflection in regard to Comte's efforts to revive past gods. Nowhere is the historic failure of civic festivals more evident than those decreed by the temporary revolutionary government following 1789, when the new calendar included holiday replacements for the traditional religious ones.[19] While this urhistory of the public collective festival succeeds in devaluing such efforts by stressing the intentional nature of legislated endeavors, it does not necessarily contribute to a revaluation of the pervasive biases against spontaneous outbursts of effervescence either. In response, I would argue that this conventional genealogy does not call into question the stereotypical depictions inherited from crowd psychologies of collective behavior as regressive or atavistic, just as it leaves unchallenged the sentiment that favorable reactions to collective movements are symptomatic of nostalgia for premodern and therefore anachronistic social formations. Sociology's counter to both positions demonstrates the speciousness of the spontaneous/intentional dualism since effervescence generated through the sacred/profane contrast is no less effective for being the outcome of a social structure. Neither entirely spontaneous nor directed, but the result of tensions and transgressions, such outbursts stand as irreducible to a single set of factors.[20]

The reconstruction of the notion of effervescence within the internal history of Durkheim's work presented in this study provided an alternative genealogical perspective: by setting his first major exploration of its effects within the Middle Ages, Durkheim explicitly located his example of effervescence in the prehistory of modern bourgeois society, thus circumventing its most controversial and repressed episode—1789. Whereas both he and LeBon cite the St. Barthelemy of the aristocrats as the foremost instance of the crowd's moralizing effect, the more pervasive and comprehensive, even global, consequences of the revolution of 1789 have been explicitly traced to its effervescence. Indeed, by relating the specificity of those events in terms of effervescence, Robert Darnton was able to capture the revolutionary spirit of 1789 as a sense of infinite possibilities. The global nature of possibilism—experienced as "epistemological exhilaration"—refers to transformations that would touch upon virtually any and every aspect of individual and collective being.[21] While this globalism may appear extreme, we recall Mauss's description of the morphological transformation of Eskimo society from one season to the other, when the contrast between the sacred and the profane did not leave any area of existence untouched.

Whereas Durkheim appeared increasingly despondent regarding the ability of collective representations to galvanize effervescent effusions, it is now possible to argue that it is less the case that those eruptions do not occur in modern societies than that they are not recognized as such. The ethnographic detour facilitates a reconsideration of the repressed memory of the effervescent, totalizing nature of the revolutionary dynamic of 1789, for instance, in terms that had become intolerable to the bourgeois society of fin-de-siècle France. Similarly, the explosive, totalizing character of the events of May '68 defy conventional critiques that such momentary elations are evanescent, since they are credited with transformations so profound one politician summed up their effect as "Plus rien ne sera comme avant," or "nothing will be the same." Like 1789 the May revolution sought to refashion the entirety of the social order by transforming its foundations in the nature and quality of social relations. Disconcerting to observers, the animus of May '68 participants was directed against the manifestation of power relations through the regulated use of language, an obvious affront to centuries of conditioning by the civilizing process. Acknowledging the impossibility of sustaining "utopian energy" for very long, Darnton nonetheless describes how it is such privileged moments can modify the symbolic dimension of social interaction:

> Thus, in the midst of an overwhelming sense of "possibilism" and the sweeping force and movement of the events, we stopped in our tracks, and in the face of the enormity of the event we felt bound to everyone around us. For a few instants we ceased to see one another through our roles and perceived ourselves as equals, stripped down to the core of our common humanity. Like mountaineers high above the daily business of the world, we moved from vous to tu.[22]

The globalism of May '68 challenged traditional categories by attracting members of virtually all major social and professional groups. Equally resistant to temporal erosion (though not always to the recuperative forces of the media and advertising), the panoply of collective representations generated by the movement—whether in the form of slogans, images, or critical notions—illustrate the ambitious claims made for effervescence from Durkheim to Bataille.

With its 1969 publication following the events of May '68, *The Ritual Process* historically validated Durkheim and Turner and indicted social scientists overly invested in a reifed, static notion of structure to the detriment of the process underlying its formation. As Chamboredon has argued, the most serious threat to sociology's vitality and power for renewal is to restrict its focus to groups already coalesced into established entities. Moreover, by neglecting process, the sociologist risks eliding the political dimension of such arrangements:

> [O]ne thus notes that institutional analysis, under the crystallized form that it takes in particular institutions, makes it difficult to apprehend social orders as "negociated" arrangements, thereby obliterating the political dimension of such phenomena.[23]

Because it deals with forces of cohesion that are outside and independent of individual awareness, sociology then risks having to "restore" to social agents the significance of the movements in which they participate. By refusing to view structure as inevitably repressive because it functions through constraint (a position erroneously attributed to Durkheim), this assessment is consistent with the approach to the taboo/transgression relation developed within the Collège.

Tiryakian's positions are also noteworthy for their recognition of the political implications of the effervescent May '68 events.[24] Because these events were precipitated by sociology students, they revived scholarly debate regarding Durkheim's academic role and personal influence in directing sociology away from explicitly political issues and, especially, solutions. Among the various images of the discipline's founder, one finds the Durkheim who sublimated his rejection of paternal Judaism ("I am a Rabbi's son") into prophetic Third Republicanism or the one who channeled adolescent socialism (see the period of the Ecole normale supérieure and his friendship with Jaurès) into a "scientific moralism." What both constructs claim is that for varying ideological purposes in the discipline's history, Durkheim intentionally shunned the controversy of politics and downplayed the potential stigma of ethnic origins in order to promote a new "science" of society.

In this, the first study to foreground effervescence in the Durkheimian oeuvre, the controversial notion was subsumed under the more comprehensive category of the collective to include reference to representations or categories that allow for a rethinking of the nature of the individual's relation to the social in a manner consistent with Durkheim's position that they not be reified into static entities. The collective also encompasses group experiences and interactions. As such, I would like this rereading of Durkheim to be a contribution to the project Fredric Jameson envisioned at the conclusion to his own historical panorama of the political unconscious, one that would explore a "logic of collective dynamics" by means of categories that propose something other than "the mere application of terms drawn from individual experience."[25] One consequence of reversing conventional genealogy and reading *Elementary Forms* from the Collège's point of view is to show Durkheim's centrality to the specifically French emphasis on the social that is a given among its most radical thinkers in the postwar period.

Resistance to the collective strain of French social thought has been especially entrenched among Anglo-American scholars who reject what they perceive to be an exaggerated focus on the social leading to an ultra-determinism. Evans-Pritchard was one of the first to denounce Durkheim's allegedly excessive preoccupation with the social as "madness." Steven Lukes counterbalanced his mentor's allegations with the observation that Durkheim's "ruthless" desire to relate everything back to society is nonetheless responsible for some of his most important insights regarding the limits of social determination.[26] Stuart Hall attributed the sources of Foucault's social determinism from "below" to the Durkheimian influence in French social thought.[27] And Pickering credits a Durkheim revival in the 1960s to the need for an alternative to "free subjectivity" among American and British leftists. As a continuation of and complement to research initiated in the 1970s, when it was widely believed that the lifting of prohibitions would result in greater personal and collective liberation, the present study would necessarily have to explain why it was that Bataille arrived at a diametrically opposed conclusion.

In a 1968 epilogue to his prewar study, Elias drew upon Durkheim's legacy in a manner convergent with the arguments forwarded by Turner and Tiryakian. At a moment in history when worldwide protest movements erupted from the sociocultural contradictions engendered by the economic transformations of the postwar period, Elias reiterated his basic premise that the correlation between personality and social structures must be assessed as the product of long-term, interdependent processes. At issue was the then-dominant sociological view, exemplified by Parsons, which considered the individual as real or actual, whereas the social was ultimately devalued as an epiphenomenon, and change appeared as the outcome of an accidental, externally activated malfunction of a normally homeostatic system. The contribution of the ethnographic detour was to reconsider such eruptions—and especially their effervescent quality—as evidence of permanent social phenomena that compel modern society to reconsider its sources by providing an experience of "[u]nbearable intensity, where the very being of sociality risks destruction through sacrificial [*dépense*] expenditure, but where it also never ceases to renew itself by drawing upon this fount of free energy for the permanent condition of its existence."[28]

Guided by their formulation of a sacred sociology, contributors to the Collège transgressed the confines of their bourgeois *habitus* to devise alternative modes of communication and understanding. As *moralistes* within the strong French essayistic tradition exemplified by

Montaigne, the authors cited in this study recast his model to fit their historical moment. All are hybrid writers;[29] but more than a revision or testing of the protocols of discourse, their writing is characterized by a tension within that impels the sociological revolution beyond the criticism of lacks and gaps to contemplate possibilities derived from the comparative approach. By enlisting the sacred—a notion at once familiar and exotic—the Collège initiated a daring probe into the microlevel of existence that would not be repeated until the early 1960s, when the resurrection of many prewar texts animated the theoretical adventures surrounding the events of May '68. The consequences of that pivotal manifestation of effervescence reinforced our argument that the revitalization of rituals associated with the tension between the sacred and the profane must be appreciated in relation to the long-standing effects of the civilizing process as an endemic feature of French political as well as social life.[30] As recently acknowledged by the historian Muchembled,

> An observable tendency since 1968 increasingly affirmed in the 1990's, is the privileging of the warmth produced by "informal" collective gatherings in contrast with those of established organizations, or the spontaneous contact of crowds over the hieratic coldness of too fixed commemorative celebrations, such as the bicentennial of the Revolution in 1989.[31]

Despite the regnant assumption since Marx that "all that is sacred has been profaned" or Habermas's contention that the avant-garde exhausts its negativity in trivialized modes of profanation,[32] sacred sociology eschews both such profanation as well as resacralization in terms of the "right" sacred. Instead, it advocates a dynamic reinvigoration of the opposition between the sacred and the profane, thereby affirming that a group, cohort, or generation must reinvent its experience of the social in terms of a sacred attuned to its needs and historical specificity. Unphased by the heterodoxies of the Collegians, Lévi-Strauss exonerated them from dismissal as amateurs because "French sociology does not consider itself an isolated discipline, working in its own field, but rather as a method, as a specific attitude toward human phenomena. Therefore one does not need to be a sociologist in order to do sociology."[33] Indeed, the sui generis identity of sacred sociology subsumes the demystifying traditions of Marxism and psychoanalysis while remaining indissociable from the collective representations it generates by means of the ethnosurrealist detour. As social and cultural criticism, sacred sociology both exposes the social basis of the sacred while asserting the need for collective representations and rituals capable of revitalizing social forms through the dynamic of collective energies. The sacred thus stands as a social phenomenon neither to be revered for its venerable antecedents in antiquity nor reviled for its association with primitives—both gestures robbing it of relevance to the present.

Notes

Unless indicated otherwise, translations throughout the text and notes are my own.

Introduction

1. In his report prepared for UNESCO in 1954, Claude Lévi-Strauss addressed the apparent disparities among various nations regarding the place of anthropology within the social sciences. A subsubsection entitled "Ethnography, Ethnology, and Anthropology" offers the following useful clarifications:

"In all countries, it seems, *ethnography* is interpreted in the same way: It corresponds to the first stages in research—observation and description, field work. The typical ethnographical study consists of a monograph dealing with a social group small enough for the author to be able to collect most of his material by personal observation. . . . In relation to ethnography, *ethnology* represents a first step toward synthesis. Without excluding direct observation, it leads toward conclusions sufficiently comprehensive to preclude, or almost to preclude, their being based solely on first-hand information. . . . [E]thnology includes ethnography as its first step and is an extension of it.

"For a considerable time, and in several countries, this 'duality' was regarded as sufficient unto itself. This was especially so in those where historical and geographical considerations predominated and where the opinion prevailed that synthesis could not range beyond determination of the origins and centers of cultural diffusion. Other countries—France, for instance—held to the same view but for different reasons; the final stage of the synthesis was left to other disciplines—sociology (in the French sense of the term), human geography, history, and sometimes even philosophy. Thus, . . . in several European countries the term anthropology was left undefined and was therefore limited to physical anthropology. . . . [T]erms like *social anthropology* or *cultural anthropology* are linked to a second and final stage of the synthesis, based upon ethnographical and ethnological conclusions. In this sense it may thus be said that there is the same connection between anthropology and ethnology as that, described above, between ethnology and ethnography. *Ethnography, ethnology, and anthropology do not form three different disciplines, or three different conceptions of the same branch of study. They are in fact three stages, or three moments of time, in the same line of investigation, and preference for one or another of these only means that attention is concentrated on one type of research, which can never exclude the other two"* (353). Claude Lévi-Strauss, "The Place of Anthropology in the Social Sciences and Problems Raised in Teaching It," in *Structural Anthropology* [vol. 1], translated from the French by Claire Jacobson and Brooke Grundfest Schoepf (Garden City, N.Y.: Anchor Books, 1967), 352–53, emphasis added. For added clarification of the meaning of French sociology in this study, see chapter 2, section entitled "Sociologie à la française."

2. Denis Hollier, ed., *The College of Sociology (1937–39),* translated from the French by Betsy Wing (Minneapolis: University of Minnesota Press, 1988), xxiii.

3. See Claude Lévi-Strauss, "French Sociology," in *Twentieth-Century Sociology,* ed. Georges Gurvitch and Wilbert E. Moore (Freeport, N.Y.: Books for Libraries, 1971), 503–37.

4. Jean Wahl in *College of Sociology,* ed. Hollier, 102, translation modified.

5. Nor do I propose an exhaustive overview of the Collège texts and their authors. The focus on Bataille, Caillois, and Leiris is justified by their respective contributions to the phenomenon variously referred to by Lévi-Strauss as "anthropological thinking," Caillois as the "ethnographic revolution," or what I have termed, especially in relation to Durkheim and Mauss, the "sociological revolution."

6. See Jean Baudrillard, *L'echange symbolique et la mort* (Paris: Gallimard, 1976); Jean Starobinski, *Les mots sous les mots, les anagrammes de Ferdinand de Saussure* (Paris: Gallimard, 1971); Marcel Mauss, "Essai sur le don. Forme et raison de l'échange dans les sociétés archaiques" (1923–24), in *Sociologie et anthropologie* (Paris: Presses Universitaires de France, 1950).

7. See James Clifford, "On Ethnographic Surrealism," *Comparative Studies in Society and History* 23 (1981): 539–64.

8. Robert A. Nisbet, *The Sociological Tradition* (New York: Basic Books, 1966), 243.

9. Ibid., 244.

10. Randall Collins, *The Sociology of Philosophies: A Global Theory of Intellectual Change* (Cambridge: Belknap Press of Harvard University Press, 1998).

11. Mark Traugott, "Durkheim and Social Movements," in *Emile Durkheim: Critical Assessments,* ed. Peter Hamilton, vol. 2 (London: Routledge, 1990), 198–206; Hans Joas, "Durkheim's Intellectual Development: The Problem of the Emergence of New Morality and New Institutions as a Leitmotif in Durkheim's Oeuvre," in *Emile Durkheim, Sociologist and Moralist,* ed. Stephen Turner (London: Routledge, 1993), 229–45.

12. For the most recent statement of this dilemma in Durkheim, see Camille Tarot, *De Durkheim à Mauss, l'invention du symbolique. Sociologie et sciences des religions* (Paris: Editions La Découverte et Syros, 1999).

13. Robert Hertz, "La prééminence de la main droite. Etude sur la polarité religieuse" (1909), in *Sociologie religieuse et folklore,* preface by Georges Balandier (Paris: Presses Universitaires de France, 1970), 84–109.

14. Hans Mayer, "The Rituals of Political Associations in Germany of the Romantic Period"; Anatole Lewitzsky, "Shamanism"; Roger Caillois, "The Winter Wind"; and Georges Bataille, "Attraction and Repulsion II: Social Structure": all in *College of Sociology,* ed. Hollier, 262–78, 248–61, 32–42, and 113–24, respectively.

15. Jeffrey Alexander, *The Antinomies of Classical Thought: Marx and Durkheim,*

vol. 2 of *Theoretical Logic in Sociology* (Berkeley: University of California Press, 1982); Alexander, "Rethinking Durkheim's Intellectual Development: On the Complex Origins of a Cultural Sociology," in *Emile Durkheim: Critical Assessments,* ed. Peter Hamilton, vol. 1 (London: Routledge, 1990), 355–81.

16. Steven Lukes, *Emile Durkheim, His Life and Work: A Historical and Critical Study* (New York: Penguin Books, 1973).

17. Tarot, *De Durkheim à Mauss.*

18. Elias points to this opposition when he traces the appearance of "civilization" in the eighteenth century to its antecedents in the earlier *politesse* or *civilité.* All three terms functioned to distinguish the European upper class in relation to "others whom its members considered simpler or more primitive, . . . above all, towards the 'simple people' in their most extreme form, the 'savage.'" Norbert Elias, *The Civilizing Process: Sociogenetic and Psychogenetic Investigations,* trans. by Edmund Jephcott with some notes and corrections by the author, rev. ed., ed. Eric Dunning, Johan Goudsblom, and Stephen Mennell (Oxford: Blackwell, 2000), 34.

19. See especially chapters 6 and 15 in Jean de Léry, *Histoire d'un voyage en terre de Brésil* (France: Livre de Poche, Bibliothèque Classique, 1994).

20. For the particular relation between French Protestants and the New World, I consulted Frank Lestringant, *Le Huguenot et le sauvage* (Paris: Aux Amateurs de Livres, Klincksieck, 1990).

21. "Tout cela ne va pas trop mal. Mais quoi, ils ne portent point de haut-de-chausses [All this is not too bad—but what of it? They don't wear breeches]." *Montaigne's Essays and Selected Writings,* bilingual ed., trans. and ed. Donald M. Frame (New York: St. Martin's Press, 1963), 116–17.

22. For a recent account of this process I relied upon Robert Muchembled, *La société policée: Politique et politesse en France du XVIe au XXe siècle* (Paris: Editions du Seuil, 1998).

23. Elias limits his comparison to Germany.

24. In the main, French authors of the sixteenth century fault their contemporaries for not being more effective in imparting the virtues of civility to the "savages" of the New World. Moreover, the perceived deficiency of civilized traits will harden into "evidence" of the inferiority of the newly discovered peoples. Only in the eighteenth century is this belief put to the test. For more on the relation between the idea of race and the social hierarchy, see Arlette Jouanna, *L'idée de race en France au XVIème siècle et au début du XVIIième siècle (1498–1614). vol. 1, Thèse présentée devant l'Université de Paris IV, le 7 juin 1975* (Paris: Librairie Honoré Champion, 1976), 375.

25. See, for instance, illustrations that represent Amerindians in the garb and classical features of antiquity.

26. See below, Postcriptum.

27. J. H. Elliott, *The Old World and the New, 1492–1650* (Cambridge: Cambridge University Press, 1970), 5. See, for instance, Gilbert Chinard, *L'Amérique et le rêve exotique dans la littérature française au XVIIe et XVIIIe siècle* (1913; Genève: Slatkine Reprints, 1970) or Geoffrey Atkinson, *Les relations de voyages du XVIIe siècle et L'évolution des idées. Contribution à l'étude de la formation de l'esprit du XVIIIe siècle* (New York: Burt Franklin, 1924).

28. Henri Baudet, *Paradise on Earth: Some Thoughts on European Images of Non-European Man,* trans. Elizabeth Wentholt (New Haven: Yale University Press, 1965), 26.

29. Johan Heilbron's *The Rise of Social Theory* (Minneapolis: University of Minnesota Press, 1995) provides a useful overview of the historical sources of French sociology from a more traditional viewpoint than the one presented here.

30. Durkheim, *The Elementary Forms of Religious Life,* trans. from *Formes élémentaires de la vie religieuse. Le système totémique en Australie* (1912) and with an introduction by Karen E. Fields (New York: Free Press, 1995), 1.

31. G. Bataille, "Le sens moral de la sociologie," in *Oeuvres complètes,* vol. 11, *Articles I, 1944–1949* (Paris: Gallimard, 1988), 58. This is also Marcel Fournier's conclusion in his extensive biography, *Marcel Mauss* (Paris: Fayard, 1994).

32. Johan Heilbron, "Les métamorphoses du durkheimisme, 1920–1940," *Revue française de sociologie* 26 (April-June 1985): 203. Another explanation forwarded is that "ambiguities" within the sociological project—namely, its claim to be a science of morality—"reduced it to the very unglorious status of a practical philosophy." Jean-Louis Fabiani, *Les philosophes de la république* (Paris: Les Editions de Minuit, 1988), 171.

33. Marcel Mauss, *The Gift: Forms and Functions of Exchange in Archaic Societies,* trans. from "Essai sur le don" by Ian Cunnison (New York: Norton, 1967), 2.

34. George E. Marcus and Michael M. J. Fischer, *Anthropology as Cultural Critique: An Experimental Moment in the Human Sciences* (Chicago: University of Chicago Press, 1986).

35. Mauss, *The Gift,* 2, emphasis added.

36. Edward Tiryakian, "Vers une sociologie de l'existence," in *Perspectives de la sociologie contemporaine. Hommage à Georges Gurvitch,* preface by Georges Balandier (Paris: Presses Universitaires de France, 1968); Jeffrey C. Alexander, ed., *Durkheimian Sociology: Cultural Studies* (Cambridge: Cambridge University Press, 1988); C. W. Thompson, ed., *L'Autre et le sacré: Surréalisme, cinéma, ethnologie* (Paris: Editions L'Harmattan, 1995).

37. W. Paul Vogt, "The Uses of Studying Primitives: A Note on the Durkheimians, 1890–1940," in *Durkheim,* ed. Hamilton, 1:178.

38. Dominick LaCapra, *Emile Durkheim, Sociologist and Philosopher* (Ithaca, N.Y.: Cornell University Press, 1972), 25.

39. Bruno Karsenti, *L'homme total: Sociologie, anthropologie et philosophie chez Marcel Mauss* (Paris: Presses Universitaires de France, 1997). Karsenti's otherwise admirable readings of Mauss tend to set up Durkheim as straw man for the better advantage of Mauss.

40. Raymond Aron, *Main Currents in Sociological Thought,* vol. 2, *Durkheim, Pareto, Weber,* trans. Richard Howard and Helen Weaver (New York: Anchor Books, 1970), 59.

41. In Malinowski's otherwise favorable review, for instance, we find the following: "First of all, we feel a little suspicious of a theory which sees the origins of religion in crowd phenomena." Bronislaw Malinowski, review of E. Durkheim, *Les formes elémentaires de la vie religieuse: Le système totémique en Australie* (1913), reprinted in *Emile Durkheim: Critical Assessments,* ed. Peter Hamilton, vol. 3 (London: Routledge, 1990), 217–21.

42. For a more recent assessment of the connections among these issues at the end of the nineteenth century, see Robert Nye, "Savage Crowds, Modernism, and Modern Politics," in *Prehistories of the Future: The Primitivist Project and the Culture of Modernism,* ed. Elazar Barkan and Ronald Bush (Stanford, Calif.: Stanford University Press, 1995), 42–55.

43. Cited in W. S. F. Pickering, *Durkheim's Sociology of Religion: Themes and Theories* (London: Routledge and Kegan Paul, 1984), 396. Pickering counters with a comparison between the crowd model of LeBon and the Durkheimian assembly. This comparison will be further developed in chapter 3.

44. See ibid.

45. This reading is clearly stated in Philippe Borgeaud's "Le couple sacré/profane. Genèse et fortune d'un concept 'opératoire' en histoire des religions," *Revue de l'Histoire des Religions* 211, no. 4 (1994): 387–418.

46. W. S. F. Pickering, "The Origins of Conceptual Thinking in Durkheim: Social or Religious?" in *Emile Durkheim, Sociologist and Moralist*, ed. Stephen Turner (London: Routledge, 1993), 64.

47. Jean-Claude Chamboredon, "Emile Durkheim: Le social objet de science, du moral au politique?" in *Aux sources de la sociologie*, special issue of *Critique* 40 (June–July 1984): 460–531.

48. Bourdieu qualifies sociology as a discipline that is disturbing because it uncovers hidden and sometimes repressed things: "One of the reasons the discipline is especially problematic is that its 'objects' are those for which struggles are waged—things that are hidden, that are censored, and for which people are prepared to die." Pierre Bourdieu, *Questions de sociologie* (Paris: Editions de Minuit, 1984), 20, 21.

49. Chamboredon, "Emile Durkheim," 484.

50. See Marcus and Fischer, *Anthropology as Cultural Critique*.

51. See George W. Stocking Jr., *Victorian Anthropology* (New York: Macmillan, 1987).

52. Tzvetan Todorov, *Nous et les autres. La réflexion française sur la diversité humaine* (Paris: Editions du Seuil, 1989). Todorov also rejects the notion of discourse as defined by Foucault, in favor of a return to the history of thought *(la pensée)* which then holds individual thinkers responsible for the inadequacies of their positions.

53. See Wolf Lepenies, *Between Literature and Science: The Rise of Sociology*, trans. R. J. Hollingdale (Cambridge: Cambridge University Press, 1988).

54. H. Stuart Hughes, *Consciousness and Society: The Reorientation of European Social Thought, 1890–1930* (New York: Vintage Books, 1958), 283. An updated "postmodernist" perspective regarding the place of sentiment in Durkheimian sociology can be found in Stjepan G. Mestrovic, *The Coming Fin de Siècle: An Application of Durkheim's Sociology to Modernity and Postmodernism* (London: Routledge, 1991), 53. Mestrovic's reading claims Durkheim's respect for science to be "a derivative of the cult of feeling," the latter a characteristic of fin de siècle philosophy.

1. Durkheim's Sociological Revolution

1. Durkheim, *Elementary Forms of Religious Life*, 220. Subsequent page numbers appearing in the text for chapter 1 refer to this title.

2. The challenges raised by Durkheim's Janus-like image were set forth in Harry Alpert's 1960 presentation to American readers in the following way: "Even Madison Avenue would have had difficulty projecting the proper image of Emile Durkheim. For Durkheim's complex personality was, in fact, a blending of at least two different images. One is the image of the serious, austere, forbidding, unsmiling scientist and professor who insists on rigorous application of logical reasoning and on strict methodological procedures. The other image, equally valid, is that of the fervent prophet and social critic, the passionate moralist, the intense patriot, and the ardent philosopher seeking truth with reason and clarity." Cited by Mestrovic, in *The Coming Fin de Siècle*, 52.

3. Lukes, *Emile Durkheim*, 363, 364. For details regarding Durkheim's critics, see Terry N. Clark, "Emile Durkheim and the Institutionalization of Sociology in the French University System" (1968), reprinted in *Durkheim*, ed. Hamilton, 1:104–36.

4. Nisbet, *Sociological Tradition*, 221. For a summary of the reception to *The*

Elementary Forms of Religious Life, see Pickering, *Durkheim's Sociology of Religion*, 86–89.

5. Robert Bellah, introduction to Emile Durkheim, *On Morality and Society: Selected Writings* (Chicago: University of Chicago Press, 1973), xliii.

6. Cited in Lukes, *Emile Durkheim*, 237.

7. For comparisons among the respective influences exerted by Robertson Smith, Durkheim, and Hertz on late-nineteenth-century American social theory and literature, see Susan Mizruchi, *The Science of Sacrifice: American Literature and Modern Social Theory* (Princeton, N.J.: Princeton University Press, 1998).

8. Cited in Lukes, *Emile Durkheim*, 237.

9. See Sir Baldwin Spencer and Francis James Gillen, *Native Tribes of Central Australia* (London: Macmillan, 1899) and *Northern Tribes of Central Australia* (London: Macmillan, 1904).

10. *Elementary Forms*, 36 (emphasis added). Philippe Borgeaud argues that the sacred/profane dualism is basically an "operative" invention of the French school necessary to their promotion of a civil religion. See Borgeaud, "Le couple sacré/profane," 387–418.

11. See Marcel Mauss in collaboration with Henri Beuchat, *Seasonal Variations of the Eskimo: A Study in Social Morphology*, trans. from the French with a foreword by James J. Fox (Boston: Routledge and Kegan Paul, 1979).

12. See Emile Durkheim, *Les règles de la méthode sociologique*, préface de la seconde édition (Paris: Presses Universitaires de France, 1973), xii–xxiv.

13. Ibid., 4.

14. *Elementary Forms*, 214. Durkheim's notion of the social unconscious as a "treasure" deposited in each generation provided his contemporary, the Swiss linguist Ferdinand de Saussure, with the basis for the structuralist model of linguistic development. But with the *langue/parole* (language/speech) dichotomy, Saussure displaced an imagery of currents and forces with rules and codes constituted through signs, thereby expunging structural linguistics of the controversial elements to which Durkheim would return. This is the conventional filiation forwarded to explain Saussure's "sociologism," even though as Mounin points out, the evidence for any direct influence, such as reading a Durkheimian text, is inconclusive. The contact is, at best, mediated by Antoine Meillet, Saussure's disciple and preferred correspondent. At minimum, the strong parallels testify to the pervasiveness of certain sociological notions. See Georges Mounin, *Saussure ou le structuraliste sans le savoir* (Paris: Seghers, 1968).

15. Durkheim, *Les règles de la méthode sociologique*, 7.

16. This issue is further developed in the context of comparisons between Durkheim, LeBon, and Freud regarding group psychology in chapter 3.

17. Marcel Mauss, *Oeuvres*, vol. 3, *Cohésion sociale et divisions de la sociologie* (Paris: Editions de Minuit, 1969), 143.

18. The convention among Durkheim scholars is to maintain *représentations* in French in order to indicate the complexity of a notion that does not correspond to a simple translation. The adjectives *individuelle* and *collective*, with which it is frequently associated, are also kept in French. The standard reference to Durkheim's multiple usages of the term is Lukes, *Emile Durkheim*, 6–8, as well as the complementary discussions of *faits sociaux*, 8–15. The expanded usage of the term in recent years within the new historicism and cultural studies movements, however, renders the italicization less urgent. The most frequent connotation used in this study is as a reference to categories and images, and how Durkheim perceives their value in either occulting or revealing the social basis of most phenomena. This is the basis for comparisons with the Althusserian

view of ideology defined as a spontaneous and therefore unconscious representation of the individual's lived relation to the world. Louis Althusser, *For Marx*, trans. Ben Brewster (New York: Vintage Books, 1970), 252.

19. Emile Durkheim, *The Division of Labor in Society*, trans. from *De la division du travail social* (1893) by George Simpson (New York: Free Press, 1964), 404.

20. As early as 1937, Talcott Parsons argued against pursuing the tack of the "group mind" *(conscience collective)* in favor of the more viable issue of representations. See Parsons, *The Structure of Social Action*, vol. 1 (New York: Free Press, 1968), 363.

21. Durkheim, *Suicide: A Study in Sociology*, trans. John. A. Spaulding and George Simpson, ed. with an introduction by George Simpson (New York: Free Press, 1966). For a discussion of the importance of medieval models in nineteenth-century French thought, see Nisbet, *Sociological Tradition*, and chapter 2 of this study.

22. Durkheim, *Division of Labor in Society*, 14.

23. Ibid., 167.

24. Durkheim, "Idéal moral, conscience collective et forces religieuses" (1909), in *Textes*, vol. 2, *Religion, morale, anomie: Présentation de Victor Karady* (Paris: Les Editions de Minuit, 1975), 16.

25. Several, though not all, parallels between Durkheim's "prenotions" and Althusser's view of ideology were signaled by Sheila Strawbridge, "Althusser's Theory of Ideology and Durkheim's Account of Religion: An Examination of Some Striking Parallels," *Sociological Review* 30 (1982): 125–40.

26. Durkheim, *Division of Labor in Society*, 15.

27. Ibid.

28. Ibid., 26.

29. Nye has signaled the widespread use of the biological analysis of French society and a medical solution at the time, including the fact that "a medical model of national decline had penetrated the political milieu." Robert A. Nye, "Heredity, Pathology, and Psychoneurosis in Durkheim's Early Work," in *Durkheim*, ed. Hamilton, 1:267.

30. Durkheim, *Division of Labor in Society*, 381.

31. Ibid., 129.

32. James A. Boon, *Other Tribes, Other Scribes: Symbolic Anthropology in the Comparative Study of Cultures, Histories, Religions and Texts* (New York: Cambridge University Press, 1982), 55.

33. Emile Durkheim, *Montesquieu et Rousseau: Précurseurs de la sociologie* (Paris: Librairie Marcel Rivière et Cie, 1953), 137.

34. Nisbet, *Sociological Tradition*, 87–88.

35. Ibid., 86.

36. Anthony Giddens, "Durkheim as a Review Critic," in *Durkheim*, ed. Hamilton, 1:158 n. 77.

37. Durkheim, *Division of Labor in Society*, 129. I am indebted to James Boon for pointing out that the mechanical/organic distinction "isolates not two separate kinds of society but rather twin aspects, apparent if a social solidarity is fully conceptualized from both external and internal vantages." Boon, *Other Tribes, Other Scribes*, 54.

38. Durkheim, *Division of Labor in Society*, 173, translation modified.

39. Ibid., 401.

40. Ibid., 26.

41. Ibid.

42. Durkheim, *Suicide*, 375.

43. Durkheim, "Remarque sur la nature de la religiosité" (1899), in *Textes*, 2:9. Karady concludes from this statement that the main lines of Durkheim's thinking for

Elementary Forms were already being sketched in his earliest essays to the point that they are "implicit" in the three great works of his early phase.

44. Very early in their thinking, Durkheim and Mauss posit a coincidence between the individual versus collective distinction with the sacred versus profane one, thus revealing the importance of religious sensibilities as access to an appreciation of social processes. For more on this, see their definition of *représentations* according to the essay on classification: "And in fact, according to those we call primitives, a category of things is not a simple object of knowledge, but corresponds above all to a certain sentimental attitude. All sorts of affective elements contribute to the representation we have of it. Religious emotions especially, not only impart a particular coloration, but ascribe to it all sort of essential properties. Things, facts and phenomena *[les choses]* are above all sacred or profane, pure or impure, friendly or inimical, favorable or disfavorable; which is to say that their fundamental characteristics are an expression of the way that they affect the social sensibility." Marcel Mauss, "De quelques formes primitives de classification," in *Essais de sociologie* (Paris: Editions de Minuit, 1968), 227. On the divergences between Durkheim and Mauss regarding the sacred, see Stephano Martelli, "Mauss et Durkheim: Un désaccord sur la question du sacré et une perspective relationnelle sur Simmel et la société post-moderne," in *Durkheim*, ed. Hamilton, 3:183–95.

45. Durkheim, *Journal sociologique*, introduction and notes by Jean Duvignaud (Paris: Presses Universitaires de France, 1969), 162.

46. Ibid., 156.

47. Mauss, "Variations saisonnières" (1904–5), in *Sociologie et anthropologie*, 473.

48. Hubert and Mauss, "Essai sur la nature et la fonction du sacrifice," in Mauss, *Oeuvres*, vol. 1, *Les fonctions sociales du sacré* (Paris: Les Editions de Minuit, 1968), 302–3.

49. Ibid.

50. Durkheim, *Suicide*, 318–19.

51. Durkheim, "Idéal moral, conscience collective et forces religieuses" (1909), in *Textes*, 2:17.

52. Durkheim, "Value Judgments and Judgments of Reality" (1911), in *Sociology and Philosophy*, trans. D. F. Pocock, with an introduction by J. G. Peristiany (New York: Free Press, 1974), 94–95.

53. Durkheim, "The Dualism of Human Nature and Its Social Conditions," in *Emile Durkheim: On Morality and Society*, ed. and with an introduction by Robert N. Bellah (Chicago: University of Chicago Press, 1973), 156.

54. Lukes, *Emile Durkheim*, 36.

55. Durkheim, "Dualism of Human Nature and Its Social Conditions," 160.

56. *Elementary Forms*, 246–47 (translation modified).

57. Durkheim, "Le problème religieux et la dualité de la nature humaine" (1913), in *Textes*, 2:35.

58. Emile Durkheim, *Leçons de sociologie: Physique des Moeurs et du Droit* (Paris: Presses Universitaires de France, 1950), 21, 23. For more on the political significance of the lessons, see Pierre Birnbaum's preface to Emile Durkheim, *Le socialisme* (Paris: Presses Universitaires de France, 1971).

59. Durkheim, *Suicide*, 389.

60. Durkheim, *Division of Labor in Society*, 28.

61. Durkheim, *Suicide*, 312.

62. More recently, Filloux argued that Durkheim's notion of the social is tied to feelings of dependence that are evoked by images oscillating between "a maternal pole of archaic phantasms for a nourishing society, and one that is allied to the law and its in-

terdictions." Jean-Claude Filloux, *Durkheim et le socialisme* (Genève: Librairie Droz, 1977), 172. Talcott Parsons, *The Structure of Social Action: A Study in Social Theory with Special Reference to a Group of Recent European Writers*, vol. 2 (New York: Free Press, 1968), 319.

63. Durkheim, *Division of Labor in Society*, 402–3.

64. Durkheim, "Progressive Preponderance of Organic Solidarity," in *Emile Durkheim*, ed. Bellah, 69.

65. Marcel Mauss, "An Intellectual Self-Portrait," in *The Sociological Domain*, ed. Philippe Besnard (Cambridge: Press Syndicat of the University of Cambridge, Australia, and Editions de la Maison des Sciences de l'Homme, 1983), 139. For more details, consult Philippe Besnard, "The Année sociologique team," 11–39, in same collection.

66. See Alexander, *Antinomies of Classical Thought*. A succinct statement of Alexander's positions can also be found in his "Rethinking Durkheim's Intellectual Development: On the Complex Origins of a Cultural Sociology," in *Durkheim*, ed. Hamilton, 1:355–81.

67. Parsons, *Structure of Social Action*, 1:384.

68. See Alexander, *Antinomies of Classical Thought*, esp. 379 n. 14, for a review of the literature regarding the issue of periods and phases.

69. In reference to the revolutionary significance of this aspect of Durkheim's work, Madeleine Rebérious asserts, "all facts are constructed and the sociologist's first task is to construct his material. We have not fully exhausted all the implications of this discovery, which is at the heart of *The Rules of Sociological Method* (1895). It sounds the death knell of scientism." Rebérioux, *La République radicale? 1898–1914* (Paris: Editions du Seuil, 1975), 180.

70. Durkheim, "Introduction à la morale" (1917), in *Textes*, 2:313–31.

71. Durkheim, *Montesquieu et Rousseau*, 31.

72. Robert Bellah, "Durkheim and History," in *Durkheim: Critical Assessments*, ed. Peter Hamilton, vol. 7 (London: Routledge, 1995), 46.

73. Filloux, introduction to Durkheim, *La science sociale et l'action*, ed. Filloux (Paris: Presses Universitaires de France, 1970), 54.

74. Durkheim, "Cours de science sociale" (1888), in *La science sociale et l'action*, 80.

75. Durkheim, "Sociologie et Sciences Sociales" (1909), in *La science sociale et l'action*, 138.

76. Durkheim, *Montesquieu et Rousseau*, 154.

77. Durkheim, *Division of Labor in Society*, 398.

78. The early association between sociology and socialism was considerable, even though Durkheim himself, along with other Durkheimians such as Célestin Bouglé, preferred radicalism and especially the solidarism of Léon Bourgeois. The latter provided an alternative to the potentially revolutionary positions of militant socialism. Filloux defines Durkheim's socialism more in terms of an ideology than a political engagement. He also places considerable emphasis upon the role Durkheim envisioned for sociology in the emergence of a socialist society. See Filloux, *Durkheim et le socialisme*, 259–69. For a recent summary of these distinctions, see Laurent Mucchielli, *La découverte du social: Naissance de la sociologie en France* (1870–1914) (Paris XIIIe: Editions la Découverte, 1998), 233–41.

79. Durkheim, "Philosophy and Moral Facts," in *Sociologie et philosophie* (Paris: Quadrige/Presses Universitaires de France, 1996), 114.

80. Durkheim, "Introduction à la morale" (1917), in *Textes*, 2:316.

81. Durkheim, "L'avenir de la religion" (1914), in *La science sociale et l'action*, 313, emphasis added.

82. Durkheim, "Le dualisme de la nature humaine" (1914), in *La science sociale et l'action*, 332.

83. Durkheim, "L'état actuel des études sociologiques en France" (1895), in *Textes*, vol. 1, *Eléments d'une théorie sociale* (Paris: Les Editions de Minuit, 1975), 105.

84. Vincent Crapanzano notes the appearance of "effervescence" in *Suicide* in reference to the "excitement" of the industrial age and then compares it to its subsequent usage in *Elementary Forms* without reference to the pedagogy study. See "The Moment of Prestidigitation: Magic, Illusion, and Mana in the Thought of Emile Durkheim and Marcel Mauss," in *Prehistories of the Future*, ed. Barkan and Bush, 391 n. 2.

85. Chamboredon, "Emile Durkheim," 479, emphasis added.

86. See Bernard Lacroix, *Durkheim et le politique* (Montréal: Presses de l'Université de Montréal, 1981), esp. 198–99. Lacroix limits his study to the period preceding *Elementary Forms* and makes no mention of the pedagogy lectures.

87. Lukes, *Emile Durkheim*, 469.

2. Savages in the Sorbonne

1. The claim is made by Georges Gusdorf, "Ethnologie et métaphysique," in *Ethnologie générale* (Encyclopédie de la Pléiade, 1968), 1775, cited by Michèle Duchet, *Anthropologie et histoire au siècle des lumières* (Paris: François Maspéro, 1971), 9.

2. Nisbet, *Sociological Tradition*, 15.

3. Ibid., 15.

4. Durkheim, "L'état actuel des études sociologiques en France," 78.

5. Mauss, *Cohésion sociale et divisions de la sociologie*, 405.

6. Durkheim, *Les règles de la méthode sociologique*, 106, emphasis added.

7. Victor Karady, "Le problème de la légitimité dans l'organisation historique de l'ethnologie française," *Revue française de sociologie* 23 (1982): 17.

8. Chamboredon, "Emile Durkheim," 531 n. 159.

9. Fabiani concurs that the teaching of philosophy during this period reflected "to the highest degree" the typical characteristics of the classical teaching practices inherited from the Jesuits as described by Durkheim in *L'évolution pédagogique en France* (1938), introduction by Maurice Halbwachs (Paris: Presses Universitaires de France, 1969). See Fabiani, *Les philosophes de la république*, 60.

10. Priscilla P. Clark, *Literary France: The Making of Culture* (Berkeley: University of California Press, 1987), 104.

11. Pickering attributes Durkheim's attitudes toward literature and estheticism to their lack of moral rigor, a position he sees as consistent with Durkheim's early Judaic training. See W. S. F. Pickering, "The Enigma of Durkheim's Jewishness," in *Debating Durkheim*, ed. W. S. F. Pickering and H. Martins (London: Routledge, 1994), 10–39.

12. See Antoine Compagnon, *La Troisième République des lettres: De Flaubert à Proust* (Paris: Editions du Seuil, 1983).

13. Henri Massis and Gabriel de Tarde [Agathon], *L'esprit de la nouvelle Sorbonne: La crise de la culture classique, la crise du français* (Paris: Mercure de France, 1911).

14. As early as 1892 Durkheim had opened his thesis on Montesquieu and Rousseau as "precursors" to the discipline of sociology with the observation, "Forgetful of our history, we have acquired the habit of viewing social science as foreign, and a stranger to our French spirit" (*Montesquieu et Rousseau*, 25). This, like other statements in a similar vein, can be appreciated as directed at the anti-German sentiment that colored the reception of psychoanalysis in France as well.

15. Massis and de Tarde, *L'esprit de la nouvelle Sorbonne*, 111, 105.

16. Durkheim, *L'évolution pédagogique en France,* 313, 314. Subsequent page numbers appearing in the text for chapter 2 refer to this title.

17. Emile Durkheim, "La sociologie" (1915), in *Textes,* 1:117.

18. Gustave Lanson, "L'histoire littéraire et la sociologie," in *Essais de méthode et de critique et d'histoire littéraire. Edités et présentés par Henri Peyre* (Paris: Hachette, 1965), 64; originally published in *La revue de métaphysique et de morale* 12 (1904): 621–42.

19. Lanson's nationalistic, servant-of-the-State, Third Republic refrain not only echoed Durkheim's: it also reveals why their shared antipathy for the class-based and biased classical humanism set them in the same ideological camp. When he undertook the assessment of sociology's contribution to literary history, Lanson had already published a diatribe against the superficiality of literary evaluations based primarily on rhetorical considerations. Entitled "Contre la rhétorique et les mauvaises humanités" ("Against Rhetoric and Bad Humanities") it impugns the Jesuit legacy of a reductionist classicism restricted to a set of fixed ideas that rob the venerable classics of their critical thrust. With its "venom" neutralized by the Catholic Church, classical humanism caters to an elitist few, for whom its very disdain of the practical world provides a sign of distinction. Moreover, by eschewing the methodological rigors of science (the only science encouraged being the abstract "uselessness" of mathematics), the rhetorical claim to an "art of thinking" degenerated into an art of speaking well without having "to think."

20. Lanson, "L'histoire littéraire et la sociologie," 83.

21. Ibid., 83.

22. See Compagnon, *La Troisième République des lettres,* sections 19–21 of section 1.

23. Christophe Charle, *La crise littéraire à l'époque du naturalisme, Roman, Théâtre, Politique* (Paris: Presses de l'Ecole normale supérieure, 1979), 155, emphasis added.

24. Clark, *Literary France,* 167.

25. R. C. Grogin, cited in Mark Antliff, *Inventing Bergson: Cultural Politics and the Parisian Avant-Garde* (Princeton, N.J.: Princeton University Press, 1993), 148–49.

26. Clark, *Literary France,* 99–100.

27. Durkheim, *L'évolution pédagogique en France,* 316.

28. Durkheim, "Les principes de 1789 et la sociologie," in *Science sociale et l'action,* 223.

29. Durkheim, *Elementary Forms,* 427.

30. Durkheim, *Division of Labor in Society,* 15–16.

31. Ibid., 27–28.

32. See Herman Lebovics, *True France: The Wars over Cultural Identity, 1900–1945* (Ithaca, N.Y.: Cornell University Press, 1992).

33. In contrast with the struggles of anthropology, the successes of Durkheimian sociology can in part be attributed to its official support by the Third Republic government: "Durkheim's sociological project was perfectly adept at espousing the preoccupations of the leaders of the Third Republic, especially in matters relating to eduction and social reform. One can thus appreciate the official support provided for its introduction into the French university system. . . . A comparable public enthusiasm was lacking for anthropology." Nelie Diaz, *Le Musée d'ethnographie du Trocadéro (1878–1908): Anthropologie et muséologie en France* (Paris: CNRS, 1991), 242. Lebovics is concerned that the traditional hagiography on Durkheim—his "triumph" over right-wing opposition—has effectively discouraged further investigation into the more subtle pervasiveness of the conservative doctrine into the first half of this century: "This vision of national identity represents something new, certainly with origins in monarchism but with claims about

the True France, claims upon a republican France more compelling than nineteenth century monarchism could be." Lebovics, *True France*, 19.

34. See Edward Tiryakian, "L'école durkheimienne à la recherche de la sociologie perdue. La sociologie naissante et son milieu culturel," *Cahiers internationaux de sociologie* 66 (1979): 97–114.

35. Madeleine Rebérioux points out that "[f]or a long time, the divisions fostered by the Affaire remained essentially ideological. Two discourses contended with each other and provided guidelines for action. But they correspond neither to organized political forces—this is precisely why ligues were created—nor to social classes." *La République radicale? 1898–1914*, 23.

36. Cited by Durkheim in *L'évolution pédagogique*, 198. In contrast with Durkheim's critique of imitation, Tarde placed it at the center of a sociological doctrine he generalized from the example of the bourgeoisie. Here is Arno Mayer's summary: "Though socially envious and feeling slighted, not to say affronted, lowborn individuals imitate those they idealize as their betters by internalizing their values and attitudes, which they then seek to act upon and externalize. To follow Tarde, having assimilated the reigning cultural ideas and societal objectives, both immediate and long-term, upstart financiers, entrepreneurs, and professionals imitated the tone-setting nobility's accent, carriage, demeanor, etiquette, dress, and lifestyle. While some were vague, confused, and spontaneous in their emulation, others were precise, rigorous, and studied. But whether flexible or slavish the bourgeois remained self-doubting and self-abasing. Perhaps their behavior was so timorous because deep-down they never stopped doubting their own social legitimacy." Arno Mayer, *The Persistence of the Old Régime: Europe to the Great War* (New York: Pantheon, 1981), 86.

37. Attacks against Jesuit casuistry were hardly novel throughout the nineteenth century. Muchembled traces to Boileau in the seventeenth century the accusation against Jesuit teaching of a constant "equivocation," which then became endemic to their students' way of thinking. The historian locates this "collective mental disposition of duplicity" among social élites from 1650 on, compelled to manifest signs of acquiescence while dissembling their political as well as social ambitions (Muchembled, *La société policée*, 97). Chamboredon also notes that the critique of the rhetorical domination can be situated within a long, though "dominated" tradition of critiques, directed against the lettered, rhetorical and superficial style of the university instruction of literature, which was especially pointed at the time of the 1870 defeat, when French universities suffered invidious comparisons with the German system and philosophy. See 517 n. 71.

38. A very different assessment of this aspect of Jesuit teaching is provided by Claude Lévi-Strauss, who credits them with providing students to their first exposure to an appreciation of other cultures: "When the Jesuits made Greek and Latin the basis of intellectual training, was that not a first form of ethnology? They recognized that no civilization can define itself if it does not have at its disposal some other civilizations for comparison." Lévi-Strauss, *Structural Anthropology*, vol. 2, trans. Monique Layton (New York: Basic Books, 1976), 272.

39. Elias, *Civilizing Process*, 64 (emphasis added).

40. See Muchembled, *La société policée*.

41. Muchembled acknowledges his debt to Alain Viala's important study of the role of literature in the development of French identity in the seventeenth century, *Naissance de l'écrivain: Sociologie de la littérature à l'âge classique* (Paris: Les Editions de Minuit, 1985).

42. Muchembled, *La société policée*, 122.

43. Mayer, *Persistence of the Old Régime*.

44. Elias, *Civilizing Process*, 32.

45. Ibid., 67.

46. Ibid., 43.

47. Mauss, *Essais de sociologie*, 250.

48. Emile Durkheim, *L'education morale* (Paris: Librairie Félix Alcan, 1925), 100 (emphasis added).

49. Ernst Robert Curtius, *The Civilization of France*, trans. Olive Wyon (New York: St. Martin's Press, 1932), 14.

50. Robert Wohl, *The Generation of 1914* (Cambridge: Harvard University Press, 1979), 5.

51. Ibid., 40.

52. Ibid., 37. Mayer offers a similar assessment: "As part of their effort to scale the social pyramid and to demonstrate their political loyalty, the bourgeois embraced the historicist high culture and patronized the hegemonic institutions that were dominated by the old elites. The result was that they strengthened classical and academic idioms, conventions, and symbols in the arts and letters instead of encouraging modernist impulses. The bourgeois allowed themselves to be ensnared in a cultural and educational system that bolstered and reproduced the ancien régime. In the process they sapped their own potential to inspire the conception of a new aesthetic and intellection." Mayer, *Persistence of the Old Régime*, 14.

53. Henri Hubert, cited by Fournier in *Marcel Mauss*, 246.

54. Mauss, in ibid., 347.

55. Wohl, *The Generation of 1914*, 209.

56. Durkheim, "L'état actual des études sociologiques en France" (1895), in *Textes*, 1:75, emphasis added.

57. Mucchielli documents "la mode sociologique" among the first generation of Dreyfusards, for whom the association between sociology and socialism was also significant. His nearly exhaustive overview of sociology's relation to—as well as influence upon—neighboring fields does not, however, include the literary field. See *La découverte du social: Naissance de la sociologie en France*, 109–11.

58. Robert Hertz, "La prééminence de la main droite. Etude sur la polarité religieuse" (1909), in *Sociologie religieuse et folklore* (Paris: Presses Universitaires de France, 1970), 84.

59. Ibid., 84.

60. Victor Karady, "Durkheim et les débuts de l'ethnologie universitaire," in *Durkheim*, ed. Hamilton, 7:146.

61. Robert Mandrou, *Histoire de la France aux 17e et 18e siècles* (Paris: Presses Universitaires de France, 1967), 305.

62. For highlights from some of the more (in)famous of these reports, see Claude Lévi-Strauss, *Tristes tropiques* (Paris: Librairie Plon, Collection "Terre Humaine," 1955), 80.

63. Relation de 1634 de Paul Lejeune, *Le missionnaire, l'apostat, le sorcier*, Edition critique par Guy Laflèche (Montréal, Canada: Les Presses de l'Université de Montréal, 1973).

64. Michèle Duchet, *Anthropologie et histoire au siècle des lumières* (Paris: François Maspéro, 1971), 10.

65. See Geoffrey Atkinson, *Les relations de voyages du XVIIe siècle et l'évolution des idées: Contribution à l'étude de la formation de l'esprit du XVIIIe siècle* (1924; New York: Lenox Hill [Burt Franklin], 1971).

66. "Certaines thèses historiques banalisées ne sont donc plus recevables. En particulier celle qui fait provenir l'éclat de la littérature classique de l'action de potentats éclairés: Richelieu ou Louis XIV se sont servis de la littérature autant ou plus qu'ils l'ont

servie. L'analyse historique dénonce les mythes de la relation harmonieuse entre écrivains et pouvoirs au Grand Siècle." Viala, *Naissance de l'écrivain: Sociologie de la littérature à l'âge classique*, 295.

67. Robin Horton has already stressed the innovativeness of the Durkheimian "continuity/evolution" model for the development of scientific thought. Moreover, he claims that this dimension of Durkheimianism has been subordinated to the sacred/profane opposition which is also correlated with distinctive modes of thought: symbolic, awe-inspiring collective representations in the sacred and rational, pragmatic in the profane. Where Horton errs, I believe, is in assuming that with the demise of the sacred in modern life, the first mode of thought will be superseded by the second. Rather, as I have emphasized here, Durkheim and Mauss viewed collective representations as characteristic of the ensemble of modern society, including the occultation of their social, collective sources. See Robin Horton, "Lévy-Bruhl, Durkheim and the Scientific Revolution," in *Modes of Thought*, ed. Robin Horton and Ruth Finnegan (London: Faber and Faber), 1973.

68. Massis and de Tarde, *L'esprit de la nouvelle Sorbonne*, 27.

69. Karady, "Durkheim et les débuts de l'ethnologie universitaire," 153.

70. Vogt, "Uses of Studying Primitives," 178.

71. Mauss, *Oeuvres*, 3:389.

72. Alternative readings can also be found in Mike Gane, ed., *The Radical Sociology of Durkheim and Mauss* (London: Routledge, 1992), and Frank Pearce, *The Radical Durkheim* (London: Unwin Hyman, 1989).

73. Jean Jamin, "L'ethnographie mode d'inemploi. De quelques rapports de l'ethnologie avec le malaise dans la civilisation," in *Le mal et la douleur*, ed. Jacques Hainard and Roland Kaehr (Neuchâtel: Musée d'ethnographie, 1986).

74. Pierre Bourdieu and Jean-Claude Passeron, "Sociology and Philosophy in France since 1945: Death and Resurrection of a Philosophy without Subject," *Social Research* 34 (1967): 172.

75. In light of Herman Lebovics's findings ("Le conservatisme en anthropologie et la fin de la Troisième République," *Gradhiva* 4 [1988]: 3–18) and the challenges it posed to the conventional view of Durkheimian domination of the field, the French anthropologist Gérard Lenclud was led to question whether such a thing as a national approach to the history of anthropology exists and should be recognized as such. See 72–76.

76. Victor Karady, "Durkheim, les sciences sociales et l'Université: bilan d'un semi-échec," *Revue française de sociologie* (April–June 1976): 267–311.

77. Célestin Bouglé, *Leçons de sociologie sur l'évolution des valeurs* (Paris: Colin, 1922), as cited in Heilbron, "Les métamorphoses du durkheimisme, 1920–1940," 221.

78. Karady, "Le problème de la légitimité dans l'organisation historique de l'ethnologie française," 18.

79. Heilbron, "Les métamorphoses du durkheimisme, 1920–1940," 230.

80. Ibid., 223.

81. Victor Karady, "Le problème de la légitimité dans l'organisation historique de l'ethnologie française," 17 n. 2.

82. Mauss, *Oeuvres*, 3:438.

83. Cited by Fournier in *Marcel Mauss*, 602.

84. Ibid.

85. Alfred Métraux, "Rencontre avec les ethnologues," *Critique*, nos. 195–96 (1963): 678.

86. The secret language of the Dogon of Sanga was also the subject of his thesis for the diploma from the Ecole pratique in 1938. He also obtained certificates of study from the Institut d'ethnologie, where his areas of study were linguistics and Black

Africa, along with courses at l'Ecole nationale des langues orientales vivantes (langue amharique).

87. André Chastel, "La loyauté de l'intelligence," in *Roger Caillois, Cahiers pour un temps* (Paris: Centre Georges Pompidou/Pandora Editions, 1981), 29.

88. Ibid., 32.

89. In 1936 Caillois obtained both the advanced degree in grammar from the Ecole normale supérieure and a diploma from the section on religion at the Ecole pratique. For more details regarding contacts between Mauss and members of the Collège, including Mauss's strong reservations, see Fournier, *Marcel Mauss*, 707–11.

90. This position was most emphatically expressed by Evans-Pritchard in his early review of *Elementary Forms*: "No amount of juggling with words like 'intensity' and 'effervescence' can hide the fact that he derives the totemic religion of the Black Fellows from the emotional excitement of individuals brought together in a small crowd, from what is a sort of crowd hysteria." Cited in Pickering, *Durkheim's Sociology of Religion,* 396.

91. In 1939 Svend Ranulf, a Danish student of Mauss, authored "Scholarly Forerunners of Fascism," in which he claimed that Durkheim's endorsement of corporate associations may have served unwittingly as a model for Mussolini's fasci. In Mauss's oft-quoted response, he laments the tragic turn of events as "une vérification trop forte de choses que nous avions indiquées, et la preuve que nous aurions dû plutôt attendre cette vérification par le mal qu'une vérification par le bien." Marcel Mauss, in *Durkheim,* ed. Hamilton, 1:34. For a more recent rapprochement between Durkheim and fascism see Crapanzano, "Moment of Prestidigitation," 95–113.

3. Politics and the Sacred in the Collège de Sociologie

1. Roger Caillois, "Introduction," *College of Sociology,* ed. Hollier, 11.

2. Robert A. Nisbet, *The Social Group in French Thought* (1940; New York: Arno Press, 1980), iv-v, i.

3. Gustave Le Bon, *La psychologie des foules* (1895), introduction by André Akoun (Paris: Presses Universitaires de France, 1975), 71.

4. For instance, Susanna Barrows, *Distorting Mirrors: Visions of the Crowd in Late Nineteenth-Century France* (New Haven: Yale University Press, 1981).

5. For more on this, consult Elisabeth Roudinesco, *La bataille de cent ans: Histoire de la psychanalyse en France,* vol. 1 (Paris: Editions Ramsay, 1982), 181.

6. For a point-by-point comparison between Durkheim and LeBon on the characteristics of group behavior, see Pickering, *Durkheim's Sociology of Religion,* 380–86.

7. See chapter 1 above for a demonstration of Durkheim's move to this position. The discussion of the relation of effervescence to his social and political thought can be found in both chapters 1 and 2.

8. Durkheim, *Elementary Forms,* 413.

9. Emmanual Levinas, *Ethics and Infinity,* conversations with Philippe Nemo, translated from the French by Richard A. Cohen (Pittsburgh: Duquesne University Press, 1985), 27.

10. Georges Bataille and Roger Caillois, "Sacred Sociology and the Relationships between 'Society,' 'Organism,' and 'Being,'" in *College of Sociology,* ed. Hollier, 80.

11. For the analysis of the critical role played by the multiple connotations of *conscience* in Durkheim's work, see chapter 1.

12. Bataille, "Attraction and Repulsion II: Social Structure," in *College of Sociology,* ed. Hollier, 114, 121.

13. Durkheim, *Elementary Forms,* 231–32. Translator's note: "Since Durkheim said

'resultant' *(résultante)* and not 'result,' he may have had in mind the mathematical notion of a vector sum of forces. A resultant may be defined as the single force, measured as velocity or acceleration, to which several forces taken together are equivalent. The term also has an analogous literary sense." *Elementary Forms,* 232.

14. Bataille, "Le sens moral de la sociologie," *Critique* 1 (1946): 45, reprinted in *Oeuvres complètes,* 11:63.

15. Bataille, "The Sorcerer's Apprentice," in *College of Sociology,* ed. Hollier, 23.

16. Ibid., 23.

17. Durkheim, in *Emile Durkheim,* ed. Bellah, 69.

18. Bataille, "Letter to X, Lecturer on Hegel," in *College of Sociology,* ed. Hollier, 91. The lecturer addressed is obviously Kojève, and the letter a response to Kojève's communication to the Collège.

19. Ibid., 91.

20. Caillois, "Introduction," in *College of Sociology,* ed. Hollier, 10, emphasis added.

21. Durkheim, *Sociology and Philosophy,* 86, emphasis added.

22. According to Hollier's notes to "The Sorcerer's Apprentice," this skepticism was expressed at the outset of the Collège by Alexandre Kojève. See *College of Sociology,* ed. Hollier, 398.

23. See Bernard-Henri Lévy, *L'idéologie française* (Paris: Grasset, 1981).

24. This is the title of Loubet del Bayle's study of such groups (Paris: Editions du Seuil, 1969).

25. Daniel Lindenberg, *Les années souterraines* (Paris: La Découverte, 1990), 59.

26. In the expanded version of his 1987 biography of Bataille, Michel Surya has added several strong statements attesting to Bataille's antifascist sentiments as well as philosemitism. See Michel Surya, *Georges Bataille: La mort à l'oeuvre* (Paris: Gallimard, 1992), 437–48.

27. Lindenberg, *Les années souterraines,* 58.

28. Mauss, in Ranulf, "Scholarly Forerunners of Fascism" (1939), in *Durkheim,* ed. Hamilton, 1:34. Mauss's reply, translated by Lukes, is in *Durkheim,* ed. Hamilton, 1:338–39.

29. *Durkheim,* ed. Hamilton, 338–39.

30. For a qualification of what is meant by Durkheim's socialism, see chapter 1.

31. Durkheim, *Elementary Forms,* 215.

32. See Lévy, *L'idéologie française,* 25, 205.

33. Durkheim, *Elementary Forms,* 301.

34. Bataille, "La structure psychologique du fascisme," *Oeuvres complètes,* vol. 1, *Premiers écrits (1922–40)* (Paris: Gallimard, 1970), 370.

35. Ibid., 340.

36. Subsequent critics also challenge the analytical viability of the sacred/profane distinction for the logical and methodological inconsistencies it presents, especially the blurring between the profane and nonsacred. Lukes questions, How, for instance, is the impurely sacred to be distinguished from the profane, a sacred profanation from a profane profanation? He also points to the lack of a sustained distinction between the application of the sacred/profane to a class of things set apart from others, and the way the sacred/profane dualism functions to distinguish between how individuals feel and evaluate those things, such as whether or not they feel intense respect, or religious horror, or veneration, or love toward them. Lukes, *Emile Durkheim,* 27. See also Pickering, *Durkheim's Sociology of Religion,* 164–66 passim.

37. Bataille, "La structure psychologique du fascisme," 353.

38. This is one of the lectures in which Bataille is standing in for Caillois, but initially speaking for himself, though the entire printed communication appears under Caillois's name. Apparently, the two had agreed to the topic, if not its content. Roger Caillois, "Brotherhoods, Orders, Secret Societies, Churches," in *College of Sociology*, ed. Hollier, 146, 147.

39. Roudinesco, *La bataille de cent ans*, 1:181.

40. Sigmund Freud, *Group Psychology and the Analysis of the Ego*, trans. James Strachey (New York: Bantam Books, 1960), 17.

41. I have left *meneur* in the original French because the English "leader" does not carry the same pejorative connotations. For the more neutral notion of leader, contemporary French uses the English word.

42. Bataille, "La structure psychologique du fascisme," 364. The original French reads, "Mais, de même que dans le cas de l'organisation militaire, la valeur affective propre à l'existence misérable n'est que déplacée et transformée en son contraire; et c'est sa portée démesurée qui donne au chef et à l'ensemble de la formation l'accent de violence sans lequel aucune armée ni aucun fascisme ne seraient possibles."

43. Ibid., 367. The essay on the psychological sources of fascism is a primary reference for critics who seek to substantiate their claim that Bataille was guilty of "equivocations" in relation to fascism. Indeed, according to Klossowski, the lack of a definitive condemnation may have been recognized—and regretted—by Bataille himself. Leiris attempted to resolve the alleged ambiguity by describing Bataille's position as a recognition of the superior capacity of the right over the left to exert massive influence: "My feeling is truly that Bataille was never a fascist. If you want, he was fascinated by the Nazi genius for propaganda. His wish would have been for the left to manifest a propaganda talent equal to that of the Nazis, but for the opposite goals." In Bernard-Henry Lévy, *Les aventures de la liberté: Une histoire subjective des intellectuels* (Paris: Bernard Grasset, 1991), 186.

44. Caillois, "Brotherhoods, Orders, Secret Societies, Churches," 149.

45. Caillois, "Power," in *College of Sociology*, ed. Hollier, 132. Due to illness, Caillois was replaced by Bataille, who spoke along lines similar to those Caillois had indicated in other texts.

46. Bataille, "La structure psychologique du fascisme," 370.

47. Bataille, "Le problème de l'Etat," in *Oeuvres complètes*, 1:333, 336.

48. Bataille, "The College of Sociology," in *College of Sociology*, ed. Hollier, 339.

49. Comparisons between the archaic and feudal significance of expenditure contemporaneous with Bataille's were also noted by Marc Bloch: "It is nonetheless true that, in squandering a fortune that was easily gained and easily lost, the noble thought to affirm his superiority over classes less confident in the future or more careful in providing for it. This praiseworthy prodigality might not always stop at generosity or even luxury. A chronicler has preserved for us the record of the remarkable competition in wasteful expenditure witnessed one day at a great 'court' held in Limousin. One knight had a plot of ground ploughed up and sown with small pieces of silver; another burned wax candles for his cooking; a third, 'through boastfulness,' ordered thirty of his horses to be burnt alive." Bloch concludes, "What must a merchant have thought of this struggle for prestige through extravagance—which reminds us of the practices of certain primitive races?" Marc Bloch, *Feudal Society*, vol. 2, trans. L. A. Manyon (Chicago: University of Chicago Press, 1968), 311. The "primitive" source for Bloch is most probably—as it certainly was for Bataille—Mauss's essay on the gift. There, in reference to the Trobriand Kula, Mauss had indeed noted that "wealth is, in every aspect, as much a thing of prestige as a thing of utility." But then, he rhetorically queried, "But are

we certain that our own position is different and that wealth with us is not first and foremost a means of controlling others?" Mauss, *The Gift*, 73.

50. For more on this, see concluding section to chapter 4.

51. Bataille, "La notion de dépense," in *Oeuvres complètes*, 1:303.

52. Richard Wolin, "Left Fascism: Georges Bataille and the German Ideology," *Constellations* 2, no. 3 (1996): 405.

53. This view was explicitly developed by Pierre Bourdieu in his *Esquisse d'une théorie de la pratique* (Paris: Librairie Droz, 1972).

54. This is the argument forwarded by Bruno Karsenti in *Marcel Mauss: Le fait social total* (Paris: Presses Universitaires de France, 1994). As such, it offers a strong counter to the position argued by Jürgen Habermas and reiterated by Richard Wolin, to the effect that modernity demonstrates the supercession of the sacred as well as archaic modes of gift exchange.

55. In his social history of France since the Second World War, for instance, Dominique Borne points out that well until 1945, the working class was rejected as a "corps étranger." *Histoire de la société française depuis 1945* (Paris: Armand Colin, 1988), 23.

56. Bataille, "La notion de dépense," 308, 319.

57. Ibid., 318.

58. Durkheim, *Elementary Forms*, 212.

59. Erika Apfelbaum and Gregory R. McGuire, "Models of Suggestive Influence and the Disqualification of the Social Crowd" (1986), in *Changing Conceptions of Crowd Mind and Behavior*, ed. Carl F. Graumann and Serge Moscovici (New York: Springer-Verlag, 1986), 28. Cf. Moscovici, in the introduction: "We must once more recognize the admirable courage of both LeBon and Freud for having dared to provide a scientific meaning to these phenomena." And then, "no one has seriously verified these hypotheses concerning influence or suggestion" (32).

60. Apfelbaum and McGuire, "Models of Suggestive Influence," 47, emphasis added.

61. Gustave LeBon, *The Crowd*, with a new introduction by Robert A. Nye (New Brunswick, N.J.: Transaction Publishers, 1995), 76.

62. Ibid., 77.

63. Freud, *Group Psychology and the Analysis of the Ego*, 95.

64. Ibid., 70.

65. Nisbet, *Sociological Tradition*, 82.

66. Ibid., 82.

67. Durkheim, *L'education morale*, 114–15. The first lectures were delivered between 1902 and 1903.

68. Ibid., 110, 115.

69. LeBon, *The Crowd*, 56.

70. Ibid., 77, 79.

71. Boris Souvarine, "Les journées de février," *La Critique sociale: Revue des idées et des livres: Sociologie/Economie politique/Histoire/Philosophie/Droit public/ Démographie/Mouvement ouvrier/Lettres et arts (1931–1934)* (Paris: Editions de la Différence, Réimpression, 1983). In the preface to the reedition of the original issues of *La critique sociale,* Souvarine infamously denounced Bataille's alleged fascism without any substantiation. In response, Maurice Blanchot stated, "Giving homage to Souvarine, I must, however, protest against the violent, unjust, and false criticism that, in a preface to the reprinting of his review, he addresses to Georges Bataille." For Blanchot's complete statement, see "Les intellectuels en question," *Le Débat* 29 (1984): 3–28. The translation cited here appears in Steven Ungar, *Scandal and Aftereffect: Blanchot and France since 1930* (Minneapolis: University of Minnesota Press, 1995), 132. Conversely, Wolin does not challenge Souvarine's credibility.

72. See the conclusion to "La Part maudite" (1949), in *Oeuvres complètes,* vol. 7 (Paris: Gallimard, 1976), 159–79.

73. Durkheim, *Elementary Forms,* 417.

74. Bataille, "Attraction and Repulsion I: Tropisms, Sexuality, Laughter, and Tears," in *College of Sociology,* ed. Hollier, 112.

75. Ibid.

76. Bataille, "Attraction and Repulsion II," 114.

77. Hertz, "La prééminence de la main droite," 89.

78. Most revealing is that Freud's positions cannot be dismissed as a simple assimilation of the stereotypes accompanying those elements of crowd psychology appropriated for his own needs. Rather, personal letters offer evidence that his theory of group psychology stems from a long-standing and exaggerated fear of crowds, a revulsion so extreme that Marthe Robert qualifies it as phobic. Precisely because his personal obsession had no basis in any personal danger, she also convincingly demonstrates that his association between the lower classes of society and unconscious forces reinforced a sociological view that would remain consistent throughout Freud's speculations regarding the very nature of civilization. Marthe Robert, *From Oedipus to Moses: Freud's Jewish Identity,* trans. from the French by Ralph Manheim (Garden City, N.Y.: Anchor Books, Anchor Press/Doubleday, 1976), 45.

79. Georges Bataille, "L'anus solaire," in *Oeuvres complètes,* 1:85–86.

80. Emile Durkheim, *Journal, 1897–1898,* 2:163.

81. Drawing upon the materials provided by Alfred William Howitt, *Native Tribes of South-East Australia* (New York: Macmillan, 1904), 683, as well as from the Spencer and Gillen sources cited above, Durkheim once more stresses the dramatic contrast between the lackluster banality of profane existence and its correlative behavior, with the intensely demonstrative effusions that can be provoked by nearly any unforeseen "event" as well as ceremony. Durkheim thus comments, "Since the emotional and passionate faculties of the primitive are not fully subordinated to his reason and will, he easily loses his self-control. An event of any importance immediately puts him outside himself." *Elementary Forms,* 217. This does not obviate the qualitatively different effects he discerns in the collective forms of effervescence.

82. Caillois, "The Winter Wind," in *College of Sociology,* ed. Hollier, 36, 40.

83. Ibid., 40.

84. According to sources close to Acéphale, the "secret" society organized by Bataille and to which Caillois was privy, the only situation in which the tactics just described were implemented consisted in the refusal to shake hands with someone identified as an anti-Semite. In order to dispel further ambiguity, Hollier indicates in a footnote to this text that Caillois entrusted the realization of the new community to the Communist Party—the sole "worthy" successor to the Society of Jesus. Hollier, ed., *College of Sociology,* 402 n. 11.

85. Caillois, "The Winter Wind," 41.

86. Jons, "Durkheim's Intellectual Development," 229–45.

87. Mauss, "Les techniques du corps," in *Sociologie et anthropologie,* 369. The article was first printed in *Journal de psychologie* (1936) after being delivered to the Société de psychologie in 1934.

88. Mauss's position also converges with Elias's contention that the sociologicial study of personality must integrate a historical perspective. The historical dimension of Mauss's analysis is especially explicit in his conclusion to the study of the idea of the "person" and expressed this way: "But let us not be too speculative. Let us say that social anthropology, sociology, and history teach us to appreciate how human thought makes its way (*chemine* [Meyerson]); it makes its way slowly through time, across

societies by means of the most unforeseeable trajectories." Mauss, *Sociologie et anthropologie*, 362.

89. Mauss, "Questions posées à la psychologie" (1936), in *Sociologie et anthropologie*, 306.

90. Mauss, "An Intellectual Self-Portrait," 139. It would also be instructive to compare Mauss's seemingly contradictory positions regarding the sociological effects of the civilizing process with those of Freud. Marthe Robert, for instance, points out that Freud's undeniably irrational fear of the "people" did not preclude an empathic identification with their plight. Due to his own experience of material difficulties, he acknowledged that their apparent refusal to submit to the same deferments of pleasure as found within the morally disciplined "civilized" bourgeoisie could be traced to the effects of poverty and deprivation, instability and social marginalization, rather than from any innate deficiency. For more on this see Robert, *From Oedipus to Moses*, 48–49.

91. Michel Leiris, *Manhood*, trans. from *L'age d'homme* (1946) by Richard Howard (London: Jonathan Cape Ltd., 1968), 142, 192. All references are to this translation unless indicated otherwise.

92. This is essentially the thesis developed by Gerrold Seigel in his reinterpretation of the bohemian phenomenon in nineteenth-century France. See his *Bohemian Paris: Culture, Politics, and the Boundaries of Bourgeois Life, 1830–1930* (New York: Penguin Books, 1986).

93. Georges Bataille, *Oeuvres complètes*, vol. 2, *Ecrits posthumes (1922–40)* (Paris: Gallimard, 1970), 99.

94. Caillois, "Introduction," 11, emphasis added.

95. The notable exception is Caillois's notion of a sursocialization. See Hollier, ed., *College of Sociology*, xvii.

96. Bataille, "La part maudite," in *Oeuvres complètes*, 7:20.

4. Sacrifice in Art and Eroticism

1. For more details regarding contacts between Mauss and members of the Collège, including Mauss's strong reservations, see Fournier, *Marcel Mauss*, 707–11.

2. Philippe Borgeaud traces the subjective approach to religion and the sacred to the influence of Rudolf Otto's *Das Heilige* (1917). Translated into French in the late 1920s or early 1930s, Otto's view of the sacred deliberately "ignores" the points of view developed by both Durkheim and Freud in favor of an approach described as a melding of mysticism and neo-Kantianism. See Borgeaud, "Le couple sacré/profane," 387–418.

3. Michel Leiris, *L'afrique fantôme* (1934; Paris: Editions Gallimard, 1981), 78.

4. Ibid.

5. Ibid., 443.

6. Jean Jamin, "Quand le sacré devint gauche," *L'ire des vents* 4 (1981): 98–118.

7. Bataille, *Tears of Eros*, trans. from *Les larmes d'Eros* (1961) by Peter Connor (San Francisco: City Lights Books, 1989), 207.

8. Leiris, *Manhood*, 87.

9. Leiris, *L'âge d'homme*, 71 (translation mine).

10. Philippe Borgeaud has pointed out that the threshold or "parvis" to the church or temple is where theorists and historians of religion from E. B. Tylor to Eliade, via Durkheim and Otto, locate the sacred, defined as that which is neither divine or belonging to the gods, nor yet entirely profaned, or removed from their association. For turn-of-the-century evolutionists, it thus represents a state of social solidarity prior to the advent of religion defined in relation to one or more dieties. This complex and problematic—as

acknowledged by Borgeaud—etymology nonetheless allows us to appreciate the ironies of Leiris's analogy to the ancient parvis in the modern world. See Borgeaud, "Le couple sacré/profane," 387–418.

11. Michel Leiris, "The Sacred in Everyday Life," in *College of Sociology*, ed. Hollier, 31.

12. Leiris, *Manhood*, 37.

13. Ibid., 141.

14. Ibid., 140. For more on this see Michèle Richman, "Leiris's *L'age d'homme*: Politics and the Sacred in Everyday Ethnography," *Yale French Studies* 81 (1992): 91–110, and Marjorie Perloff, "Tolerance and Taboo: Modernist Primitivisms and Postmodernist Pieties," in *Prehistories of the Future*, ed. Barkan and Bush, 339–56.

15. Leiris, *Manhood*, 162.

16. Bataille, "College of Sociology," 337.

17. Only the status of economic forms caused Durkheim to hedge at a thoroughly global attribution to religion.

18. Mauss, "Les techniques du corps" (1936), in *Sociologie et anthropologie*, 365–86.

19. To be well founded, sacrifice must fulfill two necessary conditions: to draw the one making the sacrifice beyond his/her immediate self—"hors de soi"—while providing objects sufficiently close to derive a benefit from the sacrifice. As Hubert and Mauss insist, "This trait of intimate penetration as well as separation, of being both inside and external to the individual, is, to the greatest degree, the distinction of social things." "Essai sur la nature et la fontion du sacrifice," 306.

20. Bataille, "College of Sociology," 338.

21. For further insight into the relation between Bataille's proclamations and behavior, see Surya's biography, *Georges Bataille*, especially 265 for Laure's vituperations against his infidelities.

22. Laure, *Ecrits de Laure: Texte établi par J. Peignot et le Collectif Change* (Paris: Jean-Jacques Pauvert), 85.

23. Bataille, "College of Sociology," 338.

24. Bataille, *Oeuvres complètes*, 1:560n, 562.

25. Bataille notes his debt to Emile Dermenghem's use of the expression "privileged instants" associated with poetry and mysticism, in an article dating from July 1938. Inspired by the Sufis, the instant is compared to a "trenchant sword," capable of cutting the roots of the future as well as the past. Thus, continues Bataille, the sword image transmits something of the "profoundly ambiguous, dangerous, and mortal nature of the sacred." He also points out that Sartre's *Nausea* (1938) had significantly referred to "privileged situations" as well as "perfect moments." *Oeuvres complètes*, 1:560n.

26. Bataille, "College of Sociology," 338, 339.

27. Ibid., 339.

28. Ibid., 341.

29. Elias Canetti ascribes the formation of "crowds" in his very comprehensive sense as arising from this same impulsion. See Canetti, *Crowds and Power*, trans. from the German by Carol Stewart (New York: Noonday Press, 1996).

30. Bataille, "College of Sociology," 339.

31. Ibid., 339, 340, emphasis added.

32. Roger Caillois, "Puissances du roman," in *Approches de l'imaginaire* (Paris: NRF Gallimard, 1974), 230.

33. "It thus appears after the fact [*après coup*], that no longer capable of expressing something derived from outside itself, art is incontestably sacred . . . , art would not be

able to survive without the force to attain the sacred instant by its own means."
Bataille, *Oeuvres complètes,* 1:561.

34. Ibid., 11:420.

35. Jean-Luc Nancy, "Painting in the Grotto," in *The Muses,* trans. Peggy Kamuf
(Stanford, Calif.: Stanford University Press, 1996), 72.

36. Durkheim, *Elementary Forms,* 385–86.

37. Bataille, *Oeuvres complètes,* vol. 9 (Paris: NRF Gallimard, 1979), 41.

38. See Nancy: "Image, here, is not the convenient or inconvenient double of a thing
in the world: it is the glory of that thing, its epiphany, its distinction from its own mass
and its own appearance. The image praises the thing as detached from the universe
of things and shown to be detached as is the whole of the world." "Painting in the
Grotto," 73.

39. Bataille, *Oeuvres complètes,* 11:484.

40. See Bataille, *Oeuvres complètes,* vol. 10 (Paris: NRF Gallimard, 1987), 7–270.

41. Bataille, *Oeuvres complètes,* 9:135.

42. Maurice Blanchot, "Naissance de l'art" in *L'amitié* (Paris: Gallimard, 1971),
9–20.

43. Bataille, *Oeuvres complètes,* 9:13.

44. Durkheim, *Textes,* 2:115.

45. Bataille, *Oeuvres complètes,* 9:35.

46. Ibid., 39.

47. I am indebted to Jay Caplan for pointing out this anachronistic relation in "La
beauté de la mort," *Dada-surrealism* 5 (1975): 37–43.

48. Michel Leiris, "The Bullfight as Mirror," trans. Ann Smock, *October* 63 (Winter
1993): 29, 34. To avoid misunderstanding, it is important to note that the "ideal limit"
that is transgressed is the projection of human desire, a reflection of misfortune or suffering, rather than a societal norm.

49. Ibid., 39.

50. Bataille, "L'érotisme," in *Oeuvres complètes,* vol. 10 (Paris: NRF, Gallimard,
1987), 23.

51. Ibid., 19.

52. Ibid., 23.

53. Ibid., 42, 70.

54. Ibid., 89.

55. Ibid., 179.

56. Bataille, *Tears of Eros,* 207.

57. Ibid., 206.

58. Bataille, "Letter to X," 91.

59. Mauss, "Place de la sociologie dans l'anthropologie" (1924), in *Sociologie et anthropologie,* 289–90.

60. Durkheim, *Elementary Forms,* 411.

61. Ibid., 459.

62. Herein resides a crucial difference with the point of view developed by René
Girard in *La violence et le sacré* (Paris: Editions Bernard Grasset, 1972).

63. Leiris, *L'age d'homme,* 127 (my translation).

64. Jean-Luc Nancy, "La communauté désoeuvrée," *Aléa* 4 (1983): 42.

65. Bataille, "L'érotisme," 7–270.

66. Karady, "Naissance de l'ethnologie universitaire," *Mauss, l'Arc* 48 (1972): 33–40.

67. Mauss, *Oeuvres,* 1:16–17.

68. Mauss, "Essai sur le don," in *Sociologie et anthropologie,* 194.

69. Bataille, "Préface de Madame Edwarda," *Oeuvres complètes,* 10:260.
70. Claude Lévi-Strauss, *The Elementary Structures of Kinship,* rev. ed., trans. James Harle Bell, John Richard von Sturmer and Rodney Needham, ed. (Boston: Beacon Press, 1969), 496–97; translated from *Les structures élémentaires de la parenté.*
71. Bataille, *Oeuvres complètes,* 12:53.
72. Caillois, "Festival," in *College of Sociology,* ed. Hollier, 301–2.
73. Ibid., 303. Familiar only with Caillois's point of view, Borgeaud arrives at the same conclusion—that the alternation between peace and war alone constitutes the only means for expression of the sacred/profane dichotomy in the modern world.
74. Bataille, "La guerre et la philosophie du sacré" (1951), in *Oeuvres complètes,* 12:50.

Postscriptum

1. "Peut-être en étudiant ces côtés obscurs de la vie sociale, arrivera-t-on à éclairer un peu la route que doivent prendre nos nations, leur morale en même temps que leur économie. [Perhaps an appreciation of these obscure areas of social life will help us light the way to future paths for the moral life of our nations as well as for their economies.]" Mauss, "Essai sur le don" (1923–24), in *Sociologie et anthropologie,* 273.
2. Jürgen Habermas, "Modernity versus Postmodernity," *New German Critique* 22 (1981): 13.
3. Bourdieu and Passeron, "Sociology and Philosophy in France since 1945," 198.
4. The exception to this statement is clearly *Tristes tropiques,* where Lévi-Strauss offers a sustained homage to his predecessors within the French tradition of anthropological thinking emanating from Jean de Léry. See especially the conclusion.
5. Bourdieu, *Questions de sociologie,* 30.
6. Georges Gurvitch, *La vocation actuelle de la sociologie,* vol. 1, *Vers la sociologie différentielle* (Paris: Presses Universitaires de France, 1963), 27.
7. Victor Turner, *The Ritual Process: Structure and Anti-Structure* (Ithaca, N.Y.: Cornell University Press, 1969), viii, 128.
8. Tiryakian, "Vers une sociologie de l'existence," 457, 454, 456.
9. Hertz, "La prééminence de la main droite," 89.
10. A complete break with this model also entails relinquishing a "genetic" view of the elementary forms as the embryonic source for subsequent social forms.
11. Roger Caillois, "Illusions à rebours," part 2, *Nouvelle revue française* (1955): 58–70. Caillois's ferocity against anthropology is consistent with his denunciation of the College as well.
12. This is the central criticism I would make regarding the prescriptive nature of the Marcus and Fischer approach to "anthropology in the service of cultural criticism." The weakness is in large part a consequence of their working primarily within the Anglo-American tradition of monographs, where comparisons are not an integral part of anthropological reflection.
13. Tiryakian, "Vers une sociologie de l'existence," 451.
14. François Héran, "La seconde nature de l'habitus. Tradition philosophique et sens commun dans le langage sociologique," *Revue française de sociologie* 28 (1987): 387.
15. The term "interest" is recent and comes from the technical vocabulary of accounting, Mauss points out. "In the morality of Antiquity, and the the most Epicurean, it is the good and pleasure that is sought, not material utility." See Mauss, "Essai sur le don," 271.
16. Bataille, *Oeuvres complètes,* 7:20.

17. Jürgen Habermas, *The Philosophical Discourse of Modernity: Twelve Lectures,* trans. Frederick G. Lawrence (Cambridge: MIT Press, 1996), 236.

18. See Karsenti, *L'homme total,* chap. 1.

19. See Mona Ozouf, *La fête révolutionnaire, 1789–1799* (Paris: Editions Gallimard, 1976).

20. I am grateful to Randall Collins for pointing out that "the difference between formally instituted rituals and commemorations and those which arise spontaneously, thereby building genuine effervescence, is addressed in recent sociological literature dealing with the emotive dimension of social movements" (personal communication). See, for instance, James Jasper, *The Art of Moral Protest* (Chicago: University of Chicago Press, 1997).

21. Robert Darnton, "What Was Revolutionary about the French Revolution?" *New York Review of Books,* January 19, 1989, 3.

22. Ibid., 10.

23. Chamboredon, "Emile Durkheim," 494.

24. See Edward Tiryakian, "Emile Durkheim," in *A History of Sociological Analysis,* ed. Tom Bottomore and Robert Nisbet (New York: Basic Books, 1978), 187–236.

25. Fredric Jameson, *The Political Unconscious: Narrative as a Socially Symbolic Act* (Ithaca, N.Y.: Cornell University Press, 1981), 294.

26. See "Emile Durkheim Today," roundtable discussion compiled by Terry N. Clark, in *Durkheim: Critical Assessments,* ed. Peter Hamilton, vol. 4 (London: Routledge, 1990), 363. Lukes also signals the extension of this preoccupation with the social by the French School of Sociology among Durkheim's followers, including Mauss.

27. See Stuart Hall, "The Toad in the Garden: Thatcherism among the Theorists," in *Marxism and the Interpretation of Culture,* ed. C. Nelson and L. Grossberg (Urbana: University of Illinois Press, 1988).

28. Karsenti, *L'homme total,* 127.

29. For more on Durkheim as a hybrid writer, see Rodolphe Gasché, *Die hybride Wissenschaft/Zur Mutationdes Wissenschaftsbegriffs bei Emile Durkheim und im Structuralismus von Claude Lévi-Strauss* (Stuttgart: J. B. Metzler, 1973).

30. Jeffrey Alexander has also placed the sacred/profane contrast at the center of a Durkheimian revival within Cultural Studies. See Alexander, ed., *Durkheimian Sociology.*

31. Muchembled, *La société policée,* 308.

32. Habermas, "Modernity versus Postmodernity," 5.

33. Lévi-Strauss, "French Sociology," 505.

Index

MICHÈLE H. RICHMAN is associate professor of French studies at the University of Pennsylvania. She is the author of *Reading Georges Bataille: Beyond the Gift* and has also published articles on Roland Barthes, Emile Durkheim, Michel Leiris, and Marcel Mauss.